A Belly Full of Bedsprings

The History of Bronc Riding

By

Gail Hughbanks Woerner

ILLUSTRATIONS BY

Gail Gandolfi

EAKIN PRESS ★ AUSTIN, TEXAS

Dedicated to Cliff Woerner,
my inspiration and encouragement,
who believes anything can happen.

"Gail Woerner leads a life that all who know her envy. She spends her time in what can only be described as 'labors of love.' Once again she is sharing her passion for the West and its history with us. And, as is always the case, her attention to fact and detail make her work worthy of serious note.

"A Belly Full of Bedsprings takes us on a chronological journey through the history of bronc riding, introducing us to the men, women and animals who left their mark in the rodeo arena. It would be impossible to include everyone who ever rode a bronc, but Gail has given us a choice of some of the best. Her inclusion of anecdotes and great photos will give this book a permanent place on your bookshelf."

Patricia Hildebrand
Executive Director
ProRodeo Hall of Fame &
Museum of the American Cowboy

"Occasional European horses have from time immemorial been vicious or have bucked, jumped, or reared, but the bronc with a 'belly full of bedsprings,' pawing for the moon, breaking in two half-way up, sunfishing on the way down, and then hitting the earth hard enough to crack open his rider's liver, was a development of the Western Hemisphere."

J. FRANK DOBIE
The Mustangs

Contents

Preface

It is a thrilling peek into our past when we watch an untamed bronc gyrate in every direction in an attempt to throw a cowboy. Everyone wants to experience a bit of the exciting time when the West was untamed. In those days of the Wild, Wild West the frontier challenged the cowboy daily—a blizzard, searing summer heat, or a constant wind that seemed endless. Prairie fires or soaking rains were other tests put to the cowboy by Mother Nature. Mentally, he was also challenged with long stretches of loneliness when he saw nary a soul—nothing but the cattle and an occasional wild critter.

A cowboy's horse was his absolute necessity. The animal was purely functional, allowing him to traverse the plains from one location to the next as quickly as possible. A well-trained horse would provide the rider an efficient way to carry on daily tasks, whether it be herding cattle, mending fence, or riding the range. Just how important a horse became as a working companion was up to the cowboy. An ability to break, train, and control his mount was imperative. Some were better at it than others. When two cowboys met, it was not at all uncommon for one to challenge the other on his bronc riding skills. Proving to be the better bronc rider established his credibility.

Men have been breaking horses to ride and use as beasts of burden for more than 5,000 years. Xenophon, an authority on horses several centuries B.C., penned a lengthy treatise on the horse in his *Anabasis*. He went into detail on the rearing, gentling, riding, and judging of the horse.[1] There was not, however, any mention of bucking and pitching; that, it seems, was a peculiar equine institution of the Americas. The theory behind it is that wild mustangs preyed upon by mountain lions in the

Americas learned to pitch to rid themselves of the cat and survive the attack. Those that did survive transmitted this quality onto their progeny.[2]

In *The Mustangs*, J. Frank Dobie stated that "occasional European horses have from time immemorial been vicious or have bucked, jumped, or reared, but the bronc with a 'belly full of bedsprings,' pawing for the moon, breaking in two halfway up, sunfishing on the way down, and then hitting the earth hard enough to crack open his rider's liver, was a development of the Western Hemisphere."[1] It was not until the evolution of the rodeo in the American West that cowboys began to ride untamed horses for sport and competition. Prior to that, horses were bucked in an attempt to break their wild spirit and tame them to be predictable cow ponies, willing to respond to instructions without a blowup. On occasion, a special wrangler would be hired to do this one particular job. However, most cowboys broke their own mounts, in between tending to a multitude of other range responsibilities.

Rodeo gave the cowboy an opportunity to perform at what he loved and did best—ride broncs. Throughout the years the horses that cowboys have ridden in bucking competitions have come and gone, but not without becoming legends. Their stories have been recorded just as diligently as have those of the cowboys who rode them.

In the development of the rodeo, cowboys and their horses have changed with time, refining their skills to an art form. In fact, certain bronc owners are now breeding their stock as if they were thoroughbreds being bred for the racetrack, just to supply premium buckers to the many rodeo stock contractors and rodeo companies throughout the country.

A bronc rider needs a bucker that tests his ability, while a bronc needs a rider that will challenge his strength to buck. One cannot exist without the other. Both strive to be the best of the best.

The sight of a cowboy riding a bucking bronc is a reminder to us of the taming of the West. May it never happen!

Introduction

The cowboy, handsome and independent, can ride the meanest bronc. And the harder it bucks, the better he likes it. It is a dangerous way to make a living, but a cowboy knows that. Injury and pain will happen, and must simply be endured and ignored. Eventually, the pain will go away. He will challenge another bronc, then another, and another. He lives free to choose what he does and where he goes. It's the cowboy way!

This description of a cowboy was defined in early western dime novels, glorified in early Hollywood movies, and reinforced later in television westerns and in stories passed down from one generation to the next. But in reality there are as many descriptions for cowboys as there are cowboys. No two are alike. Each has a unique history.

Cowboys who ride rough stock (saddle broncs, bareback broncs, and bulls) differ from roping and steer-wrestling cowboys. But don't ever try to place a cowboy in a mold: He just won't fit! Cowboys are individuals who do things their own way.

Some bronc riders have been quiet and shy, men who will ride their mounts and immediately after the ride blend into the crowd without saying a word. Other bronc riders have been flamboyant, outspoken characters who wear flashy, outrageous chaps and wave and yell at the crowd while riding their broncs. They have also been every type of personality in between those two extremes.

One of the most famous bronc riders, from any era, was Casey Tibbs from Fort Pierre, South Dakota. Casey was the youngest of ten children and started on the rodeo circuit in 1943, when he was barely fourteen. His smile won him many friends and he could ride a bronc like no one else. He had been breaking horses since he was ten years old, and his ability at riding broncs was special. When he came out of the chute, he and his bronc were poetry in motion. Tibbs won his first All-Around World Champion Cowboy title in 1951, when he was just twenty-two. During his rodeo career he won all the major rodeos, six Saddle Bronc World Championships, a Bareback World Championship, and two All-Around World Champion Cowboy titles. He was handsome, charismatic, and full of the devil. He rode broncs hard and played just as hard. He was well known around the world and brought a curiosity to rodeo from a vast array of fans.

I met Casey Tibbs while attending college in Denver. He had just won the 1955 All-Around World Championship, and during the National Western Stock Show and Rodeo he was bucked off the first bronc he drew. He suffered several broken ribs and a punctured lung and was hospitalized. The student editor of our college newspaper was in a dilemma deciding what theme to use for the next issue, and I suggested a rodeo theme featuring an interview with the hospitalized World Champion Tibbs. She liked the idea and made an appointment to interview him. Since she knew nothing about rodeo, she asked if I would go along to ask the appropriate questions.

Casey charmed us both. When the interview was over, he invited me to return that evening for a visit. I arrived, in my typical college skirt and sweater, and in a few minutes in swept a gorgeous blonde visitor dressed in an expensive gray suit, a mink stole casually thrown over one shoulder. Casey introduced her as Shirley Jean, long-time friend and original cast member of the *Our Gang* comedies. After the introduction she sarcastically whined, "Yes, I was a has-been when I was eight!" (The following day, in the Denver newspaper, I discovered in the entertainment section that Shirley Jean was professionally called "Gilda" and was a striptease artist currently appearing at a local nightclub.)

As I remember, the conversation was principally between Casey and Shirley Jean. Soon, however, another visitor arrived—an Indian woman in a leather dress and moccasins, her hair in braids. She was carrying a paper sack. Casey was pleased to see Mary Two Eagle, and explained to us he had met her through her infant son years earlier at a rodeo in South Dakota where Mary Two Eagle was performing dances in the arena with members of her tribe. Casey had noticed the baby in a cradleboard propped up against a tree, crying because flies were attacking him. Casey had picked him up and kept the flies off until his mother returned. Mary Two Eagle had not forgotten Tibbs' kind gesture.

Another arrival, that of Casey's physician, came soon. Although Tibbs introduced all of us, it was quite evident the doctor was fascinated with Mary Two Eagle. He learned she had ridden her horse from South Dakota to Denver, and was going from nightclub to nightclub offering to do Indian dances for whatever money she could get. He immediately asked if she would dance for us. At first she refused, saying she had to be accompanied by a drum. But when the creative doctor brought forth a bedpan and offered to beat the rhythm on it, she accepted and began to dance. What a curious scene: A physician keeping time on a bedpan as Mary Two Eagle, in her leather costume, danced around the hospital room, and a World Champion Cowboy, a stripper, and a very impressionable young college girl enjoying the performance.

I tell this story to illustrate what an ambassador to rodeo Casey Tibbs was throughout his life, and what diverse friends he made. The twinkle in his eye and that desire to cause some devilment was as natural to him as his ability to ride the toughest broncs with ease.

Cowboys are known throughout the world. The fascination is there, whether it be on television in the heart of Tokyo, Japan, via Japanese Broadcasting by a film crew covering bronc riding at Cheyenne Frontier Days; in the Ukraine, talking with a group of Cossacks about cowboys and sharing with them American cowboy magazines; or in Moscow, presenting a pair of spurs to a Russian government official. The cowboy is everyman's hero.

Although the cowboy mystique has become universal, it would be difficult for anyone to learn how cowboying started and how rodeo evolved to be a major sport in America without reading a multitude of various books and thousands of newspaper and magazine articles. This book was written to compile that information for those who lived it, for youth interested in cowboy history, and for everyone else who has a curiosity about the American West. The true story must be passed on.

Casey Tibbs on Necktie, owned by Elra and Jiggs Beutler. This photograph was used by artist Edd Hayes to sculpt the bigger-than-life bronze standing in front of the ProRodeo Cowboy Hall of Fame and Museum of the American Cowboy in Colorado Springs.

*— Photo by Ferrell, donated by Buster and June Ivory,
courtesy of the ProRodeo Cowboy Hall of Fame.*

1

How It All Began

The earliest cowboys worked on ranches. Cattle were *the* priority in a cowboy's life. These hard-working cowboys spent their days searching for stray cows, caring for them, moving them from place to place, and eventually taking them up the trail to market. Breaking untamed horses to be used in working with the stock was a part of the job. A good horse was a real asset to a cowboy and often was the determining factor as to how successfully he worked the cattle.

Cowboys spent many hours outdoors, in all kinds of weather. At times they ate very simply and rather meagerly. Many carried all their worldly possessions with them. Some were very transitory, moving on often, working from ranch to ranch. Others stayed in one place their entire lifetime.

A few cowboys became experts at their profession. Some were outstanding at breaking horses, while others excelled in roping. Some, however, performed just well enough to get by and keep their job. Most were somewhere in between "poor" and "expert" at cowboying. It was not unusual that those who excelled in breaking wild broncs would be matched against cowboys from nearby ranches, who were also considered to be good broncbusters. After all, it was an important and prideful circumstance for a ranch to be able to boast of having the best bronc rider in the country.

After the Civil War, the term "cowboy" was first used with reference to anyone who tended and worked with cattle in the West. A cowhand had one basic piece of equipment: the cow pony. The mount usually came from an odd collection of wild mustangs, which generally roamed freely until they were gathered up for breaking at four years of age. The broncbuster was

1

either a particularly saddleworthy local cowboy, or a specialist who traveled from ranch to ranch, working for as much as $5 per head to gentle the green mounts.[5]

Lee Warren was a broncbuster "specialist" in Montana. L. A. Huffman, a photographer from Miles City, made a visual record of his work, which was featured in the volume *Cowboys* of the Time-Life Old West Series. The broncbuster's work was detailed as follows: "Warren began by roping each bronco, then snubbing it to a post (or throwing it, if necessary) to put on the bridle. Next came the saddle blanket topped by the 40-pound saddle—and it was no mean feat to swing a heavy saddle shoulder-high with one hand while holding a rearing horse with the other. Finally came Warren himself, and that is when all gut-jarring hell broke loose for both the horse and the buster. The buster always won, for the rougher the horse behaved, the rougher the treatment he received in retaliation from the rider's quirt, spurs and rope end."[5]

It was not uncommon for a cowboy to win a bucking horse contest at dawn before he began his day's work with the cattle. And he might do it again midway through the day, when it was time to change to a fresh horse. Often, a local cowboy's standing or usefulness depended on his ability to break horses, so it was natural that each ranch tested their men in bucking contests. This led to the cowboys meeting in competition, on the ranch, but sometimes in town or during festive gatherings on holidays and special occasions.[6]

According to the most reliable records, between 25,000 and 35,000 cowboys trailed around six to ten million head of cattle from Texas to points as far north as Montana between the Civil War and the turn of the century.[3] Trail drives were primarily composed of young men between the ages of sixteen and twenty-two. Most were unmarried; they usually quit trail-herding when they did marry.

Once the final trail destination was reached, it was a relief to the cowboy to be rid of the responsibility of the herd. He could sleep inside on a real bed and eat regular meals. Visiting with local people often led to challenges to see who could ride a bronc the best. Cowboys heady with pride and relieved that the trip was over, no doubt, encouraged many a bucking match. At trail's end, those cowhands also found their pockets full of newfound wealth. It became commonplace to test one's skill, and wager that wealth against all the talk that had gone before. The breaking of wild horses drew cowboys and townsfolk alike as spectators. Hats were passed, dollar bills were crumpled and thrown into the dusty corrals, and the best rider walked away with the winnings.[4]

We will never pinpoint the exact location of the first bucking contest. That fact is lost in a quagmire of muddy history. It was, more than likely, an incidental occurrence that happened as a result of a challenge. Whether a bet was placed or the winner merely had the honor of out-riding his opponent becomes immaterial. Whether the place was a ranch or the final destination of a northern cattle trail, a Fourth of July celebration under a grove of cottonwood trees or the middle of some western town is also irrelevant. What is important is that from the early days of the cattle industry cowboys that worked daily with the stock from atop a horse required a plentiful supply of fresh horses. There were always those broncs that refused to be ridden, and always the cowboy that thought he couldn't be "throwed." And from this beginning, horse versus man, cowboy against cowboy, came early bronc contests and what became known as "rodeo."

It was not until well into the twentieth century that a cowboy could consider trying to make a living by rodeoing, with no other means of support. The earliest rodeos were few and far between and were competitions between local broncbusters. Travel was limited, and most events were only publicized locally.

Among the earliest recorded rodeos was an event in Santa Fe, New Mexico, in 1847, but according to records only roping and horse races were performed. Deer Trail, Colorado, had a bucking contest in 1869; in Cheyenne, Wyoming, in 1872 a steer roping was held, and later in 1893 the first bronc riding happened there. In 1882 Buffalo Bill held a roping, riding and bronc-riding contest in North Platte, Nebraska, on the Fourth of July. That same year, Austin, Texas, presented a silver saddle to the winning steer roper.

Buffalo Bill took his contest to Omaha, Nebraska, in 1883.

In Pecos, Texas, a bunch of cowhands swapped lies in front of Red Newell's saloon. Pecos had more saloons per capita than any other Texas community at the time, and they were proud of it! Gambling tables ran all night. They decided to hold a rodeo on the Fourth of July that year. There was no admission, no arena or chutes. A thousand people attended, and $40 in prize money was posted by area ranchers. The first winner of the bronc riding was unfortunately not recorded, possibly because of the free barbecue and dancing afterward.[40]

Payson, Arizona, held a bronc-riding event in 1884. In 1886 Albuquerque, New Mexico, had a fair and the winning steer roper received a special saddle, but the winning bronc rider garnered no special prize. In 1887 an exposition was held in Denver, Colorado, which included a "Cowboy Tournament." Local news coverage of Bill Smith's ride in the saddle bronc contest conveyed: "Up in the air and down with all four legs bunched stiff as an antelopes, and the back arched like a hostile wildcats, went the animal. But the rider was there, and deep into the rowels he sank the spurs while he lashed shoulders and neck with keen stinging quirt. It was brute force against human nerve. Nerve won. A few more jumps and the horse submitted and carried the man around the corral on a swinging rope."[29]

In Prescott, Arizona, in 1888, a committee was formed to organize a rodeo, invite cowboys, and charge spectators admission to attend. Contestants were awarded prizes. This rodeo has continued annually since that first event.

In 1897 Cheyenne Frontier Days held its first celebration on September 23. Warren Richardson, first chairman of the event, reported: "Colonel E. A. Slack, owner and editor of the Cheyenne Sun-Leader newspaper, his wife, my mother and myself were returning by train from Greeley, CO where a celebration called 'Potato Day' took place, calling attention to the farm produce grown in the area. We were discussing the idea of a fall festival for Cheyenne. Since it is not noted for agriculture Colonel Slack suggested a display of riding bucking horses, roping cattle, stage holdups and anything we could think of from the earlier days of our area. 'We shall call it Frontier Days' the Colonel announced."[10] More than

15,000 people attended the first Frontier Days, which was advertised all over the United States. Special trains accommodated visitors from afar.

Richardson reported that the wild horse race and the bucking contest were the most outstanding features of the first show: "In 1897 there were many wild horses in the Cheyenne area. Twenty or thirty miles east and northwest was open country. Stallions, closely herding their mares, sometimes met at watering holes, and fights frequently resulted which were really vicious biting affairs, the stallions rearing up on their hind legs and striking with their front feet like tigers. The horses used at the first shows had never been roped, or even herded, and the cowboys who brought a bunch of about fifty to the corral at the park had a real job."[10]

One alarming incident happened during the afternoon of this first show. The wild horses had been milling around, having become nervous and excited when some were roped by the cowboys, and finally they broke out of the corral and stampeded up the racetrack. When they were opposite the middle of the bleachers, they suddenly turned and ran straight through them. People yelled and screamed and scrambled madly about, trying to get out of their way. The bleachers were knocked down, and an opening was made by the stampeding horses for them to get through. Everyone escaped and no one was seriously hurt. Dr. Jeremiah Mieger of Toledo, Ohio, a surgeon in a state insane asylum, said, "I am used to excitement, but Cheyenne takes the cake."[10]

The names of most of the cowboys who were winners at many of these early events have become lost with the passing of time. However, a few names have been remembered, such as Will Goff and Emilnie Gardenshire, an Englishman, who won the bronc riding at Deer Trail in 1869, after riding a Hashknife Ranch bronc named Montana Blizzard. The Hashknife, Camp Stool, and Milliron ranches challenged one another to a bronc riding, and Gardenshire, with the Milliron outfit, was claimed the winner. His prize was a suit of clothes.[52]

For more than a quarter of a century, Samuel Thomas Privett was regarded as the greatest bronc rider in the world. Born on a ranch in Erath County, Texas, in 1864, he was red-headed and seemed to possess all the energy, vitality, and mischievousness often attributed to redheaded folks. By age twelve, he was known as "the redheaded kid bronc rider." At thirteen, while making his own fireworks, they backfired and he was burned very badly. A friend said, "Red sure is a booger!" From then on he was known as "Booger Red" Privett. [8]

Unlike other riders of the day who kept their eyes on their broncs, Booger rode with a careless style. He would look over his shoulder and joke with spectators while the horse bucked. His style of riding was innovative, and other riders tried to copy him.

Juan Levias won the steer roping and tied for first in the bronc riding at Prescott, Arizona, in 1888. He was awarded a wooden-mounted sterling silver-engraved shield, and his steer roping time was engraved on it. This trophy, recovered years later, by pure chance, in a scrap metal drive may have been the first trophy awarded for a rodeo event.[8]

Other early Prescott winners in saddle bronc events were

Ben Blackburn in 1891, Doc Goodwin in 1893, and Eger Jones in 1895 In 1884 E. H. Phillips rode broncs in Ellsworth, Kansas. Later he rode broncs in Buffalo Bill's Wild West shows.[7] Marion McGinty started riding broncs in 1886 and won the "Champion Bronc Rider of Texas" honor at Seymour, Texas, in 1897.[7]

Also in 1897, at Cheyenne's first Frontier Days, the World Champion Bucking and Pitching Contest was won by Bill Jones, a bronc riding cowboy that came to the area on a Texas trail drive and hired on at the Milton Green ranch at LaGrange, Wyoming. His prize was $25, but the owners of the horse he rode, Warrior, also from La Grange, received $100. Fred Bath, William Cramer and Thad Sowder, all Wyoming cowboys, won this event the following three years at Cheyenne.

Broncs that got names for themselves in the early years of bronc bustin' seldom spread their reputations beyond the area from which they came. Burgett was a stallion, owned by William Brooks of Blackland, Texas, and was ridden by Jim Woods in September 1893. Foghorn Clancy witnessed the ride and said later, "I cannot shut out the picture of the ride Jim Woods had on this great man-killing stallion, in September of 1893, as being one of the greatest rides I have ever seen."[7]

Phil Meadows, reporting on the 1900 rodeo in Douglas, Arizona, said, "Broncs were gathered from surrounding ranches, many coming from as far away as Wilcox. On a bet, Methodist Jim was ridden by a traveling horse trader named Charlie Hollingshead, a short Dutchman. He rode a slick-fork, center-fire saddle with stirrups he could just tiptoe. He rode the horse and won the bet."[11]

By the end of the nineteenth century, rodeo, still in its infant stages, was popping up around the West. It was competition *and* entertainment right off the ranches—a chance for the cowboy to test his mettle. And it always drew a crowd.

2

"WE RODE 'EM TILL THEY STOPPED BUCKIN'"

By the turn of the century, rodeo was more than an occasional event in some areas of the West. Cowboys who were bronc riders were able to prove their skill at more affairs in and around their communities. It was still rare for contestants, however, to travel very far to compete. There were two reasons for this: first, they generally were made aware of only rodeos, riding or roping contests in their own area, and second, there was always the lack of transportation.

Promoters were more inclined to take a Wild West troop across the country than they were willing to promote a rodeo. During the early days, many of the good riders spent some time as members of various Wild West companies. This allowed them to be paid regularly (if they hooked up with a show that was organized and managed well) and, additionally, gave them a chance to travel and see the country while practicing their skills. Some Wild West shows even had competitive bronc riding, as well as the usual exhibition, which afforded broncbusters an additional way of picking up extra cash.

Early Promoters

For years, Buffalo Bill Cody had a dream. He wanted to show the world glimpses of the American West. He visualized an extravagant outdoor show including horses, wagons, stagecoaches, Indians, broncbusters, cowboys, roping steers, and cowgirls—all involved in things western. On May 17, 1883,

8

he finally presented his first show in Omaha, Nebraska. It was crudely presented, and Cody was disappointed. He reorganized the production, changed financial partners, and kept reworking it until the show evolved to one that thrilled the crowds in a profitable manner to all concerned. Cody's show was one of the earliest.[12]

In 1882 the citizens of Winfield, Kansas, were having an agricultural fair and they approached Colonel George W. Miller, of the famous 101 Ranch in Oklahoma, to provide some unusual entertainment. He was just finishing a cattle drive up the Chisholm Trail and still had a group of cowboys with him. Through his ingenuity, the cowboys put on an exhibition of roping and riding events, which the citizens enjoyed immensely.[13]

Major Gordon William Lillie, who was responsible for the great land rush in Oklahoma on April 22, 1889, had proven his ability at organizing large undertakings. After traveling with Buffalo Bill's Wild West Show for a time, Major Lillie, better known as "Pawnee Bill," began a Wild West show of his own. It was known as "Pawnee Bill's Historical Wild West, Indian Museum and Encampment." Pawnee Bill was a friend of the Indian when few white men were considered as such. His show featured many Indians and much of their culture. Beginning in 1889, the show toured the eastern part of the United States and in 1894 the production expanded and set sail for Europe.[14]

Zack Mulhall, an entrepreneur from the Guthrie, Oklahoma, area, began roping and riding contests in 1899. He held his first show in St. Louis, Missouri, at a county fair. Mulhall called his organization "The Congress of Rough Riders and Ropers." Mulhall then began making a tour of county fairs in the Midwest. In 1900 he and his troupe returned to Oklahoma City when Teddy Roosevelt's Rough Riders planned a reunion and hired Zack to bring his cowboys and furnish the entertainment for the Fourth of July. Several of Mulhall's offspring, including his talented daughter Lucille, were performers.[15]

It was 1904 before the 101 Ranch Miller boys attempted a second cowboy program. Colonel Joe Miller and others from the Guthrie area were in great hopes that the 1905 National Editorial Association annual convention would be held there. Miller promised editors a big Wild West show if they chose Guthrie. In the fall of that year, a roundup—sort of a trial run—was held to see that it could be done. Everyone was pleased with the results. The following year, during the June convention, a huge roundup was held at the Miller ranch. Geronimo, the grand old Apache warrior, was there, as well as a U.S. Cavalry band, a pioneer wagon train, and many cowboys and Indians. A genuine buffalo hunt was depicted, followed by broncbusting. From 1904, the Millers held their annual roundup at the ranch in a rodeo arena considered one of the finest in the Southwest, with a seating capacity of 10,000 people.[13]

Not all Wild West shows were as large as the Buffalo Bill, Pawnee Bill, Mulhall, or Miller outfits. After spending their youth working and breaking horses, Bob and Pate Boone were given as many wild horses as they could gather. Final count totaled twenty-eight, and they trailed the horses from New Mexico to Trent, Texas, with the intention of selling them. The Boones discovered buyers were scarce, so the boys began breaking them. On Saturdays and Sundays a good-sized crowd would gather from miles around to watch them work with the wild horses in a makeshift arena. Bob laughingly told Pate that they should start their own Wild West show.

In 1906 the Boones' first Wild West show was at Merkle, Texas. The charge was twenty-five cents for spectators to watch. Two shows were held, one during the day and one at night. Using a small arena, enclosed with canvas sides, the Boones drew plenty of onlookers. From Merkle they went to Abilene and the West Texas Fair, where they held a competition bucking event. Bill Kennedy won first, Willis Barbee was second, and Rapp Green, third.[16]

Other creative cowboys followed and began their own shows. Some had large casts, with many varied events. Others were small bands of cowboys and cowgirls that traveled from one small town to the next.

"Booger Red" Privett had a small Wild West show for years that went by wagon route and played small towns and villages in Texas. He had some real buckers that often dumped the local boys who attempted to ride. When he started the show, Booger Red was older than fifty, but he did not hesitate to challenge a good local rider and would top any one of his own wild broncs.[8]

Charlie Aldridge worked his first Wild West show in 1900. It was the Johnson and Emerson Show, which toured Colorado, New Mexico, and several other western states. He then moved to the Buckskin Bill Wild West Show, and in 1906 linked up with Pawnee Bill. He went to Europe with Will Rogers, and later began a career with the Ziegfeld Follies and eventually the moving picture business.[7]

Around 1902, Sam Brownell joined the Sherwin Brothers and Baker Wild West Show. Two months later, they went broke in Lincoln, Nebraska.[18] A terrible rainstorm was their demise. Their traveling show would be short-lived. Len and Claude Sherwin notified their dad, A. G., back in Sterling, Colorado, of their dilemma. He paid off their debt and sent word, "Now get home and do something worthwhile." In 1917 Len and Claude, and partner Charlie Perkins, started putting on Fourth of July rodeos at Sterling and the local Logan County Fair, which included bronc riding and loose rope (bareback) riding. Eventually, Len and Perkins dropped out, but Claude continued to produce rodeos for another ten to fifteen years.

Meanwhile, rodeo was becoming a viable contest across the western half of the country. Denver held the Festival of the Mountains and Plains in 1901. Prizes for the winning broncs were the same as they were for the winning cowboys: first place was $150, second was $125, then $100, $75, $50 and $25 (sixth place). Thad Sowder won the cowboy's first prize of $150. A big bay mare named Peggy, owned by J. M. Kuykendall, won first-place money. After returning to the ranch and a brief rest, she was put back to work in harness pulling a buggy. Peggy strongly objected to a saddle and bucked to prove it.[23] The 1902 Festival of the Mountains and Plains official program listed sixty-four riders and eighty-nine horses. Thad Sowder, champion, won first again.

Ray Knight organized the first rodeo at Raymond, Alberta,

Cowboys with the Sherwin Brothers & Baker Wild West Show in 1903. Note Bertha Kaepernik (later Blancett) in center, an early lady bronc rider who won top prizes at Cheyenne, Pendleton, and Calgary.

— Photo courtesy of Clifford Sherwin.

Canada, on July 1, 1902. All the ranches in the district were invited to send their top bronc riders and settle the argument of which ranch had the best bronc riders. Knight trailed his wild horses to town for the celebration, called "The Stampede." Some of the cowboys competing were Delos Lund, Ray Knight, Dick Kinsey, Frank Faulkner, and Jim and Dave Austin, among many others.[71] Only two events were staged—calf roping and bronc riding. Ray Knight won the roping, and Ed Corless, from the McCarty ranch, rode his bronc to a standstill, to win. Knight provided prizes.[73]

Also in 1902, Oklahoma City held a cattle convention and included a riding and roping contest. McAlester and Muskogee, Oklahoma, had rodeos in 1903. Fort Smith, Arkansas, held a contest in 1904, and in 1905 Dublin, Texas, followed suit. Rodeos were staged in San Antonio, Texas, and Dewey, Oklahoma, in 1907 and 1908.

A handbill advertising "Big Broncho Riding Contest" announced: "Oklahoma Kid from the 101 Ranch will ride against Mr. Jesse Beemer for a prize of Fifty Dollars at Chattanooga, OK Saturday, December 25, 1909. 'Miss Pastime,' a noted outlaw from off the Pastime Ranch in Arizona, will be rode by Oklahoma Kid without bridle, without stirrups and without pulling leather, Admission 10 cents and 15 cents."[24]

In Pendleton, Oregon, in 1909, a two-day broncbusting competition was part of the Eastern Oregon District Fair. Lee "Babe" Caldwell took first place and received a $45 Hamley-McFarridge saddle. The second day C. S. Tipton, a horse-breaker from Walla Walla, won the first prize, a $50 hand-carved saddle from the E. L. Powers harness store. The bronc riding was so successful that local businessmen put their heads together, gathered finances by selling stock, and through their efforts the following year the Pendleton RoundUp began. It was to be "a frontier exhibition of picturesque pastimes, Indian and military spectacles, cowboy racing and bronco busting for the championship of the Northwest."[25]

Promoting the upcoming event was paramount, and word spread like wildfire. Lightfoot, an undersized pony "that will make somebody know he has been in a bucking contest," was to be there. The Spain brothers of Telocaset agreed to bring their bucking string. Clayton Danks from Wyoming was asked to bring his broncs Steamboat, Teddy Roosevelt, and other top buckers. It was announced that "good riders and bad horses was promised and a $250 Hamley saddle was held up as the top prize." Prize money amounted to near $2,500. Seven thousand people came the first day. Bert Kelly, of Pine Creek, became the first RoundUp bucking champion.[25]

Meanwhile, in Prescott, Arizona, the annual event that had begun in 1888 was gaining momentum. Seven bronc riders competed for $300 in prize money in 1910. John Fredericks won on a horse owned by Marion Weston. The most spectacular ride was by third-place winner Logan Morris, who had won the year before. After saddling and mounting his bronc in front of the grandstand, the animal crossed the park in a series of whirlwind pitches, and went out the gate into the street. The bronc overturned a buggy before the rider brought him under control. During the excitement a delivery wagon team ran away, scattering the contents of the wagon along the street.[27]

Smoky Snyder on Pitchfork, a Perry Henderson horse at Prescott Frontier Days.
— Bate Photo, courtesy of June and Buster Ivory.

In 1912 both Los Angeles and Calgary had rodeos. The Los Angeles competition, held March 9-25, drew more than 10,000 spectators. Guy Weadick enticed four wealthy cattlemen to finance the production at Calgary by putting up $25,000 each. Ad P. Day was the first arena director. Weadick sent Day to Cheyenne to sign up fifty top contestants, and two railway coaches crammed with American cowboys rolled into Calgary three days before the event. Three internationally famous bucking horses were present: Gaviota, Tornado, and Cyclone. Cyclone had unhorsed 127 cowboys in the past seven years. He would raise himself almost perpendicular on his hind feet until the law of gravity would cause the rider to fall off. Clem Gardner, the rider of Cyclone, came within a second or two of a qualified ride when Cyclone stopped, whipped back, and went into the air. Gardner instinctively grabbed the saddle horn, which disqualified him. Tom Three Persons rode him in the finals and won by kicking him all over the lot, and when Cyclone started his rearing tactics Tom bellowed like a bull and astonished the horse. Tom Three Persons won $1,000, a handsome saddle, and a gold belt buckle. Harry Webb and Charles McKinley came in second and third.[41]

The Calgary Stampede's September 2 opening was highly publicized across Canada, the United States, and Mexico. The $20,000 in gold offered as prize money made the trip worthwhile for contestants living a distance from Calgary. One hundred twenty thousand attended the six-day event.[26]

Headlines in the Prescott, Arizona, paper in 1914 read "Broncho Busting Feature of the Day." Day winners were chosen, and they rode in the finals. The rider placing first in the finals was given the title. After deliberating for three hours the judges chose Harry Henderson, transient resident of Prescott, as the first World's Championship Broncho Busting Contest winner. Henderson claimed $600 cash and a diamond-studded gold medal. His final ride on an outlaw named Zebo cinched the win. By 1915, interest in the Prescott show picked up across the country. Bronc riders had heard of the money payoffs and the World Championship title.[27]

The first annual Cowboys Reunion was held in Las Vegas, New Mexico, on July 1-3, 1915. Rules for the bronc riding were: "Riders will draw for mounts the night before. Marshal will appoint snub men and helpers, plus pick up men. Riders to ride slick saddle, no fork over 15" allowed. Saddle to be inspected by judges. Horse will be ridden with halter and two split reins. No knots or wraps around the hand and no locked rowel spurs. Any rider to ride any horse as many times as judge requires. Judges to decide when horse is ridden. Best average ride for three days wins. If sufficient broncs can not be procured there will be only one day of riding."[24]

By 1916, the rodeo headed east. Buffalo Bill Cody produced "The Shankive" in Chicago, but it had small purses and poor publicity.[26] Charles L. Harris produced the Passing of the West, which was held in Washington, D.C. It was to present scenes of early days in the West. Jack Miller won the bucking horse contest and Charley Williams and Bud V. Byrd split honors in amateur bucking.[11] On August 5-16 a stampede was held at Sheepshead Bay Speedway in Brooklyn, New York. Prize money totaling $500,000 was advertised. Because of a streetcar strike and a polio epidemic, the event was a financial failure. The winners in each event received only twenty-four percent of what had been promoted because the sponsor reneged on the deal due to these disasters. The saddle bronc contest was won by Emery LeGrande, second went to Rufus Rollens, and third to Lee Caldwell. The bareback event was won by Rufus Rollens, then Jack Fretz and third to Claude Ames. Tillie Baldwin won the cowgirl bucking event, second to Prairie Lilly Allen, and third, Louise Thompson.[7]

The first indoor rodeo was the Fort Worth RoundUp, produced by Lucille Mulhall and Homer Wilson and held in connection with the National Feeders and Breeders Show in the Stockyards Stadium March 12-17, 1917. A total of $2,500 was offered in prizes. The highlight was Rufus Rollens' ride on Bluejay.[11] Mulhall and Wilson also produced in San Antonio that same year a show using chutes for the bucking events, which was innovative at the time. They also used a unique publicity gimmick. Stores all over the city sold souvenir steerhead pins that entitled the wearer free admission to the roundup.[26]

Tex Austin staged a MidWinter Championship Contest in

Red Lion, a Guadalupe Garcia bronc, tries to dump his rider in 1915 at Elko, Nevada.
— Photo courtesy of June and Buster Ivory.

Red Sublett, cowboy and rodeo clown, at Logan County Fair, Sterling, Colorado, circa 1918.
— Photo by Fortner Studio, courtesy of Clifford Sherwin.

Wichita, Kansas, on January 23-26, 1918. Foghorn Clancy was the secretary. In the bronc-riding event, $500 was offered in prizes, with Bryan Roach winning first, Montana Earl, second, and Tommy Douglas, third.[7]

Dick Ringling of Ringling Brothers Circus fame had a 1919 contest in Bozeman, Montana. Their motto was "She's Wild." In 1926 Bozeman discontinued the Roundup until 1941, at which time he came back with the motto "Let's Keep Her Wild!"[7]

Leo Cremer began providing stock for a little neighborhood roundup adjacent to his ranch at Melville, Montana, in 1917. He was impressed with rodeo and the large box-office possibilities, but in those days found a lack of appeal to the general public. Audiences of those rodeos had been largely confined to immediate family, friends, neighbors, and relatives of the contestants. "Few spectators were acquainted with the contest rules of the game but the most avid fans sat through five or six hours of casually run events, often enlivened, however, by a good variety of fistic encounters when some contestants well braced with 'red-eye' would undertake to whip a judge or fellow cowboy."[7]

Early Riders (1900s-1910s)

BERT WINDSOR rode from Cody to Worland, Wyoming, to ride a "bad" horse. The entire town turned out. Bert pulled on his old bat-winged Angora chaps, saddled up, and stepped aboard. No matter how hard the horse bucked, he could not buck off Bert. The town gave him his dinner for that ride and a little "dividend." Women of the town had quilted a heavy soogan blanket, and on it they had stitched: "Bert Windsor, Champion Bronc Rider, summer of 1915, Worland, Wyoming."[11]

EVERETT M. JARMAN said he was thirteen when he first entered a rodeo. It was 1916, and the rodeo was in his hometown of Chambers, Nebraska. "I was about to mount up," he recalled, "and my mother came out of the grandstand, turned me over her knee, and with my rear exposed to the crowd, she

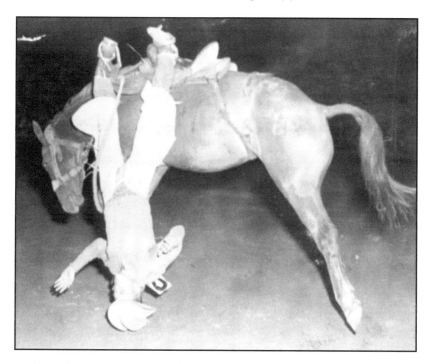

An unknown Cremer saddle bronc does his job at Nampa, Idaho.
— Courtesy of the ProRodeo Hall of Fame and Museum
of the American Cowboy. Donated by the Ivorys.

proceeded to lay it on with her purse. When she released me, I turned back and through the curious onlookers, there was my horse, Red Wing, saddled and waiting to go. I got on and she was a spinning mare. I disqualified."[11]

JOHNNY MULLENS was born in 1884 in Granbury, Texas. He worked on many large ranches and gained much experience riding and breaking broncs. His first rodeo was in Cowboy Park, Juarez, Mexico, in 1908, and he placed in the bronc riding. He joined the 101 Ranch Wild West Show that same year and rode broncs and roped steers for four seasons. Mullens realized outlaw ranch horses could be gathered at "condemned" prices and sold to producers turning a nice profit. Soon he was known as the "bucking horseman." Guy Weadick cabled for him to come to Calgary in 1912, and he was engaged to get the best livestock. For five years he was Weadick's top hand concerning the livestock.

During World War I, Mullens winded horses for inspection by allied government buyers at the stockyards in Chicago for four years. He ran the Ringling string and furnished livestock for Tex Rickards' World Series Rodeo, driving them loose down New York streets to Madison Square Garden. He rode for nearly half a century. Breezy Cox called him "the best all-around." In *Wild Bunch* magazine in 1980 a writer stated: "Johnny Mullens won't be found among champions in record books, but he was a top bronc rider and steer roper. He had too many irons in the fire to be bothered with records. He did it all— Calgary, El Paso, Madison Square Garden, Rowell and Tucson."[11]

HARRY BRENNAN (1880-1979) was born in Sheridan, Wyoming. At Ft. McKenzie in 1901, a troop of black cavalrymen was having problems with two rank horses. No one could ride them. The commanding officer offered pay to anyone who could accomplish the fete. Brennan, working for the Moncreiffe ranch nearby, completed the task and gave everyone a show as well.[20] In 1904 Brennan was the World Champion Bronc Rider at Cheyenne and had the distinction of riding the notorious Steamboat. He was called the "father of modern bronc riding" as his unique style of spurring, from the neck to the cantleboard, set the pattern for today's riders.[19]

THAD SOWDER (1874-1931) was born in Pulaski, Kentucky. His family moved to Julesburg, Colorado, where he learned to make good horses out of broncs. He was the Champion Bronc Rider at Cheyenne in 1900. He won the Festival of the Mountains and Plains contest in 1901 in Denver, and became the first World's Champion Broncho Buster. This was the first time the word "World" was used. Festival promoters gave away a cash prize and a symbolic championship belt, which, if won three times, could be kept permanently.

In 1902 Sowder won the event again on Steamboat. Sowder did not participate in 1903, as he owned a Wild West show and could not leave it to compete. Although he never won the belt three times, and the festival was eventually called off, the belt bears his name and sits on display at the Colorado State Historical Society.[19] An injury from being tossed by a bronc, at age sixteen, caused Sowder paralysis later in life. After 1905, he never rode a bronc again.[20]

MANUEL "MANNY" AIROLA (1888-1925) was born near Angels Camp, California. His family had always been horse and cattle people. His ability with horses was talked about for over fifty years after his death. Airola was considered the perfect horseman by some of the old-timers. He rode for the love of riding, but not to win prizes. He respected the broncs he rode and never feared them.

In 1914 he won the championship broncbuster's belt for Stanislaus, Calaveras, Mariposa, and Puolumne counties. It was his way of riding that impressed the elders, and they explained: "He would come bursting out of the chute on a wild-eyed, bawling, sunfishing, end-swapping bronc, raking its ribs with woolly-chapped legs, his high-crowned Stetson jammed down on his head, and waving a full bottle of strawberry soda for the crowd to see. Then while the horse bucked, squalled, rattled leather, and shook himself, Manny would drain the bottle at a single pull and never spill a drop."[17] It was not a show-off stunt but his way of demonstrating his mastery over the horse.

SAM BROWNELL (1887-1975) was born in Syracuse, Nebraska. His dad, a bullwhacker, carried freight from Omaha to Fort Fetterman, Wyoming. Sam grew up in Sterling, Colorado. At eight years of age he had a bucking burro; at age sixteen he joined a Wild West show. He won his first bronc-riding contest in Rawlins, Wyoming, in 1903.[18]

From 1904 until 1917, Sam Brownell competed at Cheyenne Frontier Days in the bronc riding and scored from second to sixth every year. But in 1917 he became World Champion Saddle Bronc Rider at Cheyenne. He later moved to Belle Fourche, South Dakota, and set up bucking contests with C. H. Wilson, owner of the famous bucker, Tipperary. Few people ever succeeded in riding Tipperary. Wilson and Brownell also furnished stock for rodeos, including the Tri-State RoundUp at Belle Fourche. Later, Brownell was a rodeo judge, arena director, worked in the movies, and became a brand inspector. He was best known for being one of the best bronc riders of his day. His tangle with Tipperary at Belle Fourche in 1918 was considered one of the hardest fought battles in any arena between man and beast.[18]

CHARLIE ALDRIDGE (1875-1951) was born on a ranch near Colorado Springs, Colorado. His first job away from home was on the TUT spread as a horse wrangler. Later, at the Diamond Tail Ranch, he developed into a great bronc rider. His first contest was in 1902, at Denver, and he played all the big ones. After a lengthy stint with various Wild West shows, he toured South America, Europe, and Africa with various troupes. He rode many bucking horses on theater stages in vaudeville, and on one occasion he suffered a broken leg when his bronc fell into the orchestra pit from the stage.[7]

CLAYTON DANKS (1879-1970) was born in O'Neill, Nebraska, and spent his young years herding cattle and breaking horses. He moved to Wyoming in 1896, but did not rodeo until 1903. The mighty bucking horse Steamboat and Danks crossed paths off and on throughout their careers. In 1903 a match between Guy Holt and Danks was held during the Albany County Fair in Laramie. The local newspaper reported: "Danks got firmly in the saddle before Steamboat was released from his blindfold. The outlaw took a good look around before commencing proceedings, then up went his back into an arch like an angry cat, his tail went between his hind legs and his head between his front legs and he was ready to begin . . . . Danks sat up straight, swung with the motion of the horse and rode splendidly. Only once, when Steamboat gave an extra sharp twisting buck at the rails, did he appear in any danger of coming off, but he righted himself quickly. Danks rode with his hands down and a strong grip on the hackamore rope, this made some people think that he was 'pulling leather' but he never touched the saddle with his hands."[20]

In a *Frontier Times* magazine article in 1962, Danks said in his opinion that Steamboat was the hardest bucker of all time. There were other buckers that did more fancy pitching, but Steamboat just kept his head down and fought. "When he gives one of those peculiar twisting jumps and comes down stiff-legged the man is rocked something painful. I had my head snapped back until I thought it was going to come off, and I felt as if my lungs were going to burst when I had ridden that horse a few jumps," said Danks.[20]

Danks won the World Champion Bronc Rider title in Denver in 1904, and two World Champion Saddle Bronc titles at Cheyenne, in 1907 and 1909. He rode many broncs, but he said Steamboat must be credited with putting lots of gold in his pockets. "When Steamboat's day was over, I think a part of rodeo ended for me, too," lamented Danks. "I missed that black beneath me the way you miss a pardner who has grub-staked you for years."[20]

Early Broncs (1900s-1910s)

Whether at a rodeo, a Wild West show, or on a ranch, a bronc is a bronc. The true spirit of the bronc was described in a 1913 issue of *Miller Brothers & Arlington Ranch Real Wild West Magazine and Daily Review*:

> In the performance of the "bucking" bronchos and their cowboy riders, it will be noticed that, among the quadrupedal concentrations of chain lightning, no two resort to the same tactics of defense. One will not permit him to be saddled and mounted before letting out the pent-up deviltry with which his hide is stuffed. Another will quietly submit to being saddled, but that is his limit to sufferance. To still another the very sight of a saddle is a signal of war. This one will start humping his back like a mad cat, and landing stiffly on all fours with the force of a pile driver. That one will lie down and stubbornly refuse to budge. Still another will rear and fall backwards with such reckless fury as to sometimes beat out his brains. A fourth will kick, strike or bite, or all this and more with savage viciousness rendering him more dangerous to a tyro than would be a hungry lion.[11]

STEAMBOAT, born in 1896 on the Foss Ranch near Chugwater, Wyoming, was sold to the Swan Land and Cattle Company in 1899. When Jimmy Danks, a Swan cowboy, and some other hands were castrating the new horses, Steamboat sustained an injury to his nose. A bone was seen in his nostril, and foreman Sam Moore cut it out. From then on, when the horse bucked he made a distinctive whistling sound—and was named "Steamboat" because of it. Unbreakable by cowboys on the ranch, he was sold to John Coble, who came looking for bucking horses in 1901. Although Steamboat was a good bucker, he was easy to handle.

His rodeo debut was October 1901, at the Festival of Mountains and Plains in Denver. Tom Minor of Idaho rode him, as did Thad Sowder. His reputation of being a good bucker spread quickly, and the following year he was at Cheyenne Frontier Days. It was known a cowboy could win a contest if he drew Steamboat and could stay aboard. For at least eight years he was considered the top bucker. Old-time cowboys agree that the peak of his career was around 1907. Cheyenne Frontier Days named him the "Worst Bucking Horse of the Year" in 1907 and 1908. His career spanned fourteen years, but the end was not good.

The Irwin Brothers Wild West Show was appearing in Salt Lake City in October 1914, and Steamboat was there. During a thunderstorm he got wire cut, and when the broncs arrived back in Cheyenne it was discovered that blood poisoning had set in. A veterinarian declared there was no way to save him, and he was put down. The National Cowboy Hall of Fame dedicated a bronze plaque commemorating Steamboat on the Hall of Fame's Roll of Great Bucking Horses December 14, 1975. [20]

COYOTE was broken by Dave Sharon in about 1915 at the Simon-Newman ranch in California. However, when he was hit accidentally by a cowboy opening a gate, he pitched his rider and forgot everything he had been taught. Jack Millerick purchased him and Coyote soon became known as the world's fastest spinning horse. Coyote was gentle to handle, but he would throw a rider fifteen feet. He was always bucked as a saddle bronc horse. Phil Stadler finally rode him in San Jose, California, July 1917. It is said he went nine years without being successfully ridden. Eddie McCarty bought Coyote in 1920 for an unheard of amount at that time— around $1,500 or $2,000.[11]

BLUEJAY, owned by E. A. Scott of Anson, Texas, was a dapple, bluish gray horse that did not look like a bucking horse. He made his owner plenty of money, and rumor had it that he went unridden for quite some time. Homer Wilson and Lucille Mulhall were producing the rodeo at Fort Worth in 1917, and made a contract with Mr. Scott to bring BlueJay to the rodeo as a feature. Wilson was to pick three riders; if the horse bucked off all three, Scott would receive $500. Wilson picked Rufus Rollens, Leonard Stroud, and Bugger Red, Jr. (Laird). Rollens was first up, and with his typical confidence and ability he poured the steel to the bucker once he was in the saddle. Rollens mastered the entire ride, but it was a ride that lived long in the memory of those who witnessed it.[28]

NO NAME *a.k.a.* FOX *a.k.a.* I DON'T KNOW *a.k.a.* RESERVATION was foaled on the H2 Ranch near Medicine Hat, Saskatchewan, in 1901. By 1908, the big sorrel gelding already had a reputation. He came out of Canada with a bucking string owned by Ray Knight and Ad P. Day. They changed his name to I Don't Know. In 1917, at Medicine Hat, the winner of the first day money had to ride him to qualify for the finals. Yakima Canutt won the day money and rode him. In the finals he drew him again, lost a stirrup, and was disqualified. Pendleton RoundUp scouts bought him for $1,100 in 1919, when he was eighteen years old. They changed his name to No Name. Earlier at Calgary, Canutt had been thrown by him, but he drew No Name and rode him to win. In 1926 No Name was retired. He died the following year and was buried along the Columbia River.[11]

PRISON BARS was foaled on the prison farm at Deer Lodge, Montana, in 1906. He made his debut bucking at four years old at Calgary, Pendleton, Couer d'Alene, and Madison Square Garden. He was easy enough to handle up to the time

the chute boys tightened up the flanking strap. Then he started to fight. Like a mountain cat coming out of a cave, he
would clear the chutes with one tremendous jump. Then he
would jolt down on those big hoofs with his head about a foot
from the ground. He held his head low all during the ride,
bawling like a range bull on the prod. He could buck twelve
times in ten seconds, but after the rider was off he was easy
to handle.

Leo Cremer took him out of the rough string for a while
and put him in amateur rodeos. After two years no one had
made a qualified ride, so Cremer put him back with the pros.
Howard Tegland rode him at Bozeman RoundUp. Prison Bars
was dirty white mixed with gray, fifteen hands high and 1,150
pounds. On November 9, 1940, he gave his last buck at Baton
Rouge, Louisiana, and he retired to Montana.[7]

BELLINGHAM BLACK was described by the 1984 National
Cowboy Hall of Fame Trustee Award recipient Harry Webb:
"Toughest, most dangerous horse I ever rode was the
Bellingham Black. I was working for Colonel Wild Bill Cody
when he purchased this outlaw in 1910. Frank Maish and I
were the only ones called on to ride him after he put Indian Dick
in the hospital. 'The Black' would have his head back in your
lap, run like a scared ape, then leap to the right or the left ten
feet. He often landed on the saddle, feet to the sky—hard to set
even if you didn't get killed. One time when it was Scout's turn
'The Black' landed with his neck doubled under him. That finished 'The Black' and we went out and celebrated."[35]

FLAXIE was owned by "Booger Red" Privett. Foghorn
Clancy said, "I remember the great ride Hugh Strickland made
on her in 1912 at the Texas Corn Carnival in Dallas."[7]

3

Origins of Chutes, Saddles, Bareback, and Cowgirls

The saddle bronc event in rodeo depicts what working cowboys did to break mounts in their daily work. An early saddle bronc contestant often brought his own "outlaw" to a rodeo to ride, or broncs were gathered from nearby ranches. Some riders exchanged "outlaws" and rode one another's broncs. Many variations of this scenario took place at rodeos.

The cayuse was snubbed in the middle of the area used as the arena, and helpers aided the rider by holding the bronc, blindfolding him, and often biting or twisting his ear to distract him from realizing that a saddle was carefully being placed on his back. Once the rider tightened the cinch to his satisfaction, he climbed in the saddle. The helpers took off the blindfold, let go, and then all hell broke loose! The horse exploded, and whether the rider stayed aboard remained to be seen. To win the competition the rider had to ride the bronc to a standstill, then, additionally, be judged to have had the most spectacular ride and the best bucker.

The Rules

Appointed judges determined who rode the best. This was generally based on the horse's ability to try to throw his rider, and the rider's ability to stick with the bronc in spite of his gyrations and fury. On occasion some judges did not agree as to which rider was the best. A prize was generally given to the best rider, and the owner of the best bucker was also awarded

27

a prize. At some contests bucking off eliminated the competitors, until a select few were left. Then they would compete again for the finals. The best rider of the finals was the overall winner. Eventually, it was recommended that the winner be chosen on an average of all his rides during a rodeo. As rodeo was evolving, winners were determined in a variety of ways from rodeo to rodeo, with little consistency.

At the 1898 Cheyenne Frontier Days, rules forbade the hobbling of stirrups. By 1901, the Cheyenne ruling required that the horse be spurred, and if a thrown rider wanted to remount, he could get back on and ride again. Year by year rules began to be more defined. In 1905 the winner was based on an average of all his rides at that rodeo.

In 1909, at Cheyenne, the names of all horses were placed in a hat and riders drew for their mounts. In 1915 riders were required to use a slick saddle with no more than a fifteen-inch swell and were required to wear spurs and chaps. [30] Also that year, C. B. Irwin and Harry Brennan teamed up and set some rules, representing the cowboys. They met with the Humane Society and the Frontier committee, resulting in "The Cheyenne Rules."[50]

Pendleton RoundUp competitor Hoot Gibson remarked years later about a 1912 event: "There was no time limit on the ride. When we got on a bronc we just stayed there until he quit bucking or we ran out of wind. Those horses kept it up for 40 seconds some times." Gibson thought the rules gave all the breaks to the bronc. "You must spur the horse with both feet; one hand must hold the reins, the other must be held in the air. A change in this position, or what is called 'pulling leather' instantly disqualified the rider."[25]

At the earliest rodeos in Prescott, riders brought their own mounts. By 1913, the rules were that three judges would be picked and riders had to ride a slick saddle with no more than a fifteen-inch form, and they could not ride without spurs or reins. A rider could ride with one or two reins, but if two reins were used they could not be fastened at the loose ends. Riders were not allowed to change hands or reins. Disqualification came from pulling leather, changing hands or reins, wrapping the reins around the hand, or being bucked off. A rider could

*Bart Clennon, known by many as a "cowboy's cowboy," handling Lee Rider at
Great Falls, Montana.*
— R. R. Doubleday photo, donated by June and Buster Ivory.
Courtesy of the National Cowboy Hall of Fame.

Ed McCarty, in 1919, on Done Gone wins championship at Cheyenne.
— Photo by R. R. Doubleday, donated by June and Buster Ivory.
Courtesy of the National Cowboy Hall of Fame.

ride without stirrups if he announced his intention to do so before the ride, and a rider could not fight his horse.[27]

In Prescott, Arizona, around 1920, saddle bronc riders began to be timed to fifteen-second rides.[27] Verne Elliott was quoted as saying, "People at Fort Worth had an indoor rodeo in 1917. Ed McCarty and I thought the Texans were crazy when they announced their intentions. They wanted Ed and I to come down and help them and I strung along as a judge. The engineers' idea was to have an indoor show, put bucking horses in chutes. The buckers up to that time had always been blindfolded and snubbed up to other horses out in the open. But the engineer built his chutes, and when the cowboys saw what they were they called them 'chambers of horror'."[42]

Yakima Canutt reminisced about the changes in rodeo: "At first we rode with two reins and there was no timing in bronc riding. In 1914 we began riding with one rein. My first ride with timing was in 1920 or 1921 at El Paso in the Tex Austin show, which I won. As I remember the timing was 10 seconds, starting when the horse cleared the chutes."[48]

There was a continual search for reliable bucking horses. The requirement to ride a horse until it ceased to buck sometimes took one minute, maybe fifteen. Horses that unseated their riders had a determination to dislodge every rider thereafter. However, when a bucker was ridden to submission, he got the idea he was being taught to accommodate himself to the man on his back. Some learned the lesson quickly, some didn't. But when they lost the urge to buck, their use in rodeo ended. One year's star performer may not buck the next year.

In 1927, in Calgary, the length of a qualified ride was cut to ten seconds and a new system of grading the performance of the horse and the rider was adopted. It not only allowed the show to run quicker but cut down the number of mounts required. An outstanding bucker seldom had its spirit broken in ten seconds, and the Stampede was able to buy the outstanding performers and assemble its own herd of bucking stock. Permanent chutes, catching pens, and corrals were constructed in the infield for the rodeo events in 1928.[39]

Consensus determined that as rodeo rules changed and

facilities improved, each contest ran more efficiently. The rodeo was not as lengthy, timewise. Instead of saddling horses in the open and thereby wasting much of the horses' strength before the riders got aboard, they began saddling broncs in chutes. Nine or ten seconds on a fresh bronc that has been "poured out" of a chute is equal to a finish ride on a bronc that has been saddled in the open.[31]

The Chutes

Through the first decade of the twentieth century the bucking bronc carried the "buster" across the contest arena until he fell off or the bronc stopped bucking. When the chute was developed and a time limit was placed on the bucking event, the event became more appealing to the spectator.[29] It has been

Not even out of the bucking chute at Camdenton, Missouri, and Jesse James, the Hoss Inman bronc, has already exploded. Inman bought this wild bronc from the E. C. Roberts rodeo string. He was the 1961 Bucking Horse of the Year.
                                    — Photo courtesy of June and Buster Ivory.

reported that in 1916 the first known side-delivery rodeo chute was designed and constructed at Welling, Alberta, Canada. Such a chute was built at New Dayton, Alberta, in 1917, and another in 1919 at Lethbridge, Alberta. The side delivery chute was redesigned by reversing the chute gate so that it hinged at the horse's head, forcing the horse to turn as the gate opened. The new design required only one man to work the chute gate and eliminated the hazard of riders' knees getting hung up. This chute design is standard today.

At the Cattleman's Carnival in Garden City, Kansas, around 1918, two fadeaway chutes were built. They were made out of two gates long enough to hold a horse, one gate on each side with about a three-and-a-half-foot gate across the front and a drop gate behind the horse. The side gates had drag pipes that rammed into the ground to hold the gate in line. Three men were needed to operate them.[51] At Cheyenne Frontier Days in 1919, front delivery or "head on" chutes were designed and used. In 1928 these were changed to side delivery chutes. Eight were built parallel to the arena and eight broncs could be loaded at one time to make the performance run more efficiently. Fort Worth also switched to the side delivery chute in 1927, and four were built, allowing the event to run faster. Fort Worth credits Verne Elliott with the development of this new type of chute.[43]

The Saddles

Before saddles were adapted to bronc riding, all saddles were "A" forks, so many of the cowboys started folding their slickers and tying them across the front of their saddle seats just behind the horn with the leather strings (latigos) found on all saddles in those days. The extra padding gave the rider a little support, and something to grip with his knees. Some saddle makers eventually came out with what were called "saddle rolls." These had padded bulges that buckled on the front end of the saddletree for knee support. All this led up to the building of swelled fork saddle trees that were used by bronc riders.[51] In 1915 Fay Ward invented the Fay Ward Bronc Riding

Tree, a saddle with a concave cantleboard, designed to make bronc riding a little easier; it was finally adapted by a saddle manufacturer and was used extensively.[7]

Saddle bronc cowboys had ridden just about any kind of saddle they had available in the event. Many had been riding old high-forked, high-cantled freak trees for some time, and were in the habit of humping over the front of their saddle. "The old freak trees were something to see," reported Gene Pruett in a 1968 *Hoofs and Horns* issue. "They were set about 4" higher in front than the saddle that eventually became the chosen saddle for saddle bronc riding. They were cut away under the swells, and you could spur clear over a horse's neck. They had a 6" cantle, and were almost a centerfire rig. Some were only 12" long and it looked like once a rider got set down in one a horse would have to turn a complete flip to get the rider out of it."[7]

Following the 1919 Pendleton RoundUp, representatives of that event, along with leaders of Cheyenne Frontier Days, the Boise, Idaho, rodeo, and the Walla Walla, Washington, rodeo went to a saddlemaker, Hamley and Company, in Pendleton, and after a discussion the combined group unanimously adopted what they termed a "committee" saddle. The standardization of a bucking contest saddle was thought to be one way of assuring more equality between riders. The committee, representing the four rodeos, ordered Hamley-designed saddles, meeting uniform specifications. Saddles were provided for the contestants in the saddle bronc competition at some rodeos during this period.

The saddle was made with round skirts, three-quarter single "E-Z" rigging (a 1915 Hamley patent), and had a flank rigging set farther back than the rear dee ring of a regular double-rigged saddle. This saddle was later designated the "association saddle." The original committee saddle had a straight-up five-inch cantle and a fourteen-inch swell fork, but this five-inch cantle had been made "laid back" to about four and a quarter inches. The fork, in almost every respect, has remained identical to the original form of the 1919 committee saddle. The modified "Ellensburg" tree was adopted as the official bronc riding saddle.[44] Eventually, Boise and Walla Walla discontinued shared possession of the saddles.

Cheyenne ordered their own, and the original six were used solely by Pendleton. Hundreds of copies were used all over the United States and Canada.[7]

Prior to the uniform saddle, cowboys were required to "spur high in the shoulders" the first jump, then "high behind the cinch" the rest of the way. They tried to ride the new committee saddle the same way. Some gave up and quit; others struggled along until they began to catch on to the new style. It became clear it was best to sit almost straight up in the saddle and take the rein longer. Riders began to spur the broncs in the neck or shoulders all the way instead of from the cinch back. They probably used a foot more rein than the old-timers did. The old way of riding, however, continued until the mid-1930s before the old "hump over the front and spur back style" began to fade out.[7]

In 1928 at Madison Square Garden, Bob Askin, Howard Tegland, Perry Ivory and Earl Thode, winners of the bronc rid-

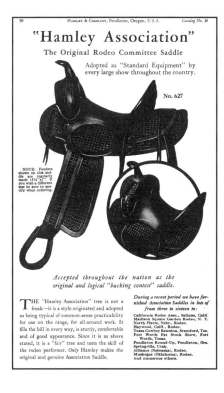

In 1919 Pendleton RoundUp respresentatives from Pendleton RoundUp, Cheyenne Frontier Days, the rodeo at Boise, Idaho, and Walla Walla, Washington, went to the local saddlemaker, Hamley and Company, and adopted the first standardized saddle for more equal competitions. They ordered six to be shared by the four rodeos. It was called "the committee (and later the association) saddle."

— 1936 Catalog donated by Jack Long. Courtesy of Dave Hamley.

ing that year, rejected the Shipley saddles provided by the Garden rodeo management and insisted on substituting Hamley association saddles. They won their point.[11]

According to Charley Beals, saddlemaker for over fifty years, as well as a roughstock competitor in his early years, a variety of saddlemakers made copies of the original Hamley association saddle. The Denver Dry Goods made a Powder River saddle that was considered the Turtles association saddle and bore the Cowboy Turtle stamp. Their model had a lower front and set lower on the horse. Burel Mulkey and Ed Curtis were thought to have assisted in the design. Casey Tibbs and Gerald Roberts, both champion saddle bronc riders, used the Turtle association saddle. Duff Severe apprenticed at the Hamley Saddle Shop on the GI Bill for nine years, then opened his own saddlery. Beals' grandson, Derek Clark, started competing in the saddle bronc event in the 1970s and used a Hamley saddle. Earl Bascom made a hornless bronc saddle in 1922. It was called the "Mulee" and was first used at the Cardston, Alberta, Stampede.[45]

Bareback Riding

Bareback bronc riding was enjoyed by daredevil cowboys out on the range. It, no doubt, entertained cowboys on ranches when a young range horse, held down for branding, was straddled by a daring cowboy who grasped a handful of mane in each hand before he was let up. Pushing with the front hand and pulling with the back hand would allow the "buster" to keep his balance pretty well.[45]

Bareback riding as a rodeo event came belatedly to most rodeo arenas, except at Calgary, where the very first Stampede held a bareback riding event in 1912. Prescott added the event in 1914, Fort Worth in 1927, and Sidney, Iowa, joined the ranks in 1929. Burwell, Nebraska, added it to the list of events in 1931. Although Cheyenne Frontier Days had bareback riding as an exhibition ride in 1920 and 1921, bareback riding was not a full-fledged Cheyenne Frontier Days event, with prizes, until 1936. In 1938 the rules at Cheyenne stated: "Surcingles will be selected and furnished by the management. No contestant will be allowed to use any other surcingles." Today cowboys own their own riggings. The Pendleton RoundUp did not include bareback riding as an event until 1948.

Charley Beals made the surcingles used by most bareback riding contestants from 1946 through 1973. In fact, about ninety percent of the bareback champions used his rigging. An advertisement in the *Rodeo Sports News* described his work: "The Rigging the Champions Use, Get the Best by Charley Beals: Double Rawhide Handhold, Rigging Body has Three Thicknesses of Leather. Can make Left, Straight, Right-Handed, or Make Handhold to Your Specifications."[52]

Around 1920, some rodeos added bareback riding; however, the winner received only half the amount of the prize that the saddle bronc winners were awarded. Sometimes, the same cowboys who exploded from the chutes on the rolling deck of a saddle bronc rode bareback as well. More often than not, however, the bareback rider performed only as a bareback rider.

The "manehold" gave way to riding with loose ropes, usually a manila rope with a honda in one end, cinched around the horse's girth, laid across both hands, one on each side of the horse's withers. The rope was tightened by the chute man and laid back across the rider's hands again. No wrap was allowed, and the rider had to grip hard, to keep it from slipping. As the event developed, the leather surcingle, a two handhold rigging, became standard bareback equipment. There was no standard size, make, or style. Different rodeo committees determined various types.[45]

A bronc without a saddle stacks all the cards against the rider. The difficulty of riding with only a surcingle provides the added thrill in the bareback event. The rider is entirely dependent on manpower as a means to conquer the wild gyrations of a cunning and shrewd animal. There are no reins and no stirrups. Horses are seldom used in bareback and saddle bronc events at the same time.

In 1934 Johnnie Schneider wrote the following account of bareback riding for the *Popular Science Monthly* magazine: "Although no points toward the national championship are awarded for riding the wild broncs bareback, this is always a thriller. We straddle a bony back in the chute, grab a half-inch rope passed lasso-like around the bronco's body and hang on with one hand. Since the wild horses are ridden without halters they have a free head to toss around as they like. As soon as they stop bucking, which usually comes at the end of ten seconds, when we quit spurring, they break into a run."[49]

The bareback event requires good balance; horses are often smaller and quicker, and without restrictions of the saddle they are freer to jump or spin or kick. The winner can often be determined by not only the rider who "keeps his balance" but who also spurs the hardest. This event also requires the rider to have his spurs over the break of the shoulders and spurring the horse when his feet hit the ground the first jump out of the chute.

Full recognition of bareback riding as one of the five major rodeo events did not occur until 1932.

The bareback horse Don't Wait, of Lester Hinds, and an unknown rider show some real acrobatics.

— Photo courtesy of June and Buster Ivory.

Women Broncbusters

Women have been a part of rodeo almost since the beginning. Lady bronc riders were documented as early as the 1880s. They were rare, and they were unique. Mary Lou LeCompte reported in her book *Cowgirls of the Rodeo* that in the 1880s sixteen women were documented as participants in rodeo or Wild West shows, including Annie Shaffer and Lulu Belle Parr. However, not all were bronc riders. Lucille Mulhall, in 1900, along with other family members, was part of her father's Wild West entourage. Will Rogers, a young trick-roping peer, has been credited with originating the title "Cowgirl" in his reference to Mulhall, but she did more roping and bull-dogging than bronc riding.[15]

In 1904 Bertha Kaepernik rode a horse from Sterling, Colorado, to Cheyenne, and put on an amazing bucking bronc exhibition. Due to her quickness to perform and her ability she has always been recognized as the woman who set the example at Cheyenne Frontier Days in broncbusting. In competition for Ladies Saddle Bronc Riding, Mrs. A. C. Clayton won in 1906 and Esther Pawson in 1907. In 1914 ladies bronc riding had a purse of $300 for first, $250 for second. The saddle bronc rules were the same as for the cowboys, except for a sixteen-inch fork and the option of riding with hobbled stirrups was allowed.[30]

At the Pendleton RoundUp, the World Championship Cowgirls Bucking Contest began in 1913. First place won $200 and a sterling silver Loving Cup valued at $75. Second place won $100. Riders drew for mounts and rode as often as judges deemed necessary to choose a winner. Riding was done with plain halter, split reins, all riding slick, no saddle forks over fifteen inches to be used. Nettie Hawn won the first year. Bertha Kaepernik Blancett won in 1914.

The Calgary Stampede had events for women at their first program. In 1916 several rodeos and events comparable were presented in New York and other eastern locations. Women bronc riders were held in much awe and fascination. Some of the other cowgirls of the times were Prairie Rose Henderson, Tillie Baldwin, and Fannie Sperry Steele. By the 1920s, some cowgirls and cowboys had earned an income well above the average salary of the times.

In 1917 Mrs. Ed Wright won the Championship Lady Bronc Riding at Cheyenne. Just weeks later, she was killed during a bronc ride in Denver. Bonnie McCarroll, a thirty-two-year-old lady bronc rider, lost her life in 1929 while riding a bronc during the Pendleton RoundUp. She was thrown to the ground and drug around the arena. The cowgirl bucking events were discontinued at Pendleton that year. Cheyenne had already discontinued their cowgirl bucking events the year before, and gradually rodeos across the country followed suit. As rodeo evolved and became more organized it seemed the cowboy and cowgirl competitions split further apart.

4

RODEOS INTO THE 1920S

The 1920s saw many additional rodeos cropping up across the West. Many continue today: Burwell, Nebraska; Grover, Colorado; Red Bluff and Hayward, California, just to name a few.

In 1921 Harry Rowell held a rodeo in Hayward on the athletic field of the Burbank School. In 1925 he moved the rodeo to his ranch in Dublin Canyon. This rodeo still continues and through the years has been recognized as one of the best in the area. Rowell had good stock and produced and promoted rodeos for other communities as well.[38]

Tucked away in the northern plains of Colorado lies Grover, a small community, sixty miles from Cheyenne and the same distance from Fort Collins, Colorado. One must still travel part of the way by dirt road to reach this town today. A rodeo was added to the Grover Community Fair in 1922, and it has been known as the "Biggest Little Rodeo in the West" ever since. Glen Snyder won the first bronc riding, and again in 1923. His winnings were $20 the first year and $25 the next. Bucking horses belonged to local residents, and $15 was paid to the owner of the best bucking horse.

Earl Anderson began producing the Grover Rodeo in 1929. He was well known for his bucking stock—Tar Baby, Andy Gump, and Cheyenne and Two-Row. Two-Row was named such, because he was accustomed to pulling a two-row cultivator in the field when he was not being used for bucking. Years that the annual event showed a negative balance Anderson was known to dip into his own pockets to keep it

Don Brownell, on an Earl Anderson horse, Andy Gump, at Greeley, Colorado.

— Photo courtesy of Clifford Sherwin.

going. Anderson also produced the Greeley Rodeo from 1930 through 1960. The Grover Rodeo was eventually renamed the Earl Anderson Memorial Rodeo.[64]

In 1918 a cattlemen's get-together was held on the A. H. Clough ranch east of Los Molinas, California. In 1921 thirty businessmen and ranchers from Vina, Chico, and Red Bluff formed the Northern California RoundUp Association and held a rodeo the last of April. In October of that year the same men decided to hold a rodeo during the County Fair. The Millerick Brothers shipped in three railroad cars of stock—forty bulls, thirty-five wild steers, and ten wild mules. Seventeen events were scheduled. The last day, more than 7,000 spectators watched the event.

Norman Cowan won first in saddle bronc riding and took home a $400 saddle; Shorty Davis won second. The entrance fee was $10. In 1922 the rodeo was held again, but not as part of the fair. Little Jeff was the best bucking horse. Happy Jack Hawn owned him, and he bucked off seven contestants including Norman Cowan. Perry Ivory won the $400, plus a belt.[67]

Homer C. Stokes conceived the first Burwell, Nebraska,

Caught in midair, Blackie Moore bucks off Lee Case's Zebra at Burwell, Nebraska, in 1940.
— Photo courtesy of June and Buster Ivory.

rodeo in 1921. Local business firms donated $25 and the local affair was held in a stubblefield on the John Shultz farm east of Burwell. Steel posts and poultry netting enclosed the racetrack. Two wagonloads of bridge timbers piled against a straw pile made a grandstand for 200 spectators. It was known as the Garfield County Frontier Fair and Rodeo until 1925. Area ranchers and farmers furnished livestock. In 1921 Buck Kraus won $25 in cash and a pair of spurs for winning the bronc riding. Tracy Shafer won second.[68]

Broncbusters of the Era (1910s-1920s)

HUGH STRICKLAND (1888-1941) was born on his father's horse ranch in Idaho. He began working with wild horses at a very young age. In 1916 he won the bronc riding at Cheyenne Frontier Days, and repeated this win in 1920. He also won at Pendleton in 1918 and 1921. His wife, Mabel DeLong Strickland, was also a bronc rider, roped steers, and competed in relay races. She won the Denver Post Ladies

Relay Race in Cheyenne in 1922 and 1923. They made quite a pair.[19]

For nearly a decade, Hugh Strickland did well in the competition, then broke his leg at Monte Vista, Colorado, after winning second in the bronc riding. It did not heal properly, and a second break to the same leg a year later ended his bronc riding career. Phil Meadows once asked Strickland which horse was the toughest he ever rode and his answer was Flaxie, "Booger Red" Privett's horse, in Texas. Strickland died suddenly of a heart attack in Burbank, California.[7]

JACKSON SUNDOWN (1863-1922), a member of the Nez Perce tribe, was born in Montana while his father was on a horse-stealing raid in the Flathead country. His family joined Chief Joseph's historic retreat from Oregon to Montana in 1877; however, they escaped into Canada. The family returned to Washington eventually and lived on the Flathead Indian Reservation, where he competed in his first rodeo.

He participated in many rodeos in Montana, Idaho and the Northwest, winning enough to make a respectable name for himself. Pendleton RoundUp was a rodeo he never missed. In 1911 Sundown, along with George Fletcher, a black cowboy, and John Spain, was in the bucking finals at the RoundUp. Sundown ended up being carried out on a stretcher. But in 1916 he won the bucking championship and the all-around at Pendleton. He wore two long braids tied under his chin and shaggy orange chaps, and he was fifty-three years old! It is said he had to ride several broncs to prove he was truly the winner. Pendleton RoundUp had never had a Native American winner before. Sundown was a colorful rider and always waved his hat in his free hand when he rode.[21]

YAKIMA CANUTT (1895-1986) was born Enos Edward Canutt in Colfax, Washington. At eleven he rode his first bucking horse, and in 1911, at sixteen, he won the five-day Colfax County Fair bronc riding. The title "Yakima" from a mix-up when he followed three bronc riders, attempting to uphold their hometown of Yakima, at Pendleton in 1914. The announcer surmised he was from Yakima, as well, and called him that, and it stuck. He won the Pendleton RoundUp All-Around in 1917, 1919, 1920, and 1923. He also won the first leg of the Roosevelt Trophy, which was awarded for having the most points at Pendleton and Cheyenne.

Canutt later went into silent movies in 1923 and completed over forty westerns. He doubled for western movie stars, such as John Wayne, and was a stunt man. Later he became an action director and is best known for his direction of the chariot spills and thrills in the *Ben Hur* epic.[48]

RUFUS ROLLENS (1891-1972) was born in Claremore, Oklahoma. Rollens was a Wild West performer early in life. In 1913 he won the World Champion Bronc Riding in Calgary, and in 1915 he won it in Miles City, Montana. On June 30, 1916, at Camp Cook, South Dakota, Rollens rode Tipperary, an exhibition bucker. The bronc cut his left front foot during the night. He was sore and lame when they brought him out, but the cut was not discovered until later. This cut would bother him the rest of his life and had to be protected with a specially made horseshoe. Rollens rode the horse, but it was said he didn't have half the horse the rider Shorty Davis had the day before.[22]

In 1916, at Guy Weadick's New York Stampede held at Sheepshead Bay Speedway, Rollens won second in saddle broncs and first on bareback. Tough buckers he rode included B. A. Scott's BlueJay at Fort Worth, and Long Tom and Angel at Pendleton. Later Rollens was involved in a bank robbery, was shot in the leg, and subsequently went to prison. When he was released, he formed his own Wild West show.

THURKEL JAMES "TURK" GREENOUGH (1905-1995) was born in Red Lodge, Montana, to "Packsaddle" Ben and Myrtle Greenough. One of eight children, he and brother Bill and sisters Alice and Margie became known as "The Riding Greenoughs." They all rode broncs and won many contests.

Turk cowboyed on ranches in Montana and Wyoming. He traveled with the Miller Brothers 101 Wild West Show and Cherokee Hammond's Wild West Show. Turk was a natural saddle bronc rider, and few people ever saw him buck off. He

From left: Old-timers Sylvester Roan, Marge Greenough Henson, Turk Greenough, Alice Greenough Orr and Hippy Burmeister, at National Finals Rodeo in 1977. All were outstanding in their events.

— Photo by Bern Gregory.

was once quoted as saying that rodeo was ideal for him because he never liked to get up early, as ranch cowboys were required to do.

Turk won the 1928 World Champion Saddle Bronc title, Pendleton in 1928 and 1943, Cheyenne Frontier Days in 1933, 1935 and 1936, and the Calgary Stampede in 1935 and 1943. After retiring from rodeo he became a stuntman in Hollywood in the 1940s. He never quit being a spokesperson for rodeo, however, and attended his last rodeo the day he died.

LEONARD STROUD (1893-1961) was born in Monkstown, Texas, started as a bronc rider in 1908. In 1917 he won the All-Around at Cheyenne Frontier Days when he successfully rode Indian Tom. He won seven firsts in 1918. Stroud was also a top trick rider and created many routines, which were copied and used by other trick riders. He created and performed for the first time the Stroud Stand Out at the New York Stampede in 1916. Also, with the horse at a dead run, he would go completely under the horse's belly, coming up on the opposite side. During his prime, he would enter as many as seven events at a rodeo. Later, he managed and directed rodeos.[19]

Paddy Ryan, top bronc rider and practically unbeatable between 1924 and 1928. Fans at Madison Square Garden were so proud of the little Irishman they used to chant his name during the rodeo.

— Photo by W. L. Stephenson, courtesy of Stan Searle.

PADDY RYAN (1896-1980) was born in Austin, Minnesota, and moved to Ismay, Montana, when he was a freckle-faced, red-headed ten-year-old. He began cowboying around Miles City by filling in on roundups when he was fifteen. He moved cows and rode broncs. He definitely preferred the bronc riding to working with the cattle. There were some tough winters during those years and much of his time was spent trying to save hides from dead cattle.

In 1916 he won prize money in a rodeo at Miles City. He went on to Moose Jaw, Saskatchewan, and Belle Fourche, South Dakota, rodeos. The 1917 winter was also bad, and hunting carcasses in snowdrifts for another winter made him determined to try something else. In 1918 he joined the army and was shipped to France. He was stationed on the Swiss border in charge of horses at a sawmill. On his days off he hunted tough horses to ride. After the war he entered the Miles City RoundUp, and the Belle Fourche, Aberdeen, Moose Jaw, and Minneapolis rodeos. He won more money than he had seen in a year working as a cowboy. His effortless style and Irish good humor made people at these events always glad to see him.

While visiting a war buddy in Nevada, Ryan heard the Dean Ranch needed a broncbuster. He went to ask for the job, wearing a cloth cap, a pinch-back suit, and patent leather shoes. The boss was skeptical, considering the clothes Ryan wore, until he rode a couple of the mustangs. He stayed on at the Dean Ranch until the horses were gentled.

In 1922 he split first, second, and third in the bronc riding at San Francisco with Norman Cowan and Hippy Burmeister. He joined the Ringling Brothers Wild West Show at Deer Lodge and stayed with them through the fall Madison Square Garden event. Yakima Canutt and Dave White won first and second and Paddy Ryan and travel partner/good friend, Bob Askin, split third and fourth in the bronc riding. With their winnings, and their Ringling Brothers wages, they each had $1,100. They headed home to Miles City. In 1923 Ryan and Askin competed in fifteen rodeos.

Ryan and Yakima Canutt were tied to win the Roosevelt Trophy going into the Pendleton RoundUp in 1924. Paddy drew the horse U Tell 'Em, and Canutt drew a good horse called Sam Jackson. Ryan won. The Roosevelt Trophy, sponsored by the Roosevelt Hotel in honor of Teddy Roosevelt, had to be won three times in order to keep it. That fall in New York, during the rodeo, Ryan was given free rooms at the new Roosevelt Hotel, situated a few blocks from Madison Square Garden. "Everything was on the house," said Paddy. "Me and Askin weren't allowed to pay for a thing. The carpet was so deep it was like walking in a snow drift."[55] Ryan became New York's favorite cowboy. Newspapers voted him honorary captain of police, Ziefeld flappers invited him to go out, and gangsters made him a guest in their speakeasies. Irish in New York used to chant his name during a Madison Square Garden performance.

From 1924 to 1928, Ryan was practically unbeatable. In the years 1927, 1928, and 1930 he won the North American All-Around Cowboy title at the Calgary Stampede. He was inducted into the National Cowboy Hall of Fame in 1978.[55]

Broncs of the Era (1910s-1920s)

TIPPERARY was born in southeastern Montana on the Elmer Wickham ranch in 1905. He had mouse-colored hair with a black mane and tail. At four years old Wickham took Tipperary to a good cowboy neighbor to break him. It didn't happen, and no one attempted to ride him again until he was ten. Wickham sold him to "Doc" Latham of Camp Cook, South Dakota. Whenever a group got together to challenge Tipperary against a good rider, a crowd would gather and bets would be made. No one could master this clever fifteen-hand, three-inch, 1,000-pound bundle of dynamite.

In 1916 Charlie Wilson bought the outstanding bucker. Wilson was known for taking good care of his broncs and chose times and places carefully for exhibition bucking of Tipperary. Most were in eastern Montana and western South Dakota.

Wilson had special rules for riding Tipperary:

Tipperary, waiting to be bucked, standing next to snubbing horse, Baldy, and owner Charlie Wilson. Fred Wilson and Elmer Clark of Amidon, North Dakota, on the right. Clark was next scheduled to ride the famous bronc.
— Photo courtesy of Paul Hennessey.

1. There would be three judges.

2. Wilson would have charge of the horse at all times.

3. Any kind of slick, single-rigged saddle could be used, except that the fork must not be over a fifteen-inch swell. Wilson would furnish halter and the rider would furnish one rein 1" wide or a 5/8" rope.

4. Tipperary was to be saddled in an open arena. The rider was privileged to cinch his own saddle. No bucking rolls, whip or quirt were allowed, nor locked spurs or hobbled stirrups.

5. The rider was to use only one rope, which was to be free at the end, not knotted or wrapped around the rider's hand. The rider could not change hands on the rope, and the other hand must be held free.

6. The rider must scratch horse at least twice in the shoulders during the first five jumps, using both feet at the same time, the scratching to be done with humane spurs.

7. Any of the following offenses would also disqualify the rider: being bucked off, losing a stirrup, pulling leather, holding on with spurs, or picking up mane.

8. Riders had to leave starting place with both feet in the stirrups; the horse must not be turned loose until rider said, "Go." The horse had to be ridden to a finish.

9. The bucking arena was to be kept clear of spectators and other obstructions and all riders excepting judges and two pickup riders.

Yakima Canutt was honored for having ridden Tipperary successfully in 1920 and 1921. In fairness, it must be noted in both rides there were disadvantages to Tipperary. In 1920 he was bucked in gumbo mud and could not execute his normal bucking ability. In 1921 Canutt lost a stirrup during the ride, seen by the audience on that side of the horse, but not seen by the judges; therefore he was not disqualified.

Tipperary was never a run-of-the-mill bucker. From the first buck to the last he always challenged his rider. He was never a competition horse. He was strictly bucked in exhibition, a challenge to those known as the best rider at each affair. He never had a flank strap on him, and he never refused to buck. He always fought while the saddle was being placed on him.

Nearly ninety riders tried to ride Tipperary, but few succeeded. Rufus Rollens rode him successfully in 1916.
Unnoticed at the time, Tipperary had cut his left front foot the
night before. The injury caused him to wear a specially built
shoe the rest of his life. Those who witnessed the ride said
Rollens didn't have near the ride as Tipperary had put on the
day before. Harold Ekberg rode Tipperary when the bronc was
twenty-one years old, September 6, 1926. Charlie Wilson died
six weeks after this contest, and Tipperary was put out to pasture and died during a blizzard in 1932.[22]

TYGH VALLEY, owned by Harry Rowell of Hayward,
California, started her career as a bucker in the dirt arenas of
the Pacific Coast around 1911. She was still bucking in 1939
and spent most of her thirty-two years "a'heavin' and
a'twistin' and a'buckin'," with her nose in the dirt and heels
overhead, a leer on her handsome face and some poor cowboy
scrambling to get away from those flyin' hoofs.[23]

*Tygh Valley, a Harry Rowell saddle bronc, tosses Dan Peterson
to the ground.*
— Photo courtesy of June and Buster Ivory.

Rowell said that before her bucking days, children used to ride her to school. They got to cracking walnuts on the horn of the saddle, and she turned into a bucker. When she became too crippled and blind to enjoy life any longer on the Rowell Ranch in Dublin Canyon, Tygh Valley passed on.

TALCUM POWDER, a flea-bitten gray, almost white, with tiny brown specks all over, weighed about 1,100 pounds. In 1916, when they started to lead old Talcum Powder from the corrals out to the snubbing horse, Bill King's father made the remark that he'd bet $50 that "Talc" would get his man. King was swarmed over by people wanting to cover all the money he had to bet. Rufus Rollens drew him, and this cowboy's reputation was one that made people crowd around to watch. King collected the money.[51]

HELL BENT, owned by Bob Barmby, weighed 1,400 pounds. Purchased in the late 1920s, he was an excellent workhorse, well broken for harness, but the sight of a saddle sent him into a frenzy of bucking. He gave contestants tough rides for twelve years, bucking off hundreds. Among his victims were Paul Carney, Pete Grubb, and Ward Watkins. Eddie Wood, on the other hand, won top money on him several times.[7]

RED HOY was a southwest Texas horse around 1911. A peculiar outlaw, he was so gentle you could place as many as three kids on his back, bareback, and let a couple of others play around his feet—and rest assured they were safe. But once saddled, he became a package of TNT, and few riders could stand the explosion. He was fast as greased lightning. Most riders seemed to make a dive down his left shoulder to exit.[7]

MADE IN GERMANY was a 1,300-pound, black gelding with a nasty disposition and had to be handled cautiously. Owner Len Carmin usually prepared him personally. He was so tough that he was kept out of the draw for a time and was used for exhibitions only. Historians say he went six years without a qualified ride. In exhibition he was ridden by the winner of the bronc riding or by someone whose name was drawn from a hat. In 1929, at Burwell, Nebraska, a young fellow's name was drawn. Realizing it was very unlikely he could ride the horse, he sold his "chance" to Earl Thode, who bought it for Turk Greenough to ride. Turk was successful, and it was the first time Made In Germany had been ridden successfully in a long time. He was inducted into the Trail of Great Bucking Horses at the National Cowboy Hall of Fame in 1984.[11]

5

THE DEPRESSION ERA

A lthough Wild West shows had been traveling to Europe for some time, 1924 was the year of the First International Rodeo, held in London, England. In the *Official Programme and Souvenir* the following statements were printed: "Because the contests embody the every-day activities in the life of a cowboy, and because the activities demand skill, strength, courage and all the other qualities that go into the making of a real man, the Rodeo is regarded by the people of the cattle-raising countries, Canada, Australia and the United States, as insurance against any possible development of a race of molly-coddles."

The article continued: "The contestants at a Rodeo are not paid performers. They do not work on a salary. They pay their own living expenses, travel expenses and entry fees. Their only hope of financial reward lies in their ability to win first, second or third place in the events they enter."[24] A total purse of 20,000 pounds sterling was offered at the rodeo held in Wembley Stadium.

This was just the first of many rodeo troupes that went to foreign countries to perform and promote rodeo. Although, from a promotional standpoint, some ventures may have been successful, they were never highly successful financially. Some troupes were left stranded in foreign countries and had to make their own way back to the United States and Canada. Unlike the Wild West shows that went to foreign countries, these troupes were generally dependent on winnings. Many of their money sources for prizes reneged or paid less than originally offered. Nevertheless, the cowboys or cowgirls always got the most out of any experience and usually had great stories to tell once they were home.

The rodeo has always fought the image of being a "show" and not a sporting event. No doubt this was caused by the early influence of the Wild West shows that covered the nation before rodeos were introduced into some parts of the country.

William J. Clemans, in an attempt to form an "All American Rodeo Team," wrote in the *Tucson Daily Citizen* in February 1931: "Although Rodeos have become popularly considered as sports events there is no question in my mind, or in anyone's mind who is

Earl Thode, first All-Around Champion, in 1929. He also won the Saddle Bronc Championship in 1929 and 1931.
— Photo courtesy of Stan Searle.

rodeo-educated, that rodeos should be ranked among the major sports. Through misuse and the ballyhooed circuit rodeo and fly-by-night shows, a misconception has arisen that the rodeo is a spectacle and not a sport. This is truly a slander to a great game, because where properly sponsored, the rodeo offers greater action, suspense and thrills for the spectator and requires greater courage, daring and technique from the con-testant than any of the major sports now so popular."[7] Mr. Clemans chose three people that year, which exemplified the best of their event: Earl Thode in bronc riding, Dick Shelton in bulldogging, and Jake McClure in roping.

The attempt to get the public to see rodeo performances as sporting events instead of western extravaganzas was ongoing. In July 1939, Cy Taillon, a famous announcer of rodeos, com-mented, "In our work today we try to emphasize the contest ele-ment and to 'build up' the cowboys as the fine athletes they are, playing at one of our original and most spectacular sports. We need a lot of work in this respect to erase the stigma left by the so-called 'Wild West Shows' invariably billed as 'rodeos'."[7]

Year after year rodeos made improvements. Prescott, Pendleton, Calgary, Cheyenne, and Sidney (Iowa) added and improved facilities annually. Better stock, better judges, and better help were recruited as the events grew. But, from one location to another, there were some very big differences. As cowboys started traveling greater distances to compete, especially after winning events in their own area, they often found distant rodeos not to be what they expected.

In 1929 rodeo committees formed the Rodeo Association of America. Headquartered in Salinas, California, the association was designed to correct the shortcomings of rodeos and to produce more continuity. One of the major complaints of cowboys was that a rodeo would routinely advertise to have a large purse for winners; yet, upon arriving and winning, participants often found the purse was smaller than advertised. This made for some very disgruntled cowboys. In order to keep high principles of fairness, the Rodeo Association of America was created. The association's other goals were to oversee competition of contestants, protection of the stock, integrity of advertising, assumption and payment of all just and fair accounts; setting rules for honest and fair exhibition in recognized events; and keeping the sport on an amateur standing while giving the public a correct representation of western life for their edification and entertainment.

Initially, for a rodeo to become a member of the Rodeo Association of America (RAA), a rodeo committee could apply for $35. Annual dues were 2% of the purse, with dues at a minimum of $35 per committee and a maximum of $150 a year.

Not all rodeos entered the RAA, but many across the country did eventually join and the sport improved. The RAA was the keeper of records for each event and points were given each competitor for their wins, going toward their year-end accounts. The era where world championships could be won by competing and winning at a number of different rodeos was over. From 1929 onward, only one all-around and one champion for each event were recognized through the RAA.

The Cowboys Strike for Fair Money

As rodeo eased into the 1930s, the depression began to overtake the nation. It was not an unusual idea for a rodeo to want to "pull in its belt" and be as conservative as possible. The contestants were finding that even if they won, the pay-off was so small it wouldn't pay their expenses. Cowboy contestants got more and more frustrated. Yet the contestants were but one of the concerns of the RAA; the association also looked after the stock, the contractors, and the rodeo committees.

Admittedly, this was not a new complaint. In 1910 at the Jefferson County Fair, held at the Stockyards Stadium in Denver, the cowboys and cowgirls formed the Broncho Busters Union. They demanded $5 a day for contestant wild-horse riders. The local newspaper, the *Denver Republican*, reported that imposters trying to enter were threatening the respectability of the ancient and honorable profession of the real cowboy.

In 1916 Fay Ward tried to organize cowboys and provide for injured and retired performers through the monthly magazine *The Wild Bunch*. He proposed an organization that would arrange their own contests and support management of the organization and the contests, as well as financially support cowboys "under doctor's orders" and families of deceased contestants. Nothing ever happened at that time, but the seeds were planted.

At the National Western Stock Show and Rodeo in Denver in 1932, M. D. Fanning talked with cowboys about organizing in order to raise the standards of the sport, and to provide a pool of funds to take care of those injured while competing. Another aim was to force certain rodeos to increase their prize money. The group boasted ninety-five members and collected $300 by passing the hat. Abe Lefton was chairman and eight committees were organized to represent each branch of rodeo. It eventually went by the wayside, but at that time conditions were right. By the mid-thirties many occupations in the United States had formed unions or organizations to improve their bargaining positions.[9]

The cowboys' frustration over low prize money continued. Attempts to discuss their feelings with various producers and rodeo committees seemed to go unanswered. A group that had been working diligently to strike during the Boston Garden Rodeo in the fall of 1936 finally decided it. This rodeo was held just after the Madison Square Garden Rodeo, and Colonel W. T. Johnson, the premier rodeo producer of the decade, produced both events. His rodeos were considered the biggest and the best, at that time, and the cowboys knew that if they could force Colonel Johnson to accept their recommendations other producers across the country would follow suit.

Hugh Bennett and others tried to talk with Colonel Johnson while at the Madison Square Garden Rodeo, but he had ignored their suggestions, paid off the winners, and moved his stock by rail to Boston and had begun to set up for the big event there. The cowboys had told him they wouldn't be there, but he thought they were bluffing.

On opening night, November 3, in Boston, sixty-one cowboys who had signed the Cowboys' Turtle Association document, refusing to compete until their demands were met, sat in the grandstand watching to see what would happen when there were no competitors for the various events. Colonel Johnson urged stable boys and hands to ride in the place of contestants so that the performance could be held for the spectators. When a lowly stable worker would buck off, the cowboys would jeer and laugh uncontrollably. It was a disaster! Johnson agreed that night to the cowboys' terms, which included increasing the purses. The cowboys promptly went back to work.

That wasn't the end of the problems suffered by cowboys or rodeos, but it was a good start toward solving them. The Cowboys' Turtle Association grew. Everett Bowman, president of the association, and an active contestant, said: "Protection of the cowboys was the reason for forming the Association: to keep shows from holding our entrance fees and to make them pay purses according to the attendance. Also, experienced and capable judges were required. Before the Turtle Association was formed, lots of boys won bronc riding on their reputation, but now it has to be on their ability."[7]

In 1939 the Southwest Rodeo Association was formed at Fort Worth. Its purpose was similar to that of the RAA and was

1938 Rodeo Association of America Board of Directors. Upper row, from left: Laurenson, Richardson, Kinney, Kressman, Frank, and Ritner. Center row, from left: Hebbron, Sadler, Maxwell McNutt (president), Sylvester, and McCarger. Bottom row, from left: Howe, Perry, Frank Moore (of Madison Square Garden), and unknown. Photo was taken at Ogden, Utah.

— Photo courtesy of Stan Searle.

organized because there was a need for a similar group in that section of the country; few Southwestern rodeos were RAA members. The Southwest Rodeo Association was open to rodeos in Oklahoma, Texas, Kansas, Arkansas, Missouri, New Mexico, and Tennessee.

In 1945, a scant nine years after its formation, the Cowboys' Turtle Association became the Rodeo Cowboys Association (RCA), and it grew even larger with more credentials and more amenities. (In 1975 the organization would change its name again to Professional Rodeo Cowboys Association (PRCA), which is the organization most present-day cowboys strive to join if they choose professional rodeo.)

On the Road to Another Rodeo

Some of the frustrations cowboys faced could not be handled by an organization. One was the problem of getting from one rodeo to another. In 1916 Weadick needed to get cowboys back to New York for his big Sheepshead Bay Speedway rodeo, so he arranged three groups of contestants, each party with twenty-five or more. The railroad furnished a free baggage car for their horses. One party left from Cheyenne, at the close of Frontier Days, another from Fort Worth, and a third party from Iowa with C. B. Irwin and the regular shipment of rodeo stock.[7]

In the late twenties, automobiles were not dependable and were grossly underpowered. Often a cowboy did not have a car and had to catch a ride with others going his way. On some occasions he and other cowboys might ride a train headed toward their destination. The roughstock riders were especially capable of "grabbin' a ride" because their equipment was light and required little space. The ones that had been winning bought a train ticket; others might just "hop aboard" when no one was looking.

Sometimes a number of rodeo cowboys would go in together and rent an Armor Palace car. The cars looked like baggage cars but were pulled by passenger trains. They were seventy or eighty feet long with compartments at each end and a 12x12-foot space in the doorway. The cowboys would turn about six head of horses over to a groom, who would look after the horses, tack, saddles, trunks, and other gear.[51]

Gib Potter, a trick roper, and Hughie Long, a saddle bronc rider, hitched a ride with calf roper Irby Mundy in the summer of 1928 from Miami, Texas, to Calgary. As told by Potter in a *Western Horseman* article, the experience indicates the trials of getting from one rodeo to another in that era. Mundy had a new Ford light delivery truck and a sturdy built horse trailer, a two-wheeler with twenty-one-inch wheels, no springs to nullify sway and bounce, and no brakes to nullify stops. The sides of the trailer stood four feet high and were made of spaced 1x4-inch hardwood. The tailgate dropped so it could be used as a ramp. The axle ran over the floorboards. The horse's head

and neck overhung the front. He was not tied, in the event of a rollover.

Mundy's horse, Happy, was a good roping horse, and any roper that he mounted had to kick in a quarter of any prize money that he won while mounted on him. Some bulldoggers also used him. Mundy was a man going places; he won the 1934 calf roping title a few years later.

Mundy and his passengers rattled out of Miami and made Guymon, Oklahoma, the first night and bedrolled. They were up at 4:30 A.M. and on their way. Near Springfield, Colorado, they stopped at Mundy's ranch, helped him with some of his chores, and left early the next morning. They averaged thirty miles per hour on highways that were mostly dirt and gravel; pavement generally was found only on main streets, two blocks long, in the larger towns. Their route led them through Lamar and on to Sterling, Colorado, and then to Sidney, and Alliance, Nebraska. The Alliance Rodeo was two days long. Hughie placed in the saddle bronc day money.

The pay was $3 a head for bareback mount money, open to saddle bronc contestants only. The arena was the infield of a racetrack, and the pickup men never had a chance. So, after the first long ride there was a scarcity of contestants. Hughie got five mounts before they cut him off. His method was to spur the pony so hard in the neck that it would chill him and slow him down. Hughie would step off and head back for the next one. In a weak moment, Hughie had loaned his Hamley Committee saddle to a couple of riders back in Texas. He was a bit perturbed to find they had put up his saddle to cover their entry fees at Alliance. Fortunately, they won enough to bail it out before Hughie got mad.

It rained and rained during that rodeo. Breezy Cox wired from Arizona to hold his bronc for him. He drew Made In Germany, and that big black laid Breezy out like a carpet. He hit the ground so hard that he didn't talk for two hours, which caused Oklahoma Curley to remark that he must be dead.

When the rodeo was over, Gib, Hughie, and Mundy traveled through Hot Springs, Custer, Sundance, Gillette, Sheridan, and Billings, and found a stall at the fairgrounds for Happy. The next day they headed for Great Falls and another rodeo. This was a big one with good stock, big crowds, and every name contestant in the business. Floyd Stillings won the saddle bronc riding. Mundy picked up some cash in the day money and in the average as well as garnering a wallet-full just through mounting. When it was over they headed on toward Calgary, with an additional passenger, Cheyenne Kizer. Later in the day a connecting rod conked out. They unloaded Happy and unhooked the trailer. After some time had passed, someone came along and offered to haul Mundy and his truck to the nearest garage. Hughie and Gib located a sheepherder and sat with him until Mundy returned.

Heading north they crossed the line into Canada at Carway. Then came the mud—miles and miles of it. They unloaded Happy, and Hughie rode him as the truck and trailer maneuvered the mud. By this time quite a caravan of vehicles had joined the group: first was Mundy's rig, followed by Billy Kingham's car and trailer; then Lloyd Saunders with his Hollywood wife and Arabian roping horse; then "Black Hat" Bob Crosby and his bay horse, Earl Thode, Breezy Cox, and Floyd Stillings; and last was a touring VIP and his wife in a Pierce Arrow limousine, complete with a uniformed Japanese chauffeur. Fortunately, the caravan finally ran out of mud and reached their destination—Calgary. Potter exclaimed that "at 30 mph, you have the time and leisure to appreciate the grandeur and magnificent vistas of the big west."[32]

Herman Linder of Cardston, Alberta, top bronc rider and rodeo producer. He won twenty-two championships at the Calgary Stampede alone. Photo taken at Penticton in 1949, just after he retired from bronc riding.
— Photo by Jim Chamberlain, courtesy of Stan Searle.

Another account of early travel was by Herman Linder. The first year that Mrs. Linder hit the road with him was 1933. They set out at the end of July from Cardston, Alberta, in a 1929 Model-A Ford with their luggage piled high in the back, including all their heavy winter clothing because they knew they wouldn't return until November or December.

By the time they reached Chicago, the car was feeling the effects of a few thousand miles of gravel roads and dust clouds. When Herman turned down into the Loop, the engine conked out. The starter wasn't working, so he jumped out and cranked the engine into life. After Chicago, they made it to St. Louis, but the engine began to sound as if it was going to fall apart. Everything was being shaken loose by the vibration. A shiny 1931 second-hand Model-A with only 2,000 miles that ran like new, priced at $200 (plus their old car), was their salvation!

Within a few years, Herman was grossing $5,000 to $8,000 a year in rodeo. In the midst of the Great Depression, that amount was a near fortune. They would cover about 100 miles every three hours, traveling across the continent on dusty roads. The larger rodeos, where they could stay a couple of weeks to a month, were a real treat for them. Small towns caused problems, as there were no motels in those days, just the odd tourist cabins, roughly made, much like farm granaries. At Sidney, Iowa, they stayed in private homes as there was only one hotel and it was always full during the rodeo.

Mrs. Agnes Linder cooked meals for herself and Herman. Most rodeo people did their own cooking. The boys who did not have wives with them or who weren't married would usually eat with the rest. The Linders always had two or three boys to dinner.

Keeping clothes clean was also a problem while on the road. Rodeo wives found themselves busy washing out socks and shirts. Mrs. Linder did washing for some of the other boys too. "I had to wash Herman's things anyway and one or two extra things didn't matter," she said.[33]

Hugh Bennett remembered, when talking about the early days, "We slept on an old mattress in the back of the car or slept on the ground or in a tent. My wife, Josie, would have to roll up the tent in record time to make it to the next rodeo."[37]

Train travel was also a way to get from one rodeo to the next for a cowboy, especially if he had horses or stock to transport as well. Often they would hop on any train and ride with their stock if it didn't have passenger cars. One special train was called the Rodeo Train, which served no other purpose than to carry contestants, stock, and everything it took to produce a rodeo from Texas to Madison Square Garden. In 1932 Colonel W. T. Johnson, rodeo producer, wanted to get his World Champion Rodeo stock and menage to New York and hired a special through train of closed cars. He put 500 head of livestock aboard, and whooped it up right through to New York, halting rail traffic, clearing tracks, altering schedules, backing passenger trains off on sidings, and generally playing the devil with three different railroad lines, reported the *San Antonio Light*.[57] The cost to Colonel Johnson for the trip— one way—was $23,804.

Johnson also sent most of his staff, along with nine carloads of livestock, to Chicago by special train. The train departed from San Antonio, stopped in Fort Worth, and then in Oklahoma, to pick up contestants and additional equipment. A 1936 Boston Garden program stated: "It costs about $25,000 to move the stock from Johnson's ranch in Texas. All steel baggage cars are equipped with electric lights for horses. It takes about 50 hours to make the trip, traveling at a rate of about 50 mph, with no stops, except to water the engine."[72]

Everett Colborn had been Colonel Johnson's arena director, and when Johnson quit producing rodeos in 1937, Colborn took over for the new owners. The Rodeo Train continued to run, carrying cowboys and cowgirls thousands of miles. The only difference was that it originated from the small Edna Hill community near Dublin, Texas. Feed, tack, and equipment were boxed, packed, and carted off to New York. It loaded in Dublin, stopped to pick up passengers in Fort Worth, unloaded to rest the stock in Iowa, then roared into New York City. All along the way people met it, wished the riders well, and cheered them on.

The train consisted of nineteen stock cars, two baggage cars filled with equipment, one chair car, one or two sleeping cars, and one dining car. It was completely a private train with no other purpose than the rodeo.

Frank Alvord, arena secretary at Madison Square Garden, owned a café on Fort Worth's northside, and had contracted with Colborn to feed the people on the train. (The Santa Fe Railroad did not provide much of a dining car in the early years. It was simply an empty galley car with a large table down the center and benches on either side.) Alvord had butchered a steer in Dublin and planned on a basic beef menu. Flaxie Fletcher kept track of who ate and when. It was a hopeless task, as people wandered in to eat whenever they chose, and sometimes they didn't stay long. "Fred fixed these steaks, and they covered the whole plate," said Flaxie. "They turned out to be tough and no one could cut them with their knives. The lights went out briefly and when they came back on everyone was holding their steaks in their hands and trying to eat with their fingers."[34]

For shipping stock, one normally thinks of cattle cars, but these were not cattle cars. They were all express cars. The expresses, or palace cars, were fully enclosed, with special stalls built for saddle horses. There were sixteen saddle horses in each car. Some thirty bucking horses were packed together in the others. All in all, they took nearly 200 horses to New York, remembered Lanham Riley, who worked his way there by helping feed the stock. In addition, there were the steers, calves, and bulls. The safety of the animals was paramount,

and the train had to make a stop along the way to let all the stock off to water and rest. Fort Madison, Iowa, became a regular layover.

Once they arrived in New York the stock was unloaded at 49th Street, near the Hudson River. The bulls were trucked to the Garden. The horses, steers, and calves were driven right down the street.

The 1937 Madison Square Garden Rodeo was Colborn's first big-time production. Paul Carney, of Galeton, Colorado, was the star of the rodeo, winning the saddle bronc riding and bull riding; Kid Fletcher of Hugo, Colorado, won the bareback bronc riding; and Brida Gafford, of Casper, Wyoming, won the cowgirls' bronc riding.

The rodeo ended on a Sunday night about 10:00 or 11:00. By 1:00 A.M. the stock was loaded back onto the train. The crew worked all night, generally finishing up around 10:00 A.M. Then the cars were hooked up and the Rodeo Train left New York City for Boston. It was just an overnight trip. On Tuesday, the train was unloaded at the Boston Garden. On

Wednesday and Thursday, everyone involved got a chance to rest. By Friday, it was another parade and the start of another two-week rodeo. When the train returned to Texas, two months had passed.[34]

Women in the Saddle

Lady bronc riders always had much appeal with the spectators and rodeo fans. Their dress was always colorful and unique, and many were beautiful girls—Vaughn Krieg and sister, Gene Creed, Lucyle Richards, and Alice and Marge Greenough among them. However, the competition changed after the late 1920s. Some rodeos still held exhibitions and paid lady bronc riders to ride. Madison Square Garden, on the other hand, held lady bronc riding through the 1930s.

The women who chose this unique profession in the 1920s, '30s and '40s were excellent athletes, and caused quite a stir wherever they went. Colonel W. T. Johnson recognized their ability to attract publicity and used attractive cowgirls to promote his rodeos whenever possible.

Alice and Marge Greenough learned bronc riding at home in Montana. Their dad, Packsaddle Ben, expected all his children to be self-sufficient and capable of breaking and riding horses. The girls remembered staying at a line shack, when only ten or eleven years old, tending cattle, breaking horses, and caring for themselves, with an adult coming by, rarely, to check on them. Chuck Henson, Marge's son, said he remembered hearing his mother laugh loudly as she rode broncs across the arena, she enjoyed it so much. Alice was World Champion Lady Bronc Rider four times and later had her own stock contracting business and produced rodeos in the Montana region.

Women competitors were not leaving rodeo. In 1948 a group of women met in San Angelo, Texas, and formed the Girls Rodeo Association, which eventually became the Women's Professional Rodeo Association (WPRA) and held all-girl rodeos across the country.[26] Today the organization sponsors the barrel racing events at 700 to 800 PRCA-sanc-

Corinne Williams riding Invermere, a Beutler Brothers saddle bronc, at Phoenix, 1962.
— Photo by Devere Helfrich, donated by Bill Cheshire.
Courtesy of the National Cowboy Hall of Fame.

tioned rodeos annually and has between 1,500 and 2,000 members. A sister organization, which shares offices with WPRA in Colorado Springs, Colorado, the Professional Women's Rodeo Association (PWRA), holds between twenty and twenty-five all-girl rodeos a year and has about 200 members. At an all-girl rodeo the events are bareback riding, bull riding, breakaway calf roping, tie down calf roping, steer roping, and barrel racing.

Corinne Williams was an exception when the women began their own organization in the late 1940s. She stayed with the RCA, as she wanted to bulldog steers and this was not an event in the all-girl rodeos. After having stints with several Wild West outfits, Williams gave exhibitions of bulldogging and bronc riding. Don Bell, historian from Wyoming, told the author, "She was a good hand, and always took the advice given her by the experienced cowboys of her day."

Broncbusters of the Era (1930s)

In 1939 Cy Taillon, in *Hoofs and Horns* magazine, made this comment:

> It is interesting to note the reaction of rodeo fans in different sections of the country. In the South and Southwest, roping seems to command the major interest and from these sections come the game's finest handlers of the hemp.
>
> In the north country where the boys have their mittens on five months out of the year, roping bows to bronc riding as the major attraction and as a natural result this section has produced such immortals as the late Pete Knight, Paddy Ryan, Bob Askin, Floyd Stillings, Burel Mulkey, Nick Knight, Ray Mavit, Stub Bartelmay, Turk Greenough, Bill McMackin, Bob Walden and scores of other top bronc peelers. If my memory serves me right, Earl Thode, one of the finest to ever swing a spur, also came out of this country, later to make his home in sunny Arizona.[7]

Taillon's astute comment is substantiated below, by the number of different locales from which the 'busters originated.

PETE KNIGHT (1903-1937), born in Philadelphia, moved with his family to Stroud, Oklahoma, and then to Crossfield, Alberta, Canada in 1914. The very next year he began to break and gentle horses. He entered his first rodeo in Crossfield in 1918, where he set about winning second in saddle bronc riding on both days.

He entered the Calgary Stampede in 1923, but during the parade his horse slipped and he broke his leg, preventing him from competing. In 1924, however, he again entered Calgary and lost the saddle bronc title by less than half a point to Pete LaGrandeur.[41] He won the championship at Edmonton Exhibition and Stampede, plus $1,000 that year. In 1926, at Winnipeg, he won another championship and $1,500. He won the 1932, 1933, 1935, and 1936 Champion Bronc Rider of the World at Calgary.[19]

Pete Knight was one of the first Canadian bronc riders to master "bicycling"—moving both feet forward to the horse's

Top saddle bronc rider Pete Knight, going off Duster at Rowell Ranch Rodeo, Hayward, California, 1937. He died on the way to the hospital from injuries he sustained from this ride.
— Photo courtesy of June and Buster Ivory.

shoulders for the first five jumps, then kicking high behind for another five jumps. Some judges said they'd not seen a rider spur a horse as savagely ahead of the cinch as Knight. He was strong as a bull.

Knight was respected for being one of the best bronc riders of the day, but he was also respected as one of the best guys in rodeo. At the top of his career he was killed. At Hayward, California, on May 23, 1937, he came out of the chute on a bronc named Duster, a Harry Rowell horse, and when he was thrown the horse stepped on him. He died from an internal hemorrhage, leaving a widow, Ida Lee "Babe" Avant Knight, and baby daughter, De Anna Thomasine.

When Knight, the top bronc rider of the day, was killed, the shock of the rodeo world was indicated by the letters, poems, and testaments sent to *Hoofs and Horns* magazine. Pages were filled with words from cowboys, rodeo officials, and friends. Maxwell McNutt, president of the Rodeo Association of America, wrote:

The fire of his courage thawed a trail through the snows of Canada; and on he rode. The prairie about Cheyenne, the Rockies of Colorado, the rolling hills of Oregon, Nevada's sage brush, California's sunburned valleys, the Mesquite and cactus country of the great Southwest, and all they had to offer succumbed in turn to his indomitable will. Changing conditions alike of climate and of way of life were no hindrance to this man of super serenity and calm; he conquered all. Yes, on and still on he rode, he scored favor, south no quarter. He obliterated the international boundary line and for the years 1932, 1933, 1935 and 1936 was World Champion Bronc Rider, in a word he dominated Continental Horse-America.[7]

EARL THODE (1900-1964) was born in South Dakota, and one of his earliest chores was breaking horses for his father. He started rodeoing in 1920, and in 1927 he won the Bronc Riding Championship at Cheyenne. He won the title again in 1931, 1932, and 1934. In 1929 he was the first to win the Rodeo Association of America All-Around Championship. He also won the Saddle Bronc Championship at the Calgary Stampede in 1929 and 1938.

William Clemans picked him as the best bronc rider in 1931, and later recalled that day: "It was the finals of the bronc riding championship and Thode had drawn the top horse of the string. He came out of the chute and whammed both spurs into the bronc's shoulder and looked back over his shoulder to show his utter indifference to the horse's ability. From my view he had his left spur hung in the cinch. After the ride I said to him, 'You didn't spur on my side.' 'No', he said, 'there were no judges on that side.' Had the judges been on both sides as they should have been he would have been scratching on both sides."[24]

Thode drowned in a boating accident near his Vernon, Arizona, home in 1964.

LEO "PICK" MURRAY (1902-1978) was born in Colbert, Oklahoma, and reared on a ranch. His dad and brothers, Leonard and Bobby, were all top rodeo cowboys. His first rodeo was in 1919, at Tishomingo, where he roped calves, rode steers, and bulldogged. By 1923, he was also riding broncs, the event in which he would specialize, and won his first saddle bronc prize at the 101 Ranch Rodeo in Marland, Oklahoma. He joined the 101 Ranch Wild West Show but left every year to rodeo, much to the disappointment of the show's leader, Colonel Zack Miller. By 1930, "Pick" was on top and won the bronc riding championship at the big Madison Square Garden rodeo, followed by a win at Fort Worth the next spring. He won the Belle Fourche bronc riding several times, and at Salt Lake City won the Bing Crosby Trophy along with the bronc riding title. He was also runner-up to the RAA All-Around Cowboy title.

In a bad accident, Murray broke his arm and then managed to break it several more times. He had to shift arms and use his right arm in order to hold on to the bucking rein. This threw his balance completely off, but Murray learned to adjust. He rode several top buckers, where others had failed; Midnight and Five Minutes to Midnight (three times in one year) were among them. In 1937 he won four bronc-riding titles. That same year he was asked to judge the bronc riding at Madison Square Garden and Boston Garden. He was inducted into the National Cowboy Hall of Fame in 1987.[7]

JERRY AMBLER (1911-1958) was a native of Minburn, Alberta, Canada. His dad owned one of the largest horse ranches in Western Canada. Jerry was in the saddle by age two. He entered the United States to rodeo in 1932, at Butte, Montana, but he was bucked off and broke his wrist. At Bigger, Montana, he won first and second day money, and finished second in the finals. Later that year, he made the eastern rodeos and won first day money in New York and second day money in Boston. In 1935 he won sixteen rodeos.

Ambler won many events and titles, including the 1941 North American Bull Riding Championship, an event he won three times in a row at Calgary. He won the North American Bronc Riding Championship twice, a first in bronc riding at both Madison Square Garden and Boston, third at Cheyenne, second at Pendleton, and so on. He had tough luck in 1944, when he broke his arm. That put him out of the running for the rest of the year, but in 1945 he was back. By 1946, he had won the World's Saddle Bronc Riding Championship a full 4,000 points out in the lead.

There are two basic styles of bronc riders—those who ride by brute strength, and those who ride by balance. The great majority of bronc riders are in between the two extremes, a combination of balance and strength. Jerry Ambler rode with balance form. At times during his rides he was in contact with the saddle on little more than the area of a man's hand, and with his knees totally free from leather, spurring with long, sweeping strokes far ahead and far behind. This system has distinct advantages. Much of the terrific jerk and snap of the saddle is lost, and the ride is smoother. Moreover, the rider has his legs free to concentrate on spurring, in the case of strength riders; the whole jerk of the saddle is passed on through the body of the rider. Balance riding has, however, a distinct disadvantage: It's just hard to do. A rider can choose to ride by strength, with more chance of staying on his horse yet with less chance of winning the money, or to ride by balance, with less chance of riding but more chance of winning if he does ride. Ambler chose to ride by balance. He once told a potential bronc rider, "If you're going to ride broncs, come out wild and ride like Hell. If you won't ride wild, stay off altogether."[47]

FRITZ TRUAN (1916-1945) was born near Seeley, California, and began rodeoing when he was nineteen years old. He rode saddle broncs, bareback, and was a bulldogger. Fritz had many friends and loved to laugh and joke. He was a flamboyant cowboy and did everything in a big way. He won the World Champion Saddle Bronc Riding in 1939 and 1940. He was also All-Around Champion in 1940. His ability as a bronc rider was well known throughout the rodeo world.

At the 1941 Madison Square Garden rodeo, Fritz shared a room with twenty-three-year-old Wally McConnell from Boise, Idaho. Wally was a third-year competitor but had never been to Madison Square Garden before. After nineteen days of grueling competition, the body starts having aches and pains that do not affect a rider at a short rodeo. Wally had been up in the bronc riding nine times, and had bucked off four. Fritz

Three All-Around Champions: (from left) Burel Mulkey (1938), Fritz Truan (1940), Paul Carney (1939), and Nick Knight, also a top saddle bronc rider of the 1930s.
— Photo courtesy of June and Buster Ivory.

discovered Wally's next draw was the notorious Hell's Angels. He knew Wally was not able to ride this outlaw, but was to proud not to try. Fritz knew it would take something clever to stop Wally from trying, and possibly getting a serious injury. Fritz and Everett Colborn, rodeo producer, collaborated and decided to try the following: Fritz burst in to his hotel room, cussing a storm and appearing hopping mad at Colborn. "That son-of-a-gun called me a cheese champion and said I couldn't ride Hell's Angels! Before I knew it I had bet him a hundred dollars I could. I forgot, kid, you had drawn him. But you're out of the finals, and you can't ride him as sore as you are, so be a good pal and lend me that Cayuse tonight. I'll smack Mr. Everett Colborn for a hundred bucks." And with that Wally agreed to do him the favor. Truan made a ride that would be talked about for years to come.

Sergeant Fritz Truan, United States Marine, died in com-

Alvin Gordon on Hell's Angels, an Everett Colborn bronc.
— Photo by R. R. Doubleday, donated by Jack Long. Courtesy of the National Cowboy Hall of Fame.

bat at Iwo Jima during World War II. The Marines were making a mighty attempt to take Hill 382, and while his peers were being told to stay down he charged up the hill, taking a bullet in the neck and dying immediately.[7,53]

ALVIN "ALVIE" GORDON (1910-____) was from Couer D'Alene, Idaho. His family moved to Athena, Oregon, near Pendleton, when he was a small boy. His mother rode broncs at Pendleton in 1918, 1919, and the early 1920s as Lauretta Schrimpf. At fourteen, Alvie started bulldogging, but the steers kept growing and he didn't, so he switched to saddle bronc and bareback riding. In 1937-38 he was the captain of the American team that won the saddle bronc championships in Australia.

Chuck Martin described Alvin Gordon in 1940 as a bronc rider that concerned himself with making a ride. He had balance, knee-lock, spur-savvy, and plenty of brains to outthink the horse. With his strong, powerful legs, he used a knee-lock, which was seldom broken, but it also left his legs loose and free from the knees down. Gordon's spurs never stopped scratching from chute gate to whistle. He also used his right hand on the hack-rope; he did not choke the rope, but rode entirely by knee-grip and balance. A bronc wouldn't be found pulling Gordon out of the saddle when the critter came apart and swallowed its head. He was not a flashy rider, but quiet, serious, and methodical. And he was a thorough craftsman.

Alvin Gordon listed the following horses as the toughest in the country during his day: Will James, Hootchie Kootchie, Lee Overalls, Crying Jew, Short Cut, Five Minutes to Midnight, Ham What Am, Big Jess, and Stork. He won the International Bronc Riding Championship at Tex Austin's London Rodeo in 1934.[7] Later he ran chutes and was in charge of the stock for Colborn. He was also the bronc riding representative for the Turtles.

HERMAN LINDER (1907-____) was born in Wisconsin. His family moved to Cardston, Alberta, in 1918 and purchased land. As a kid he rode bucking steers and horses. In 1924 he entered his first rodeo at Cardston. In 1929 he won both the Canadian Saddle Bronc Riding Championship and the Bareback Bucking Horse Riding contest at the Calgary Stampede. He won the Canadian All-Around Cowboy Championship in the years 1931 through 1936, as well as 1938. He won the North American All-Around Cowboy Championship in 1932, 1934, 1935, 1936, and 1938. Twenty-two championships went to him at the Calgary Stampede during his career.

Herman Linder was on the Canadian Rodeo Team sent to Australia in 1936 and in 1938. In 1933 he won the Bareback Bronc Riding Championship at Madison Square Garden, and received his first prize saddle. He took the saddle to bed with him the first night for safekeeping. Subsequently, he won prizes in the United States, Canada, Australia, and England.

In 1939 he retired from competition and put on rodeos in Canada. During the early 1940s, he bought horses for stock contractors, such as Leo Cremer, Everett Colborn, and the Rings. Many of the horses that turned out to be fine buckers came from Long Time Squirrel, an Indian who ran horses on the Blood Reservation that bordered Cardston. Some of the broncs were Fiery Cross, Bear Park, and Chief Tyhee. [7,11,33]

Herman continues to promote rodeo and is always in favor of anything that improves the sport. Tater Decker was overheard at National Finals a few years ago telling a group of cowboys that Herman Linder and Gerald Roberts were both top-flight bronc riders, but they were not flashy. Just all business!

Broncs of the Era (1930s)

CRYING JEW—Cuff Burrell, rodeo stock contractor, of Hanford, California, heard of a horse that was causing his owner much grief by kicking, bucking, and tearing up his farm machinery. Burrell found him to be a good bucker and purchased him. Since the former owner was Jewish and complained so loudly about how much damage the horse had done and how much it had cost him, Burrell named the bronc Crying Jew, after his former owner.

At thirteen years of age, in 1939, the bronc was Burrell's top bucker. He was nervous, high-strung, and consistent. The most consistent thing about his bucking was that he always came out of the chute with his forefeet in the air. He was a chute fighter that nearly always gave a man a bad go away from the gate. After he left the chute gate he varied his performances with plenty of tricks. He dumped many of the top bronc riders of the day. During the 1938 season he was successfully ridden only twice out of twenty-five times in the chute. He was a natural.

Raised in Fresno County, California, he was a bay with a white strip down his face, a Roman nose, white hind feet, and weighed about 1,300 pounds.[7]

WILL JAMES was one of Leo Cremer's best broncs. The big black gelding was named after the man who bought the horse at an auction ring for $25 and gave him to Cremer, saying the big black looked like a promising bucker. Around

1930, the horse was at the top of Cremer's string. It didn't happen often, but the cowboy who could ride him would most likely win first day money. He threw Leo "Pick" Murray, who went on to ride fourteen horses at Madison Square Garden in New York to win the world championship.

Ray Gafford, of Casper, Wyoming, rode Will James in 1935, at the Livingston RoundUp, and won the bronc riding finals before a record crowd of 13,000 while his fiancée, Brida Miller, entertained the dudes with her exhibition bronc riding. Shipping broncs from place to place made it necessary for Cremer to brand them, above the tail and across the rump. Will James carried the number "21." Rodeo cowboys in a 1940 poll voted him one of the top five bucking horses in the world.[54]

MIDNIGHT was born on the plains of Alberta, Canada. After bucking his owner, Jim McNabb, off several times as a saddle horse, he was taken to the Calgary Stampede, where he

Famous bronc Midnight displays his winning form.
— Photo taken from a 1938 Madison Square Garden
program. Courtesy of June and Buster Ivory.

was an instant sensation as a bronc. Peter Welsh bought him for $500 and later sold him to rodeo producer Colonel Jim Eskew. In turn, Eskew sold Midnight and Five Minutes to Midnight to Ed McCarty and Verne Elliott for $500.

Midnight was half thoroughbred and half Morgan. He was gentle and easy to handle, when someone wasn't on his back. McCarty and Elliott led him in Frontier Day parades. But when he came out of the chute, he came with a fifteen-foot leap, and when he landed, he came with head down and all four feet stiff. They say the shock of the impact was what unseated the boys on the first leap out. He was a strong horse and weighed between 1,200 and 1,300 pounds. In 1930 the cowboys wanted Midnight barred from competition. It didn't happen.

About 1932, Midnight began to show signs of ringbone, probably due to the jolt of his front legs in his strong bucking. The next year it was announced that he would be retired at Cheyenne Frontier Days. Turk Greenough won the saddle bronc championship at Cheyenne that year after he was thrown by Midnight. After a couple of years' retirement on Verne Elliott's Colorado ranch, the horse was frisky enough to make a trip to England to be part of a rodeo promotion there. After the tour, they retired him again. He died in 1936 and was buried on Elliott's ranch. Later, when he was inducted into the National Cowboy Hall of Fame, his remains were moved to the Oklahoma City site where visitors to the museum could see his grave.[7, 50, 54]

FIVE MINUTES TO MIDNIGHT was spotted with other wild horses at the Alberta stockyards, headed to a cannery and certain death. He was bought and put in a wild horse race, but he did not allow anyone to ride him. Peter Welsh then purchased him. The Canada Kid, Lee Ferris, barely rode him in the bronc riding, and he was seldom ridden after his career was launched.[54]

Welsh went broke in 1928 and sold Five and Midnight to Colonel Eskew, whose assessment of the two black outlaws was "too rough to ride." Eskew sold the pair to McCarty and Elliott in 1929. Whereas Midnight was a large horse and bucked with brute force, Five was small, only 895 pounds, but

Five Minutes to Midnight, top bronc, tries to outwit Don Nesbitt.
— Photo by Lainson Studio, Denver, Colorado.
Courtesy of June and Buster Ivory.

active as a cat. He was considered a thinking bronc, because if he wasn't bucking his rider off one way, he'd change his style mid-buck and do something just as bad another way. His small size was compensated for with determination and cleverness.[50]

It was said that he was ridden fourteen times in twenty years of professional bucking. He bucked off between 1,200 to 2,000 riders. In 1936, at Portland, Oregon, the rodeo committees drug a sack of 1,600 silver dollars into the arena, the prize for anyone who could ride Five. They gave it a good try, but no one collected.

Five Minutes to Midnight was retired in 1945, and died in 1946. He arose from a $10 plug to a $5,000 star rodeo attraction. Like Midnight, he was buried on the Elliott ranch in Colorado, then was moved to the Oklahoma City Cowboy Hall of Fame after he was inducted. [11]

HAM WHAT AM *a.k.a* JIMMY SIMPSON *a.k.a* SALTY DOG—This horse's career began sometime before a 1927

Indianapolis State Fair, when a young rider, named Sammy Smith, was dragged to death by him. Hughie Long and Gib Potter witnessed the tragedy. Potter recalled in the *Wild Bunch* (December 1987), "Sammy's foot just went through the stirrup. He hung up and was kicked to death. It was an accident. This horse was not mean in any way, though afterwards, as always happens, he got a reputation." Long remembered that Sammy had run-down heeled boots. "We kept telling him it was dangerous to ride bucking horses in boots like that. He didn't listen, when the horse went for the fence his boot shoved clean through the stirrup. The horse snatched him off the fence and charged away with him. His rib cage was popped open and he was dead by the time we could get the horse under control."

His name was then changed to Salty Dog and the rodeo "spieler" called him "the killer horse." In the early thirties he was sold to McCarty and Elliott during the Fort Worth rodeo, and they changed his name to Ham What Am.[11]

During a Tex Austin show at Gilmore Stadium in Los Angeles, three top bronc riders were the final contestants:Doff Aber, Pete Knight, and Earl Thode. The six final horses were Ham What Am, Duster, C. Y. Jones, Crying Jew, Five Minutes to Midnight, and Goodbye Dan. Ham What Am played no favorites—he bucked each rider off during the finals.[23]

HELL'S ANGELS was born in 1926 and raised by a farmer in Montana. Doug Rutledge tried to break him to ride. He rounded up horses on him for two months, and he bucked every single day. His mother was a pinto, the father a Percheron, owned by Lew E. Parks. He was sold to Buck Yarber in 1933, when he was seven. He bucked the first time in Jackson, Wyoming. Mike Hastings bought him in 1933 and bucked him at Butte, where he bucked off Eddie Curtis. At Indianapolis he threw three bronc riders; in New York he bucked eleven times, and eleven riders failed to make the whistle; then in Boston he bucked off five more riders. After that show Hastings sold him to Colonel W. T. Johnson, and eventually the horse went to the World's Championship Rodeo Corporation. He was not successfully ridden more than twenty times between 1933 and 1942. However, Fritz Truan was the exception: He rode him five out of seven times up.

Vic Schwartz said, "Hell's Angels is a stout, powerful horse, a slow bucker with tremendous force in his jumps. He keeps a man off balance most of the time driving him out of the saddle by sheer power." He never left the chute without kicking the top board with his hind hoofs. In 1939 Ward Watkins hung up on him at Madison Square Garden and survived being dragged around the arena one and a half times.[7]

Hell's Angels caught distemper at Buffalo, New York, in 1942 and was discovered dead in the railroad car at Hannibal, Missouri, as they were heading back to Texas. He was inducted into the National Cowboy Hall of Fame in 1966.[11]

HELL-TO-SET was picked up with a string of horses out of Utah by Jack Dew in 1935, for $62.50. "Dogtown Slim" Leuschner bought Dew's broncs in 1937. It has been said "Hell-to-Set's papa was a train wreck and his mama was a Wyoming blizzard." He was a good bucking horse.

Every time he was mounted he learned new tricks. At first he bucked in a straight line, with his head between his front feet. He went high and landed hard. Some of the best cowboys got off before they were ready, but a few discovered if they took a deep seat and pulled hard on the halter rope, they could let Hell-To-Set win the money for them.

Then at Las Vegas in 1935, Harry Knight inadvertently taught the horse a fancier way of making cowboys walk. Knight, champion bronc rider, was doing well for the first few jumps and decided to show the judges how a bronc could be handled by a top hand. He reached up and caught his spur in Hell-To-Set's shoulder. The outlaw suddenly threw his lead away, around to the right, meanwhile continuing with his rapid up-and-down motion. This made the halter useless for holding on, but it also gave the horse's torso a twisting action that was great to see! Harry took to the air and walked back to the chutes.

From then on Hell-To-Set always tossed his head back toward his rider, always on the right side, and then later on either side. A year later Knight tried to ride him again. Again he walked back to the chutes.[59]

6

GROWING PAINS: THE WAR YEARS

As the 1940s developed, rodeo advanced in popularity and became a major drawing card across the country. Organizations such as the Cowboys' Turtle Association (CTA) and the Rodeo Association of America (RAA) were getting more organized and improving their representation of the sport. By 1940, the Cowboys' Turtle Association had 1,100 members, including cowgirl bronc riders, trick riders, trick ropers, clowns, and announcers. The dues went from $5 to $10 a year. The CTA accepted RAA's rules for contests. However, the Turtles did ask stock contractors or contract acts that were CTA members or providing stock for a CTA event not to work "open" shows. For example, the historic Prescott, Arizona, rodeo was an amateur show in 1940 and CTA President Everett Bowman wrote an open letter in the *Hoofs and Horns* magazine, stating that this rodeo would "put them [cowboys] in bad with CTA." He also reported that the Livingston, Montana, and Reno, Nevada, rodeos had not been approved by CTA, as their purses were too uneven.[7] Competing cowboys could only enter rodeos sanctioned by the Cowboys' Turtle Association or jeopardize their standing in the association.

At the 1940 Turtles' annual meeting, held at the Belvedere Hotel in New York during the Madison Square Garden rodeo, Alvin Gordon was chosen to be the saddle bronc representative and Chet McCarty was picked to represent the bareback riders. The Denver Rodeo was just around the corner, and the Turtle Association had asked the Denver

committee to add calf roping to their list of contested events. Denver didn't exactly refuse but let the group know they did not want to add this event. The board of directors of CTA took a vote. The results: 5 to 2, not to work the Denver Rodeo. When the Denver officials were advised of the results, calf roping was added, and the Denver Rodeo for 1941 was reported as an accredited rodeo for CTA members. The Turtles, who had earlier required stock contractors who supplied stock to CTA rodeos not to supply stock to an amateur show, released the stockmen from this requirement.[7]

The Rodeo Association of America (RAA) was also suffering growing pains. Even though they promoted all members (rodeo committees) to have major events "open to the world," they agreed that they would not accept, for contesting, any person who was unsatisfactory to both the Turtles and RAA. Rule changes were publicized whenever necessary. For example, RAA reported that in the saddle bronc riding rules, following the phrase "horse must be spurred first jump out of the starting place," it added, "and rider must continue to spur throughout ride to the satisfaction of the judges."[7] Many new ideas were voiced; some became rule changes, and some did not.

Not all rodeos became members of RAA. In 1940 an animal rights group carrying placards during the rodeo, stating "Rodeo unfair to animals," harassed one California rodeo. The following day, lawsuits were filed by the group against the rodeo committee, and also against the Rodeo Association of America. Although this was not a sanctioned RAA rodeo, and the lawsuit against RAA was dismissed as quickly as this fact was realized, the rodeo committee did ask the RAA to help them pay the legal fees incurred over this incident. RAA also had other issues with which to contend, such as rodeo committees that did not get the purse information to RAA in time to circulate prize amounts thirty days prior to the event, which was a requirement of the members. Enforcing this issue, with close to 100 RAA-accredited rodeos a year, was not an easy task.

Purses were improving by 1940. Saddle bronc total purses were $1,600 in Cheyenne and Calgary that year. Houston had a purse of $1,435, Pendleton and Ogden offered $1,000

Louis Brooks, bareback and saddle bronc champion, departs from Colborn's Pet.
— Photo by R. R. Doubleday. Courtesy of the National Cowboy Hall of Fame.

and Colorado Springs had $900. Belle Fourche, South Dakota, Wolf Point, Montana, Filer, Idaho, Sheridan, Wyoming, Burwell, Nebraska, and Silver City, New Mexico, all had a $600 payoff. The bareback riding purses were not as good— yet. Calgary's total purse was $300, Cheyenne's was $650, and Houston paid $735.

It was a time for organization, and others in the rodeo world followed suit. On February 25, 1941, at Hanford, California, the Cowboys' Amateur Association of America was formed. Membership was $10 a year—$5 to be used for running the organization and $5 to be placed in a fund to help compensate for cowboys' injuries or deaths. This group copied many of the Turtles' original rules. It was an organization strictly for amateurs. Once a member won $500 in any one year, he automatically became a professional and could no longer be a member.

Dr. Leo Brady, of Endicott, New York, a fan of rodeo for twenty-five years, proposed the formation of Rodeo Fans of

From left: Wag Blessing, bareback bronc and bull rider; "Pink" Boylen, RAA director from Pendleton, Oregon; and Bud Linderman, All-Around competitor.
— Photo by A. Sponagel. Courtesy of Stan Searle.

America in 1941. This organization gathered members rather quickly and did much to promote rodeo, especially in areas of the country where rodeos were not often held.

Fred S. McCargar, secretary of the RAA, published an open letter in the *Chicago Tribune* to answer questions about rodeo in 1942. Here are the questions and his response:

> 1. How many rodeos are held each year in the United States and Canada? *Answer*: There are approximately 150 recognized rodeos. Some are exclusively rodeos, some are rodeos held in conjunction with fairs, or stock shows.
>
> 2. What is the attendance at these rodeos? *Answer*: The question is impossible to answer because there is no way to determine how many people attending a fair or stock show are there for the rodeo.
>
> 3. How many contestants enter rodeos? *Answer*: The average of a show is around 100 contestants. Shows that have low entrance fees attract larger numbers of local contestants who like to compete against world champions.
>
> 4. Which and where are the ten biggest rodeos? *Answer*: Based on the amount of money paid to the contestants per event they are: Los Angeles Coliseum Rodeo, one performance; Cheyenne Frontier Days, five performances; San Bernardino National Rodeo, two performances; Salinas Rodeo, four performances; Madison Square Garden, New York, twenty-six performances; Tucson Fiesta de Los Vaqueros, three performances; Iowa Championship Rodeo, Sidney, four performances; Reno Rodeo, three performances;

Klamath Falls, Oregon, Rodeo, three performances; Pendleton RoundUp, four performances, and Lewiston, Idaho, RoundUp, three performances (tied). Taking the rodeos according to the total purse paid to the contestants, they rate as follows: Madison Square Garden, New York; Chicago Stadium Rodeo; Boston Garden Rodeo; Minneapolis Aquatennial Rodeo; Cheyenne Frontier Days; Houston Fat Stock Show and Rodeo; Grand National Exposition, San Francisco; California Rodeo, Salinas; Calgary Exposition and Stampede; (three-way tie) Iowa's Championship Rodeo, Sidney, Auditorium Rodeo, Buffalo, New York, and Cleveland Arena Rodeo.[7]

The following month rule changes were circulated. For bronc riding, "add to first paragraph the following: 'Where three judges are used, one judge to mark horse and two judges to mark the ride, the three figures only to be added to determine the total points.'" For bareback riding, the following was added to reasons for granting re-rides: "If horse fails to buck, re-ride to be granted at the discretion of the judges. Horse must be spurred in shoulder first jump out of chute."

Cowboys Overseas

By 1942, World War II was raging. Many rodeo cowboys didn't wait to be called; they enlisted and went to war. The *Hoofs and Horns* magazine became an important tool to convey information regarding what was happening in the country toward defense, but also what was happening with the cowboys overseas. In April 1942 headlines read: "Real Job Lies Ahead For Rodeo Profession." The article stated: "A colonel in the army told me only yesterday that he felt that the rodeo was one of the finest morale builders for the army of any other community event. He urged that every rodeo be held that possibly could be, and that admissions to soldiers be made just as low as possible." In some cases this was not possible, and rodeos had to be canceled, as the manpower left at home was busy working in defense plants. But many rodeos were still held; in fact, some cowboys who were in the armed forces would come to the rodeo and compete in uniform. It was a real flag-waving time in the history of the United States, and as one person reported, "Cowboys risk life and limb rodeoing. Courage combined with skill are essentials of success in the rodeo arena. Is it any wonder these boys make fine soldiers for Uncle Sam?"[7]

Hoofs and Horns was filled with reports on where cowboys were stationed, their addresses, and letters from the boys overseas and those stationed at military bases across the country. Lists of names as they enlisted were printed, and month by month the lists grew longer. Magazine covers were often drawings of cowboys in uniform, or donned in red, white, and blue. Rationing of gas and tires caused problems in traveling to distant rodeos, but most of the cowboys found a way. Hitchhiking became popular, and anyone who did not stop and pick up a boy in uniform might be considered downright un-American.

Camp Roberts, California, held a successful rodeo on the base, and other camps throughout the country were encouraged to do the same. Some cowboys stationed overseas put together rodeos in various countries—Italy and India among them. They had to do some real improvising where the normal stock was not available.[7]

Foghorn Clancy, an early rodeo announcer, and often a reporter to various rodeo-oriented periodicals, wrote in the October 1943 issue of *Hoofs and Horns*:

> All through the years, because it is a he-man's sport, because it is a great drama of real life, because its actors are real and unique, and because it unfolds more thrills in a given length of time than any other sport, Rodeo has continued to grow right up to the time the Japs landed their sneak-punch on Pearl Harbor.
>
> Many difficulties have beset the rodeo game since the start of this present war—shortage of contestants on account of the vast numbers entering the armed forces, gasoline and rationing. But the cash customers have, as usual during a war, more money to spend than ever and therefore the rodeos being staged this year where the customers can get transportation to get to them, are breaking all records for financial returns and attendance.

We are winning this war. But let's not forget that while we labor to win the war, we should also do all that we can to keep Rodeo alive and healthy. We can do both, and out there on the far-flung battlefields are buddies of yours and mine. They are looking forward to the day when they can return to their homes and to the rodeo arena. They are charging us with keeping the game alive and healthy until they return. President Roosevelt has outlined a plan for taking care of service men upon their return from the war when it is over, so let us do our best to take care of our returning cowboys. Let's have Rodeo going bigger and better than ever, and they will thank us for it.[7]

One cowboy who did not return from World War II, having sacrificed his life for his country, was Fritz Truan. On February 28, 1945, he was killed on Iwo Jima.

Reorganized Rodeo

Many changes took place in rodeo in 1945. The Cowboys' Turtle Association changed its name to the Rodeo Cowboys Association and moved their headquarters from Phoenix to Fort Worth. Medical and life insurance was offered to its members, in case of injury or death in an approved rodeo, for $12 a year. Everett Bowman, who had been the president of the organization since 1936, resigned. In an article printed in *Hoofs and Horns*, June 1945, he stated: "I told everyone when it was suggested that we hire a business representative that they could count me out. I was never in favor of such an extravagant idea, and I did not think it would work. I always felt that any time the boys could not run their own business it was time to quit. . . . I still think our cowboys are plenty capable of running their own business." He went on to say that the business manager the Turtles hired, Earl Lindsey, was to make a salary of $7,500 a year, plus all expenses of traveling, hotels, and meals. Bowman said when he resigned there was $7,497 in the Turtle checking account, and $20,000 invested in United States Government War Bonds.[7]

The National Rodeo Association, formerly called the

Jim Shoulders, five-time All-Around Cowboy of the World, rides a Beutler Brothers bareback horse at a Capitol Hill Rodeo, Oklahoma City, in 1948.
— Photo by James Cathy, courtesy of
June and Buster Ivory.

Southwest Rodeo Association, and the Rodeo Association of America was in the midst of a merger. It was decided that one organization could now handle the affairs of all professional rodeos. On April 28, 1946, members voted unanimously to merge. A rodeo commissioner was to carry out the policies of the association and work with contestants and the cowboy rodeo associations. The new merger was named the International Rodeo Association (IRA). On March 16, 1947, International Rodeo Association representatives and Rodeo Cowboys Association (RCA) representatives met and agreed on one set of rules for rodeo competition throughout the country. Rodeo was becoming a big business!

Vignette of a Cowboy's Start

Pat Thompson was raised near Hershey, Nebraska, and tried every task required of a cowboy. As a teenager he competed in local rodeos on bareback broncs and bulls. The year he was eighteen he added saddle bronc riding. The young cowboys around Hershey all talked about "the Daddy of 'em all—Cheyenne" and how they were going that year, for sure, and enter their favorite event. Pat made plans too.

When the time came, the local group had dwindled one by one, as the boys made excuses for not going. One had to help with haying, another had injured his arm, and so on. In fact, everyone had backed out except Pat. He put his belongings in a paper box, tied it with twine, bought a bus ticket, and headed to Cheyenne. The year was 1947.

When Pat stepped off the bus in downtown Cheyenne, his eyes were as big as saucers. He just knew those cowboys and Indians were going to have a fight right there in front of him! Pat proceeded with caution. His exposure to the big city and celebrations the size of Frontier Days was lacking, but he was not to be waylaid from his objective: the saddle bronc event at Cheyenne Frontier Days.

He paid the entry fee and got ready for his event. Just as he put on his chaps, with his name sewn on the bottom corner, they called him to ride. He was up. He rode his first mount. Several of the cowboys told him it was a good ride. He could hardly wait until the event the next day, when he could ride his next bronc.

A little more confident the following day, he at least knew where to be. Pat had his chaps on and was ready when they called his name. He rode to the whistle again, meaning he would be in the finals.

Pat could hardly sleep the night before the finals. He drew an outlaw bronc, called Wind River. The ride started out good, but just before the whistle Pat hit the dirt—bucked off. He was so embarrassed he made his way out of that arena as fast as he could. The first thing he did when he got away from people was cut the letters "PAT" off his chaps. Maybe no one would recognize him as the kid that bucked off just before the whistle.

Pat Thompson bucks off Wind River at 1947 Cheyenne Frontier Days Amateur Bucking Finals. Deb Copenhaver won it that year, and other contenders were Buck Rutherford and Les Gore.
— Photo courtesy of Pat Thompson.

Pat went back to Hershey with empty pockets. Those dreams he had before Frontier Days about winning didn't happen. And on top of that disappointment now he had to tell his friends what had happened. He just knew they'd laugh themselves silly. Much to Pat's surprise, in a day or two, everyone in Hershey, Nebraska, was treating him with a great deal of respect. The old-timers would wave when they saw him. The hometown guys considered him a hero! Pat Thompson had ridden all the way to the finals at Cheyenne Frontier Days, "the Daddy of 'em all." And he had drawn Wind River, that ornery cayuse that everybody knew. "Why, that bronc had bucked off the Lindermans and all those top broncbusters!" the old-timers would marvel. "And 'our' Pat had almost ridden him to the whistle, by golly!"

This story could be about three-fourths of the cowboys that compete at small-town rodeos across the nation. They don't travel far to compete, they have jobs and responsibilities

Buster Ivory being congratulated by the Christensen Brothers, Oregon stock contractors, on winning the bronc riding at the Cow Palace, San Francisco, 1952.
— Photo by George W. Baker, courtesy of Stan Searle.

that prevent it, but they do participate around home and read the papers and keep track of the minority of the cowboys who make rodeoing a full-time job. Pat Thompson never became a full-time roughstock rodeo contestant—he became a top-rated quarter horse trainer and rancher—but he still vividly remembers competing at "the Daddy of 'em all."

Buster Ivory started rodeoing in 1938 at MacArthur, California. He was working on a ranch for $30 a month and someone suggested they go to the local rodeo. Ivory entered the bull riding and the steer stopping. He won the bull riding and split first and second in the steer stopping, collecting $58. That was almost two months' wages on the ranch, and he collected that in one afternoon! It wasn't long until Ivory was a full-time rodeo contestant.

The Winners' Circle

In 1944 the final winners of the saddle bronc event at the following rodeos were: Denver—Vic Schwartz; Houston—Bill McMacken; Fort Worth—Louis Brooks; Calgary—Bill Linderman; Salt Lake City—Louis Brooks; Cheyenne—Bill McMacken; Great Falls—George Yardley; Pueblo—Bill Linderman; Pendleton—Bob Burrows; Philadelphia—Ralph Collier; Madison Square Garden—Shirley Hussey; and Boston Garden—Paul Gould.

Bareback riding event winners at some of the rodeos holding that event were: Houston—Jerry Brown; Salt Lake City—Louis Brooks; Cheyenne—Louis Brooks; Great Falls—Jack Wade; Pueblo—Hank Mills; Boston Garden—Howard Brown; and Madison Square Garden—Louis Brooks.

In this era the basis for point awards toward championships was one point for each dollar in prize money won. The RAA did not give points on that part of the purse made up of added entry fees, but the RCA did. There was a discrepancy between the two organizations, and as a result the winners for each organization were often different.

In 1945 the Rodeo Association of America Standing of Leading Contestants was as follows:

All-Around: Bill Linderman (15,303 points)
     Bud Linderman (14,832 points)
     Gerald Roberts (12,209 points)

Bronc Riding: Bill Linderman (5,962 points)
     Bud Linderman (4,607 points)
     Bill McMacken (4,584 points)

Bareback Bronc Riding: Bud Linderman (6,842 points)
     Bill Linderman (5,813 points)
     Gerald Roberts (3,442 points)
     Hank Mills (3,086 points)

The Rodeo Cowboys Association Point Award System for 1945 was as follows:

All-Around: no championship awarded

Bronc Riding: Bill Linderman (7,104 points)
    Ken Roberts (5,660 points)
    Bud Linderman (5,244 points)
    George Yardley (5,240 points)
    Bill McMacken (4,854 points)

Bareback Bronc Riding: Bud Linderman (8,131 points)
    Bill Linderman (6,919 points)
    Gerald Roberts (4,983 points)
    Hank Mills (4,340 points)
    Pat Gould (3,898 points)

Broncbusters of the Era (1940s)

GENE RAMBO (1920-1988) was born in San Miguel, California, where his dad, a ranch manager and good bronc rider, taught him to break and ride colts when he was only seven years old. He started his rodeo career at seventeen, and the following year won money at Prescott when he placed in the bronc riding. During the next ten years he competed in practically all events.

He won the RAA All-Around Championship in 1946 and 1948. In 1948 he won first in bareback bronc riding, second in bulldogging, third in saddle bronc riding, and fourth in calf roping. To win the '48 crown, Rambo traveled about 30,000 miles and entered no

Gene Rambo being awarded the 1958 All-Around Champion Cowboy buckle by Pete Cronin, with Levi Strauss, donor of the buckle.

— Photo by George W. Baker,
courtesy of Stan Searle.

less than thirty contests. He stood five feet, ten inches and weighed 180 pounds. He was hard as a rock and stayed in perfect shape, and had an amazing amount of energy.

Longtime friend Don McMillan said of Rambo: "At Salt Lake City in 1947 Gene was riding a wild bareback bronc that plunged headlong into the arena fence just at the whistle. The horse bounced back, dead as a gutted jack-rabbit, leaving Gene hanging on the top of the fence badly bruised and shirtless. Despite these bruises and a deep wound in the palm of his hand, Gene went on to work in three events that afternoon and three that evening. Then, he sat around until 2 A.M. to be paid off, took a shower, loaded his horse and drove to Cheyenne, a distance of 480 miles. I was with him during all this and it liked to wore me out just watching him."

Rambo said the toughest ride he ever had was on a horse of Doc Sorenson's named Fox, at Ogden, Utah. Rambo was a modest, easygoing fellow, who was well liked by the rodeo gang and praised by rodeo fans.[7]

BUSTER IVORY (1923-____), a native of Alturas, California, worked on ranches and at fourteen entered his first rodeo, winning two firsts. Although he didn't rodeo full-time until two years later, he knew what he wanted to do. He competed in saddle bronc, bareback, bull riding, and occasionally team roping.

In 1942 he broke his shoulder in eight places, and was out of competition for a year. In 1945 he won the bareback riding at Denver and ended the year winning the same event at the Cow Palace, plus many in between. He had a good year in 1946, but in 1948 he was bucked off a horse called Red Ryder at Salinas, California, and broke his neck. He was hospitalized for six months. The doctor's orders to stay away from bucking stock kept Ivory working in saddle shops and western stores, although he did judge rodeo. In 1950 he was riding saddle broncs again. The first rodeo was at Palm Springs, and he split first and second. He won the Christensen Brothers trophy awarded to the high point winner at their thirty-five rodeos.

Ivory never won the awards he was capable of winning

Buster Ivory shows perfect saddle bronc riding form on Buck at Roseburg, Oregon, 1957.
— Photo by Devere Helfrich, donated by June and Buster Ivory. Courtesy of the National Cowboy Hall of Fame.

because he was too busy with additional responsibilities for rodeo. He was secretary of the RCA from January 1953 until 1957; livestock director for the National Finals Rodeos (NFR) from its inception for twenty-six years; NFR chute boss for three years; livestock superintendent for the 1958 World's Fair American Wild West Show and Rodeo in Brussels, Belgium; livestock superintendent in 1967 at the World's Fair Rodeo in Montreal; and the general manager in 1970 of the Rodeo Far West that toured Europe. He has been a representative in one way or another for many years.[35, 53]

BILL LINDERMAN (1920-1965) was born near Bridger, Montana, where his family was in the cattle business. Bill entered the big-time rodeo business at Denver in 1942. He began by riding saddle broncs and bareback, but eventually included bulldogging and calf roping as well. He won the North American Champion Cowboy title at Calgary four years in a row. In 1945 he won the All-Around Cowboy

Bill Linderman readies his saddle bronc riding equipment.
— Photo courtesy of Jack Long.

Championship of the World, and won it again in 1950 and 1953. He was World Bareback Champion in 1943, and Saddle Bronc Champion in 1945 and 1950. He also won the Steer Wrestling World Championship in 1950.

Bill Linderman was six feet tall, 175 pounds, and handsome. When his rodeo injuries kept him from competing, he helped rodeo grow by representing the sport and becoming an integral part of the organization. He was president of the RCA for six years and later held the office of secretary-treasurer for four years.

He died in a plane crash at Salt Lake City on November 11, 1965. Linderman was one of the original honorees inducted to the ProRodeo Hall of Fame in Colorado Springs in 1979.

BUD LINDERMAN (1922-1961), younger brother to Bill, was also born on the family homestead near Bridger, Montana. He made quite a splash when he entered the competitive rodeo game by winning the first five shows he entered. In 1941 he began traveling with Fritz Truan and continued until Truan entered the service in 1942. At eighteen he was fourth in the All-Around standings at year's end. He won the Bareback Championship of the World in 1945 and IRA World All-Around Cowboy title in 1947. He was one of the top five in bareback or saddle bronc from 1945 through 1950. In 1951 he was seventh in the All-Around. He was second in the All-Around in 1945, being beaten by a few hundred points by his brother, Bill, and repeating this same scene in 1947 when Gene Rambo beat him in the All-Around race by eight points!

Bud Linderman was a versatile competitor, and in addition to all three roughstock events, he was a calf roper and bulldogger. Some of his friends from that era said Bud was a natural. He could do, with little effort, what others had to work very hard to accomplish. One example was relayed of Bud entering a calf roping after drinking all night, and he was still "full of liquor" when it was his turn. The boys helped him up onto the roping horse and he rode out, tossed his loop, tied his calf, and beat everyone else.

During World War II, Cecil Wright, correspondent for "California News Items" in the *Hoofs and Horns* magazine, wrote the following in his column: "Bud Linderman did fourteen days on bread and water for going A. W. O. L. from the Navy detachment at Treasure Island. When asked how it was to live on bread and water, Bud said, 'Boy, after about three days, that bread tasted just like chicken.'"[7]

LOUIS BROOKS (1916-1983) was born at Fletcher, Oklahoma, and, due to his dad's death, was reared by his grandparents. He went to cowboying early in life, working for various ranches. His first rodeo was in Pawhuska, Oklahoma, in 1936. When he started contesting he entered everything, and could win in every event. But eventually he quit bull riding, and he said his saddle bronc and bareback ability improved 40% within thirty days. He was All-Around Champion Cowboy in 1943 and 1944, Champion Bronc Rider in 1943 and 1944, and Champion Bareback Rider in 1942 and 1944. Some of the top horses he rode were Amos, T-Joe, Hell's Angels, and Hootchie Kootchie.

When Brooks retired from rodeo in 1945, a scant nine-year career, he went into ranching and raised Brangus cattle. He was inducted into the National Cowboy Hall of Fame and the ProRodeo Hall of Fame.[19]

DOFF ABER (1908-1946) of Wolf, Wyoming, grew up riding horses. At nineteen he was already a professional saddle bronc rider. This was the only event he entered. He won the bronc riding at the 1935 Tex Austin Rodeo in Los Angeles, pitted against top riders Earl Thode and Pete Knight. In 1939 he won Cheyenne, 1941 Pendleton, and 1942 Cheyenne and Calgary. In 1941 and 1942 he was the RAA Saddle Bronc

Doff Aber, 1941 and 1942 Saddle Bronc Champion of the World, from Wolf, Wyoming.
— Photo courtesy Stan Searle.

Champion. Aber went to thirty-eight rodeos in 1941; he placed in the finals in twenty-four of the thirty-eight—eighteen in succession. Clifford Westermeier said, "When Doff talked bronc riding a light would come into his eyes." Westermeier's book, *Man, Beast, Dust,* was dedicated to Aber, who died in 1946 on his Fort Collins, Colorado, ranch in a jeep accident.[23]

BUREL MULKEY (1904-1982) was born at Clyde, Idaho, and learned to ride on the family ranch. He entered his first rodeo in 1929, and became Saddle Bronc Champion in 1937 and 1938. He was All-Around Champion Cowboy, as well, in 1938. He was said to give his all no matter if the horse was a good bucker or a "dog."[19]

Mulkey and mischief went hand in hand. He and friends were always playing a trick or thinking up something hilarious as they traveled the rodeo road. He and Nick Knight, often called "The Gold Dust Twins," were inseparable before they both married. It is told that after they had arrived in a new town they would go to the local tavern or café and visit with locals. Once they knew the names of other locals they got a kick out of saying, "Hey, did you hear about Mr. _____ getting into trouble with his wife, when she caught him with that girl, _____?" Of course, it was all untrue, but Mulkey and Knight would roar over their tricks on the unsuspecting locals.

Broncs of the Era (1940s)

BADGER MOUNTAIN was born on a ranch near Douglas, Washington, and proved to be an outlaw—unfit to be a saddle horse, and unfit to be a workhorse. The Willems Brothers took him to a rodeo at Waterville and he threw every rider there for three days. For two years he continued to buck off everyone who tried to ride him. In 1931 Leo Moomaw acquired him, and Badger Mountain bucked at major rodeos for twenty years. During much of his bucking career the Ring Brothers of Wilbur, Washington, owned him.

When they first started bucking this big bald-faced, bay bronc, he would leave the chute as if he were packing the mail. He traveled fast, crooked, and hard. As time went on, his front feet must have bothered him, for he changed his style. He would come away from the chute fast, but go up on his hind legs, swinging his shoulders into a wicked twist, and would fight his head like a Brahma. The farther he was ridden the faster and rougher he would get. Bronc riders without a heavy rein would likely pull him over, but he was an honest horse and seldom hurt a man. Known as a clever horse, he loved rodeo the way some men love golf. He was too lazy to work for a living pulling a plow, and smart enough to find a way to avoid it.[7]

Badger Mountain died in a chute, although he had been retired for three years. A vet was to work on his teeth in the chute. Apparently the excitement of being back in the chute after all those years was too much for the twenty-nine-year-old horse.

COME APART was foaled in the spring of 1945 on the Claud Lewis ranch in Big Horn County, Wyoming. His mother was a sorrel thoroughbred mare. In 1948 Andy Gifford, who ranched at Crystal Creek and was a stock contractor, bought him. He had been broken by Ken Kimbrough, who worked for the Lewis ranch, and he used the colt all the time. Something happened after Andy bought him, because Andy had to walk back to camp several times. He then put him in the bucking string.

Merle Fales, of Cody, Wyoming, bucked him at Cody Nite Rodeo, under the name Trail Tramp, and he was just better than average. He then was put in Cremer's string as a saddle bronc, but the 1,350-pound, sorrel streak-faced gelding made very little impression. When Cremer bucked him in the bare-back string at Chicago, no one could ride him. Come Apart found bucking people off, without a saddle, came easily and frequently. Shortly thereafter Cremer was killed in a car accident, and Harry Knight shipped all the Cremer stock to his ranch at Fowler, Colorado.

"Come Apart was athletic, long-backed and double tough," said Leonard McCravey, "there was no way to stop him." A writer for the *ProRodeo Sports News* said, "It's easy to see why they named him Come Apart—he lived up to his name every time a chute gate was opened. He pulled apart cowboys' ribs, snapped their wrists and rearranged their forearms. He jerked gloves right out of the rigging, and the stitching right out of the gloves. And when he got done turning cowboys upside down, he turned them inside out. For the power that this horse possesses was like no other."[53]

Few riders qualified on him, but if they did, they knew they would be in the money. One exception to that statement was Jim Houston; he drew him four times and successfully rode him all four times. And Bert France made a qualified ride on him:

> At Houston, Come Apart was probably one of, if not the rankest horse alive. . . . He was not a workhorse type; he looked more like a tall roping horse. Well muscled and straight legged, he had small, alert eyes and ears. In order for a man to complete a ride on the famous horse, he had to come 'a cluckin' (or spurring). You couldn't hold 'um in 'em, for his strength was such that his own power would rip your feet high above your head and tear your hand from its grasp, and send you flying high.
>
> There have been, and still are, many good and rank bareback horses, but Come Apart in my estimation, ranked in the top five of all time greats, and Bert knew it! He had tried the sorrel before, but without success. Now he was ready. . . .
>
> A thought of Bert's boyhood rushed through his mind, then he scooted up on his hand, and nodded, hesitating a split second—then Come Apart jumped, and hit the ground, at the same time kicking high, almost standing straight up on his front legs. He kicked so hard his hocks cracked like a rifle shot, but his power failed to loosen Bert's spurs, and they stayed planted deep, in the sorrel's brisket, and Bert knew

he was safe. Again the horse jumped, seeming to be trying to go through the roof of the coliseum, and little Bert drug hair plumb to his riggin. It looked as though his knees would break, from bending them so hard. His body leaned back, till the back of his hat pushed against Come Apart's rump, bending his hat brim up. When ol' Come Apart hit the earth again, Bert's short shanked spurs sunk to the band in the sorrel's tough hide. A smile almost came on his face as the ride continued, for he knew he'd triumphed. At the whistle, Lefty Wilkins drove his horse into Come Apart and snatched the halter and little Bert slipped off and eased over Lefty's horse's rump, and to the ground.

The grandstand thundered, clapping and stomping their feet so loud that when Cy announced the score, it was impossible to hear. Finally the applause began to quiet, and Cy blared, "Listen to this score, Ladies and Gentlemen, an unheard of 193!" and the crowd began to roar again.[58]

Mrs. Harry Knight considered Come Apart her favorite. He bucked for twenty-seven years and was just as hard to ride late in life as when he was young. He was bit by a rattlesnake, south of Pueblo, Colorado, in 1970, and died instantly.

JOKER was a great-grandson to Man-O-War, and brother to High Tide, and at one time he was in a wild horse string owned by Fred Krogan of White River, South Dakota. He was purchased by Archie Anderson from the Cleary ranch in Winnemucca, Nevada.

Joker, owned by Harry Knight, and Christensen Brothers' War Paint tied for RCA Bucking Horse of the Year in 1958. He bucked off thirty of the thirty-three riders who attempted to ride him in his last season. He had been in the bucking string ten years.

On a return trip from a Harrisburg, Pennsylvania, rodeo it was discovered he had a slight head injury. He developed an infection and died of lockjaw.

Death came at Fort Madison, Iowa. Joker was fifteen at the time of his death.[52]

WAR PAINT was foaled on the Klamath Indian

Reservation. Orrie Summers brought him in from the reservation and he was bought by Christensen Brothers. War Paint was picked as the Bucking Horse of the Year in 1956, the very first year this honor was awarded. He won the title again in 1957, and tied with Joker in 1958. War Paint was eleven in 1958, and had been bucked in California and the Northwest for eight years. Hank Christensen said, "He has no distinctive way of bucking, he just keeps trying." They had War Paint insured with Lloyds of London for $10,000, which was a lot of money in that day. Insuring a bronc was a first for rodeo.

After unseating Jim Botham at the Emerald Empire RoundUp at Eugene, Oregon, War Paint was retired and unsaddled in the arena in 1958. He had traveled 540,000 miles across the United States and Canada, and out of twenty-eight starts that season had had twenty-five buck-offs.[7, 11, 52]

CHIEF TYHEE, a sorrel with a flaxen mane and tail, and a lot of white in his face, was bought by Herman Linder from Long Time Squirrel on the Blood Reservation, near Cardston, Alberta. Linder sold him to Everett Colborn. He was a stout horse, solid and very fast, but would try to hurt the cowboys in the chutes.[11]

WIGWAM, a strawberry roan gelding, was foaled on the Spencer Ranch in South Dakota in 1942. Broken as a two-year-old to be a saddle horse, he was used by kids. When the ranch cowboys began to ride him, rebellion ensued. In 1946 he was sold to Roberts Rodeo Company in Kansas. Milt Moe at Topeka rode him once the first year. Jerry Ambler, at Saint Joseph, Missouri, did not ride him again until September 1948. Those who won on him were Gerald Roberts, Casey Tibbs, Jack Buschbom, and Ken Roberts. He was strictly a saddle bronc, weighed 1,250 pounds, and his bucking included a high kick and turnback and a tailspin.[7]

STARLIGHT was born in 1934 in Nevada. During 1940 Fritz Truan rode him successfully.[23] Harry Rowell brought him to the rodeo arena. Truan said that without a doubt he was the worst horse to ride in the business. He had a way of rearing into the air and then coming down on his forelegs with his withers heading right into the heavens. But he was not routine, and twice as temperamental![7]

SCENE SHIFTER was foaled on the Jack Hitt ranch at Malta, Utah. Hitt's son broke him to ride. One time a horsefly bit the bay, and he bucked his rider off. After several other attempts to ride him to no avail, he was sold. He went from one to another for a while. During the four years he was owned by Parley Hall and Earl Hutchison, of Hillside Rodeo Company, he bucked off sixty-two out of seventy-two that drew him. Harry Rowell purchased him in the mid-1940s. He bucked straightaway. *Hoofs and Horns* reported, "Heard Bill Ward made one of the greatest rides of his career on him to win the bronc riding at Red Bluff in 1946."[7]

HOOTCHIE KOOTCHIE was owned by Leo Cremer. Shirley Hussey came out on this bronc who had been ridden only twice in twenty attempts. The horse pitched high and did a hula dance on the peak of his jump. He came down hard in front and kicked high behind, but Hussey scratched him right up to the pay window for first day money in Salt Lake City, 1940.[7]

DEER LODGE SPECIAL, owned by Jake Johnson of Perma, Montana, was purchased from a stock rancher in Deer Lodge Valley. Bill Linderman made the only successful bareback ride ever made on this ten-year-old grey. Linderman won money at Polson, Montana, in 1947, on him. The horse quit bucking whenever the whistle blew, and would trot off, content in a job well done.[7]

7

BORN AND BRED TO BUCK

Without the bucking horse, the bronc, or the outlaw we would never have had broncbusters or roughstock events in rodeo. The early-day wild mustangs provided this need, but as the huge herds were depleted it was necessary to find other sources. A few men who bred horses and saw the need for horses that would buck in rodeo have helped develop the much needed bronc.

Reg Kesler, an early competitor and a stock contractor for more than fifty years, from Sterling, Alberta, told the author, "A good bronc is like any top athlete; he has to have the desire, of course, but he always has to have a lot of HEART." Kesler went on to say, "Watch a good bronc, he'll buck even when he's in a pasture, with no human beings in sight. He just loves to buck."

World War I created a great demand for horses in Europe, and many nations sent representatives to Montana and the grasslands of Canada to buy horses. Cowboys rode or attempted to ride each horse. The representatives from various countries would often make their decisions based on these rides. This is how some of the broncbusters of the day gained experience.

In eastern Montana, South Dakota, Wyoming, and Alberta, Canada, the plains were dotted with wild horses during the early part of the twentieth century. By the 1930s, the plains were covered with these outlaws, and with a drought and the depression something had to be done about this overabundance of untamed horses. By this time, these bands were a combination of mustangs, draft horses that had been mortgaged by unsuccessful homesteaders that had returned east and turned them loose, plus remount horses and some horses that had wandered off the Indian reservations. These horses were destined to die of starvation because of the great number of horses in this area, and the lack of grass and water.

The United States government made an agreement to supply Russia with horse meat, which at that time was treated as a delicacy in that part of the world. The Chapple Brothers Cannery (CBC), active in Illinois and farther east, was providing this horse meat. They moved their operation closer to the source of horses in the late 1920s, to gather horses for their plants. Horse gatherers working for the CBC outfit were paid well—between $40 and $45 a month. Normal ranch pay was $1 a day. But working for the Chapple Brothers was not easy. A CBC cowboy started his day at 3:00 A.M. and ended it at 8:00 or 9:00 P.M., seven days a week.[56]

Running wild horses was not a job for every cowboy. Racing across the badlands and ravines and keeping up with these outlaws while riding full-speed took quite a bit of daring, and a lot of luck. If a cowboy was hurt, he had to heal fast. Historian and former horse hunter for the Chapple Brothers Cannery, Dick Glenn, said at one time there were more than 60,000 horses running between the Yellowstone and Missouri rivers. The Chapple Brothers Cannery stayed in the area until 1937.

Meanwhile, rodeo grew. Miles City RoundUp began in 1913. By the mid-1930s, practically every little community in the West held a rodeo. Stock contractors from everywhere came to this northern plains area to buy potential bucking stock.[56]

In 1947, at Billings, Montana, Bill Linderman and Don Wright held a bucking horse sale. More than 400 range and spoiled horses were ridden for $10 mount money for saddle broncs, and $5 mount money for barebacks.[35] Stock contractors from all across the nation attended. In addition to a couple of carloads of bucking horses, Everett Colborn, of Dublin, Texas, also bought a pinto saddle bronc for $500. The sale was a huge success. The following year there were 664 horses bucked and sold, and Colborn was again the volume buyer.

Deb Copenhaver on Snake, a top horse of Leo Moomaw and Joe Kelsey, at Penticton, 1949.
— Photo by Jim Chamberlain, courtesy of
June and Buster Ivory.

In 1950 Les Boe, owner of the Miles City Auction Company, and his son-in-law, Bob Pauley, bought some yearling steers and got thirty-five head of bucking horses in the deal. They had no use for the horses, and knowing how successful the Linderman-Wright sale at Billings had been, decided to hold a bucking horse sale in Miles City. They also bought 200 head of pinto studs and spread the word for other folks in the area to bring their horses to sell. They borrowed ten bronc saddles from Montana stock contractor Leo Cremer, and contacted all known stock contractors. Although they had planned a one-day sale, it took several days for the horses to be bucked and sold. The total was somewhere between 900 and 1,800 horses.

Cowboys got $10 and $5 mount money. It was good pay in those days, and numerous fights broke out among the bronc riders over who was to ride which horse out of which chute. Despite the confrontations, the sale was a success and Boe and Pauley decided the sale should be held annually.[56]

After a few years, paying mount money to the riders ceased; however, bronc riders continued to come to ride. It was an ideal way for young, beginning riders to practice bronc riding. Rodeo schools were unheard of at the time, and other than an occasional local rodeo, where a rider could ride one or two head of stock, if they didn't break horses for a living, opportunities to gain experience as bronc riders were limited.

The sale became world famous and through the years was featured in a variety of magazine and newspaper articles. Leading stock contractors relied on the Miles City sale to provide a continual flow of new broncs to their numbers.

In 1952 Alice Greenough's 66 Ranch was volume buyer with a purchase of sixty-eight head, and Leo Cremer bought fifty-eight. In 1954 Everett Colborn paid a high price of $250 for a horse consigned by Ed Vaughn. By 1955, the sale was RCA-sponsored, and Charley Mantle won the saddle bronc contest with Dick Johnston first in the bareback riding. In 1957 Alvin Nelson picked up $981.20 by winning both saddle bronc and bareback events.

In 1960 the famous sale bucked a horse out of the chutes every minute and a half, for a total of 276 horses. The Tooke Rodeo Company in 1961 paid $350 for a horse consigned by Frank Woods. During the 1966 event, well-known area bronc riders Jim Tescher and Alvin Nelson were pitted against each other in a matched bronc ride. Nelson got hurt on his second bronc, and Tom Tescher stepped in and rode Nelson's last bronc. Jim Tescher had the highest score.

In 1969 Harry Knight paid a record price of $875 for a bronc. Ten years later, Jack Bloxham, buyer for Mike Cervi, of Sterling, Colorado, paid $2,000 for the top horse. By the 1980 sale, 302 horses sold, averaging $500 a piece. In 1981 Marvin Brookman paid $3,000—another record—to Arnie Lesmeister for a saddle bronc. Lyn Jonckowski won the ladies' bareback riding. A total of 243 mounts averaged $644.

Although those who started this annual event are gone, the affair is still a feature for Miles City. Numerous stock contractors continue to attend and buy potential bucking stock. This well-known part of the West has provided top buckers for more than a hundred years.[56]

Bucking Horse of the Year, Big John, dethrones Kenny McLean at Denver, 1963. Jack Bloxham sold this saddle bronc to Harry Knight.
— Photo by Devere Helfrich, donated by June and Buster Ivory. Courtesy of the National Cowboy Hall of Fame.

Other bucking horse sales have been held; in fact, in 1986 a Bucking Stock Sale was started during the PRCA National Finals in Las Vegas. It has since been held annually, and the sale offers part of the proceeds to the ProRodeo Hall of Fame in Colorado Springs, and is considered one of the Hall's most profitable fundraising activities. At the present time it sells saddle broncs, bareback broncs, bucking bulls, pickup horses, and fighting bulls. Since most major stock contractors are in Las Vegas at the time of the sale it is an ideal way to get "preferred buyers" to the auction.[53]

One of the major spokespersons for the promotion of the bucking horse during the 1950s was Casey Tibbs. The following examples show his support.

A letter to the editor of *Hoofs and Horns* magazine, in the May 1957 issue:

> In a recent issue of your publication I noted the same old argument—the old time buckers tougher than today's

horses; or could today's bronc rider ride the wild one that stood on his hind feet. I believe I can answer this question for you. I have been in the game over twelve years. My first years at places like Great Falls, Montana. They never had anything but wild horses, and most of them had never been corralled more than a couple of times in their life. I'm sure everyone in rodeo remembers Wild Horse Rickter. This man seldom had a horse that was halter broken or that wouldn't tear the chutes down. Most people in Dakota are familiar with the Madison string. I remember when they used to bring a lot of wild horses but the money was still on the Hickory Dicks, Comanche's and the Maybe's, if they rode them. The wild horse is an explosion horse and doesn't have the power or strength to throw it at you like a horse that has been bucked a lot. Also, an old bucker learns a few nasty tricks now and then. But the one thing for sure is a horse that stands on his hind legs is not part of a bucking horse and the only way he can throw you is if you think he is coming on over backwards and you loosen up. I will admit some of these horses are crowd pleasers. When some kid gets lucky and wins the championship in 15 or 20 years from now, I hope they accept him as Champ and not say he couldn't have ridden with Tibbs. When a good cowboy or bucking horse comes along, give them credit.[7]

The question is continually being tossed around, especially among the old-timers, as to whether the bucking horse of today measures up to the outlaw bronc of yesteryear. In the *Rodeo Sports News* of June 1, 1957, Casey Tibbs, RCA vice president, at the time, wrote an open letter to Verne Elliott, top rodeo producer and stock contractor:

While passing through Denver the other day, I stopped at the Rodeo Cowboys' Association office. In looking over some newspaper clippings I came across an interview from you on bucking horses, mainly condemning the horse of today and saying we might have to start bucking automobiles. Being the great producer of rodeo that you are, I can hardly imagine you saying this. But let's get back to the bucking horses.

I know that "Five Minutes to Midnight" and "Midnight" were great horses and you loved them so much you nearly choked up every time you talked about them. There are still a lot of tough bucking horses and they all eat hay and their mothers all give milk the same as they did thirty years ago.

Also let's take into consideration how many times the bucking horse of today is used. A lot of them are used around 50 times a year. The old horses were never exposed to cowboys more than 15 times in actual competition in one year. Naturally these horses today are going to be ridden more often.

Another point I'd like to bring out, the number of horses it takes today in comparison with thirty years ago. There are about five times as many rodeos and five or six times as many cowboys. There are probably that many more bucking horses being used today than then, and while there are not as many as could be used, rodeo is too big and well-founded for the problem not to be solved when the time comes. Possibly as you suggest, by raising bucking stock.

We could go on and argue this forever, and still never get everyone to agree either way. It's like the argument about who was the toughest, Dempsey or Marciano. How are you going to prove it?

In closing I'd like to add one more thing. You said rodeo had been good to you. I think you have been good to rodeo. If you continue in rodeo you may solve the problem yourself. So after all these years don't you think it sort of unfair to suggest to the public the thought of no more bucking horse, or having to buck automobiles?[52]

Much of what this response talks about did happen. Many of the top stock contractors did start their own breeding program for bucking horses. The biggest frustration with this solution is the time it takes and the acreage required to have a successful program. Bucking broncs are not even tested or required to show their ability until they are at least four years old or older. It takes a minimum of eighty acres per animal to raise these horses properly. Realizing that not all progeny will produce the buck, or the personality required to take their honored place in a contractors' bucking string, means a lot of time. And land is tied up with questionable long-term results. It also means stock contractors still cannot rely on what they have in their own pastures, but are continually looking for new broncs. With

War Paint, owned by the Christensen Brothers, won the first "Bucking Horse of the Year" award. This photo by Devere Helfrich, shows John Ivory aboard at the 1962 Pacific International.
— Donated by Bill Cheshire. Courtesy of the National Cowboy Hall of Fame.

the number of rodeos being held since the 1950s, the number of horses required for roughstock events is staggering.

In 1956 Tibbs suggested a "Saddle Bronc of the Year Award," which was picked up and sponsored by the *Rodeo Sports News*, the newspaper of the Rodeo Cowboys Association. It was to be voted on by the top ten saddle bronc riders for 1956, at the end of the year. It would be awarded at the National Western Stock Show and Rodeo in Denver the following January. Horses nominated were required to have been in bucking action during the immediate calendar year. *Rodeo Sports News (RSN)* would give the winner a silver mounted bucking horse halter, distinctive and recognizable, but still functional, to be worn when the horse was drawn.

The first award went to War Paint, owned by Christensen Brothers, of Oregon. He also won the award the following year, 1957. Although Beutler Brothers of Elk City, Oklahoma, was providing the stock for the Denver Rodeo in 1958, Christensen's brought War Paint to Denver for the presentation. This was a major publicity feature and the Denver arena was full of photographers, reporters, and technical people from three television networks who came to witness the event. [52]

Alvin Nelson, 1957 World Champion Saddle Bronc Rider, was also there. Ready to be inducted in to the Armed Forces, Nelson was given permission to be in Denver to give an exhibition ride on War Paint. Nelson had not been around the award-winning bronc and was not familiar with how he bucked. The top ten riders who had voted on him had said, "he was a good, honest bucker." Deb Copenhaver and Tibbs helped Nelson get ready. The chute gate opened, and War Paint made his traditional high jump out of the chute, went into his furious buck, and Nelson was off in two seconds.

It was reported a few months later in *Rodeo Sports News* that War Paint had also dumped Tibbs, at a matched bucking in Red Bluff, California.[52]

Horsemen Known for Good Bucking Stock

FEEK TOOKE (1909-1968), AND SON, ERNEST—Earl and Bessie Tooke, and their six boys, Frank, Fay, Dick, Red, Bill and Feek, were at every rodeo in and around Ekalaka, Montana. In 1931 they built an arena and a couple of bronc chutes on their ranch and began putting on rodeos. Later they supplied stock for the Miles City, Baker, Billings, Deadwood, Belle Fourche, and Hettinger Rodeos. They also leased stock to Leo Cremer and provided rough stock for the 1938 Chicago Rodeo.[35]

In the early 1940s Feek decided to breed horses, having the disposition necessary for rodeo broncs. He bought a registered Shire stud called King Larego, who sired a colt named Prince. He also bought a mean-spirited Arabian saddle horse named Snowflake. "Snowflake was the meanest horse, that was broke to ride, that I'd ever met," said Ernest. "If you walked up to him, it was four hoofs in the air and the mouth wide open. It was necessary to rope and throw the little Arabian just to put on or remove a halter."[35]

Tooke had the right combination between Prince's orneriness and Snowflake's mean streak. He crossed Snowflake's daughters to Prince and Prince's mares to Snowflake. Tooke soon had a bloodline of bucking horses to be envied in all rodeo circles.

Prince also sired two half-brothers, General Custer and Timberline. General Custer sired Major Reno and Sheep Mountain, who have all made their impact as bucking horses in rodeo. Ernest told of one of his greatest thrills at the Miles City Bucking Sale, when five of the top bronc riders were matched: Jim and Tom Tescher, Pete Fredricks, Alvin Nelson, and Dean Armstrong.

> It was muddy and the riders in the match were riding the other contractors' horses fairly easily in the mud. Alvin Nelson, a World Champion, was mounted on our big stallion, General Custer. "Custer" was a full-blood Shire and weighed about 1,800 pounds. He was the rankest bucking horse for his size I will ever see.
>
> Alvin got seated in the saddle, they opened the chute gate and "Custer" bucked Alvin down the third jump. Jim Tescher hadn't been bucked off a horse in three years; he was matched against Gray Wolf. "Wolf" was one of "Custer's" colts and weighed about 1,700 pounds. Jim lasted about six seconds, then he was bucked off. This was a tremendous accomplishment to have bucked down two of the best in professional rodeo, in spite of bad conditions.[56]

The Tooke-bred horses have been or have sired many of the top bucking stock since Feek's 1940s endeavor. Sunset Strip once bucked off twenty-four cowboys in a row; Bald Hornet was ridden only twice in nine years; Indian Sign threw such a fit in the arena that pickup men did not dare go near him until he settled down. Major Reno twice cost Larry Mahan the average at National Finals.[56] Beutler & Gaylord Rodeo Company, of Guthrie, Oklahoma, bought the Tooke horse herd in 1991—ninety-two mares and twelve studs. There are many Tooke offspring broncs in rodeo today. Clem McSpadden, rodeo announcer and spokesperson for the sport, is keeping a herd of Tooke yearlings for Beutler & Gaylord on his ranch that will begin their bucking careers in a few years.

Mel Potter, of Rodeo, Inc., asked Feek Tooke to represent Potter and go to National Finals in 1968, to flank the Rodeo, Inc., broncs and accept a plaque for Sheep Mountain, owned by Potter, who was the 1967 National Finals Top Saddle Bronc. Unknown to Tooke, Potter had a special plaque made for Tooke, since Sheep Mountain was born and bred on the Tooke ranch.

Clem McSpadden made the presentation at National Finals, and he noticed when Tooke rode into the arena, this man who spent his life with horses was not sitting his horse properly. But with the business at hand McSpadden dismissed his concern and the presentation was made. Tooke rode out of the arena. By the time McSpadden reached the alleyway, Tooke was lying on the ground. He was rushed to a local hospital but was soon pronounced dead. "Feek Tooke was years and years ahead of his time in breeding bucking horse stock," McSpadden said.

HARRY KNIGHT (1907-1989) was born in Quebec City, Canada. His first competitive sport was racing dog-sled teams. He also worked on ranches and wrangled horses. His first rodeo was at Sundre, Alberta, in 1925, where he rode his first bronc. He continued competing until 1941, and considered Five Minutes to Midnight and Fiddle Face as the two toughest broncs he ever rode. He was the 1926 Bareback Champion at Calgary, and the Novice Bronc Rider for 1926 and 1932. He contested for fifteen years. When a severe injury in 1933 curbed his competition, he began judging rodeos.

Knight was associated with top stock contractors throughout the rest of his rodeo career: the Clemans, Gene Autry, Everett Colborn, and Leo Cremer. Three of his own saddle broncs—Jake, Joker, and Big John—were RCA Bucking Horses of the Year.[11]

EDDIE VAUGHN (? -1974) was born in Fairfax, South Dakota, and was engaged in farming until drought and grasshoppers totally discouraged him. He became a major supplier of horses to the Miles City Bucking Horse Sale, traveling the country buying and selling horses. Danny Looman often accompanied Vaughn and always wondered why Vaughn would ask him if he locked the car, once they arrived at their destination to buy horses. Looman later discovered Vaughn kept $10,000 in cash under his car seat. Often, when they would buy horses, the sellers were not willing to take a check.

Doug Wall also worked for Vaughn and remembered trailing some horses from Angela to Miles City. Wall's saddle horse suddenly played out. Vaughn always kept his saddle horses mingled in with the broncs. "I picked out a little sorrel and one of the other riders roped him. He bucked a little, but settled right down once I put my saddle on him," Wall recounted. They arrived in Miles City and ran the horses down Main Street, and Wall noticed Vaughn standing in front of the café with his mouth wide open. They got the horses to the sale yard and Wall was just finishing unsaddling his horse when Vaughn pulled up. "Where are you going?" asked Vaughn. Wall answered, "I'm going for a beer, why?" Angrily, Vaughn answered, "Well, you just rode my best bareback bronc to town!"[56]

Vaughn purchased a good horse at a bucking horse sale Jim Shoulders held at an early National Finals. Mike Cervi liked him and wanted to buy him from Vaughn. Vaughn said no, he wasn't ready to sell him. But Cervi was persistent. Finally, Vaughn said it would take $1,700 to buy him. Cervi said he'd flip him double-or-nothing for the horse. The coin was tossed, and Cervi won. He named the gray horse Vaughn's Folly.[56]

EDDIE McCARTY (1888-1956) started his rodeo career in 1909 at Cheyenne Frontier Days by winning the steer roping. By 1910 he began his lifelong career as a "horse man"— he won the wild horse race. But he was versatile, winning the bulldogging in 1914 and the saddle bronc riding in 1919.

McCarty had a knack for picking good bucking horses. He raised them on his Chugwater, Wyoming, ranch. In 1917 he joined partnership as a stock contractor with Verne Elliott, and that partnership continued until 1940. They were always known for their outstanding broncs.

After McCarty sold his interest in McCarty and Elliott to partner Verne Elliott, he returned to his ranch for a while. But it wasn't long before he had put together another tough string of saddle bronc and bareback horses, with Doc Sorenson of Idaho, and produced Cheyenne Frontier Days.[70]

Cecil Henley takes a spill off White Slave, a Doc Sorenson bronc. Sorensen often held a "White Horse Cavalcade" at rodeos where only white or gray broncs were bucked.
— Photo by Snyder, courtesy of June and Buster Ivory.

The hundred-year celebration of Cheyenne Frontier Days in 1996 included a McCarty horse and empty saddle as a tribute to the man who helped make Frontier Days what it has become.[70]

RAY KNIGHT (1872-1947) was born in Payson, Utah, but the family moved to the grasslands of Alberta, buying land with money from an enterprising silver and lead mine in Utah. They went to Europe and bought 300 head of the best horses they could find, both draft and light breeds. Ray furnished stock for rodeos in Raymond, Alberta, and places close enough to trail stock. He also supplied stock for the first Calgary Stampede and continued to do so for the next thirty years.

Ray's father had a contract to purchase large areas of land in southern Alberta, if they would break up 3,000 acres the first year for farming. They ran 46,000 head of sheep, 15,000 head of cattle, and more than 3,000 head of horses. At the time they were breaking and selling light horses to the army for cavalry re-mounts.

Ray did much for rodeo and always looked for better ways to do things. He introduced calf roping and chariot races into Canadian rodeo. The chariot races eventually evolved into chuckwagon races. He also invented bull riding with a saddle and Roman races. He was a calf roper and judged bronc riding at Madison Square Garden. Ray Knight has been called the Father of Canadian Rodeo.

8

ON THE ROAD AND IN THE PAPERS: 1950S

As the 1950s came into view, after more than half a century of rodeos, the sport was well on its way. Rodeos were held in just about every little town, big city, and wide spot on the road west of the Mississippi, and were well represented east of the "big muddy" too. The last twenty years had seen great accomplishments in the development of the sport. Yet there were still problem areas of rodeo, and new ways of doing things continued to be tested.

One of the most important areas to be developed during that decade was that of public relations for the sport. By 1952, RCA had decided to publish their own newspaper, called *Rodeo Sports News*, and in November it came hot off the presses, reporting all upcoming RCA-approved rodeos, rodeo results, and articles on rodeo personalities and various phases of rodeo, plus advertising for all people and things related to this phenomena.

The Rodeo Information Commission was formed, with the sole responsibility of providing the media, primarily newspaper and magazine editors, with factual information pertaining to rodeo. By 1955, the Associated Press and United Press, major wire services, began carrying the Point Award Standings. The commission also contacted 500 newspapers and thirty free-lance writers and gave information about the RCA and its integrity for the sport of rodeo.[52] How many periodicals actually printed the releases is not known, but at first very few responded.

The technology of television and its popularity also

A major publicity coup for rodeo was when this photo of Casey Tibbs appeared on the cover of Life *magazine, October 22, 1951.*
— Photo courtesy of Moe and June Pratt.

brought about a new way of watching a rodeo. In 1953 and 1954, WBAP aired national coverage of the Fort Worth Rodeo through the National Broadcasting Company. Although this was a great way to allow the public to see the sport, the concern came that too many fans would stay at home and watch rodeo for free, rather than attend the events.[43]

On September 14, 1957, more than 38,620,000 Americans saw a one-hour telecast of the historic Pendleton RoundUp, sponsored by General Mills cereals. Carried on 168 CBS stations, it was the first television coverage to ever show an outdoor rodeo. Jack Stangier, president of the Pendleton RoundUp, adjusted the rodeo so that the five top scoring contestants in each event would compete on their last head, and markings were announced immediately. Clark McEntire won the All-Around, Alvin Nelson the Saddle Bronc Riding, and Bob Cullison the Bareback Riding.[52]

Publicity prior to this event included an article on the upcoming telecast in the September issue of *Reader's Digest*; the "Lone Ranger" and "Wyatt Earp" television programs promoted it; and General Mills offered a write-in premium gift of a book, titled *World Championship Rodeo*, compiling facts on rodeo, its history, biographies, and background stories.

By 1958, RCA was determined to keep television coverage limited to two presentations per year. There was too much concern about television exposure overkill. Examples of other sports were cited, such as boxing, which had lost much of its small "smoker" match attendance.

Other business on the rodeo table during this time primarily concerned three subjects: improved judges and judging; matched ridings; and allowance of permit holders to RCA rodeos.

Regarding the criticism that had followed rodeo judges, ever since the first person judged a contest, it was determined that in roughstock events judging was "a matter of personal opinion." To correct and eliminate talk implying that judges score some contractors' horses higher, or are partial to certain riders, it was recommended that judges be moved from area to area, thus judging stock by a variety of stock contractors, as well as judging a more varied group of riders. Judges for rodeos with purses of $1,000 or more needed to be pre-approved. The board also considered other criteria striving for fair judging.

Matched bronc ridings became very popular during this time. The concerns of the association were these questions: Can there be too many matched ridings? What was best for the sport of rodeo? It was finally determined that too many in a given area were not good as they were often in direct competition with RCA rodeos. Any organization wanting to hold a matched riding was now required to submit a request and be given written authorization from the committees of each RCA rodeo in the area, for thirty days before and after the event.[52]

One matched riding which started at that time and has continued to be held annually is the Home on the Range Annual Champion Ride Match, at Sentinel Butte, North Dakota. The event is held on the grounds of Home on the Range, a home for disadvantaged, pre-delinquent and delinquent adolescents, under the auspices of the Catholic Diocese of Bismark, North Dakota. Encouraging visitors to come see the home and spread public visibility, the match was the brainchild of area bronc riding brothers Tom and Jim Tescher in

Jack Vaage, bareback rider, on unknown bronc, at El Monte, California, rodeo, 1952.
— Photo by Raymond L. Pound, courtesy of Stan Searle.

1957. Father Fahnlander, who was serving the Sentinel Butte parish at that time, became very involved. In fact, for many years he would travel to the National Western Stock Show in Denver to invite top cowboys to the event. The basic format has always featured bronc riding. Other events held in conjunction with the saddle bronc event have varied through the years. There have been matched calf roping events, ladies' barrel races, bull riding, team roping, and steer wrestling. Top-ranked riders in the field are invited. Although riders from all parts of the country participate, cowboys from North and South Dakota, Montana and Wyoming feel it is almost mandatory to be there for this annual event. Currently, a major conflict with the PRCA Dodge City finals, which are held the same day, causes a rider within reach of a moneyed spot at Dodge City not to miss those finals in their quest for PRCA points. Home on the Range staff and residents understand this, and are truly proud of their area heroes in rodeo, although on occasion they are forced to miss the Champion Ride held in August. Saddle bronc prize money in 1993 was $12,000. It is not unusual for the winners of the matched ride to donate their winnings back to the home.[62]

The RCA Permit System was developed in 1957 to promote newcomers into rodeo. Those who gathered experience at high school, college, and other such non-RCA approved rodeos could then decide whether or not they should consider going into professional rodeo. A permit could be purchased for $5 and the holder could compete in RCA-approved rodeos until he placed in the money. Once a holder placed in the money, regardless of the amount, the permit would become void, and the permit holder was not allowed to compete at RCA rodeos as a nonmember. Becoming a full-fledged member required paying a $100 initiation fee. Permit bearers were in no way members of the Rodeo Cowboys Association, and were not covered by RCA insurance, but were subject to all RCA rules while competing at approved rodeos. In February 1958 the headlines of *Rodeo Sports News* reported: "Permit Holder Wins Bull Riding at Phoenix." Jimmy Clary of Purcell, Oklahoma, had won $1,325. In May, the *RSN* reported: "Two More Permit Holders Win."[52]

Other issues of the era included insurance for all RCA members. The insurance covered injury or accidental death in the arena, while competing, performing, or working an approved rodeo. The association boasted no fatalities in 1954; however, $50,000 was paid out to cover injuries that occurred during the year.

Written into the *Official Rule Book* was a new rule that there "will be no trading out or placing of contestants." Formerly the rule allowed cowboys to trade positions after the stock and position had been drawn. This allowed cowboys to juggle their schedule and enter more rodeos held on the same dates. When this subject was reviewed by directors, taking into consideration the paying customer and news media, it was determined that the customer is the one who makes rodeo possible for all and it is to these fans that everyone in rodeo owes their attention. The spectator was the one most cheated by the practice of trading out, and eventually everyone would have felt it, as there is so much intense competition for the entertainment dollar.[52]

Amidst all the scrutiny and the efforts to improve rodeo and make it better in all ways, Houston announced it would hold a *nonapproved* rodeo for 1958. RCA, as was its custom, reviewed all rodeos and evaluated purses. When a rodeo appeared to have an increased number of fans and the revenue to improve the purse in each event, RCA would recommend it. Generally, the rodeo committee would agree, and purse amounts grew. When Houston officials were asked to increase their purses, they declined. It was a known fact that the rodeo had made approximately $300,000 the year before, and the RCA board did not think their request was unreasonable. Houston officials did not comply, however, and RCA refused to approve their rodeo. The Houston rodeo of 1958 was held without the professional cowboys.[52]

Competition was keen between players in 1954, and saddle bronc riders Deb Copenhaver and Casey Tibbs were at the top of the heap. Tibbs bet Copenhaver $1,000 that he would win the World Saddle Bronc Championship even though Copenhaver was $2,500 ahead of Tibbs at the time of the bet. Copenhaver took the bet. When the year was over, Tibbs did indeed win the World Champion Saddle Bronc title with $23,052 to Copenhaver's $20,388. At the awards ceremony, Tibbs was given the champion buckle and a check for $1,200. Copenhaver was given a check for $1,000 for winning second. Later he said, "I took that $1,000 check and handed it right over to Casey. It was probably the only time in history a guy won first and second in the World in the same year."[52]

That same year, 1954, Eddy Akridge and his best friend, Buck Rutherford, were running neck and neck for the bareback championship. They traveled together, helped each other in the chute, then competed against each other. Before the year was over they made a deal. Whoever won the World Championship would keep the champion buckle, but would give the friend the World Champion saddle that was always awarded. Eddy Akridge beat Buck Rutherford by $7 ($14,983 to $14,976). Ouch![52]

Travel Fun and Misfortune

Cowboy travel had expanded greatly by the 1950s. It was the custom for several cowboys to get together and split expenses, whether the mode of travel was by car, train, or

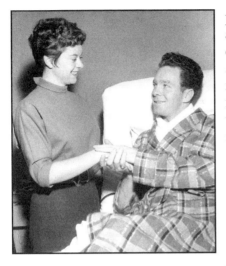

Author Gail Woerner and All-Around Champion of the World, Casey Tibbs, at a Denver hospital, January 1956, after he was bucked off by a bronc, sustaining several broken ribs and a punctured lung.
— Photo by Harry Smith, Colorado Woman's College photographer.

plane. Cowboys weren't always successful in their events, at the pay window, so if one contestant was winning he might pay several friends' entry fees, and in turn, when they got in the money, they would reciprocate. Once Bill Linderman said, "In rodeo, if a competitor's broke, we'll not only loan him transportation and entry fee, we'll throw in a saddle. Besides we'll tell him how the horse he draws bucks." A reporter called it "frontier honesty."

Airplane travel to and from rodeos was still new, having begun in the mid-forties. The clever broncbuster figured out if he got a point for every dollar he won, the best way to get to be a champion was to get the most dollars, and that meant expanding one's self beyond a single rodeo and making it to as many as he could physically make. Air travel was expensive, and often several would pool their money and share the expense.

Buster Ivory told that early in that era he and Carl Olson, Glen Tyler, and Wag Blessing decided to charter a twin-engine airplane and leave Reno, travel to Calgary, on to Salt Lake City, then to Ogden and Cheyenne, to compete in each rodeo and split the expenses. It was decided Ivory was to handle the travel arrangements. "I know you guys," he said, "you'll all change your mind before the plane takes off, so if I'm going to handle it give me your money now." They did, and Ivory scheduled the plane for the following morning. By the next morning Blessing and Tyler had gone a different direction, and Ivory couldn't find Olson. Knowing that Olson liked to gamble, Ivory started checking casinos. It wasn't long before he found him hunched over a crap table. Olson had not only lost most of his money; he was still drunk from the night before! Ivory escorted him out and they high-tailed it to the airport.

While waiting for the pilot to ready the airplane, Olson decided to have a bite to eat. Ivory said the place was not fit to eat in, but Olson didn't seem to notice. Ivory, realizing they weren't going to have all the expected passengers, told the pilot he could take his wife along. They hadn't been up in the air long when Olson started to turn green. No one was paying much attention, until suddenly Olson opened the airplane door, and the forced air nearly sucked him out of the plane. Ivory said he believed Olson's toes, hanging over the edge of the door, saved him. "I, and the pilot's wife, both tried to get him back in the plane," said Ivory, "but I was laughing so hard I was not very helpful. Finally we got him back in his seat, and the door closed. We asked him why he did such a dumb thing." His answer was he didn't want to throw up in the cockpit.

"A piece of metal came off the wing later, and I pointed it out to the pilot," Ivory recalled. "The pilot said, 'Oh my God!' and we landed at Helena, got it repaired and headed on." They met a storm at Lethbridge and went straight through it instead of going around it. When they landed there were holes in the wings, metal around the motor had dents from hail, and some windows had been cracked. Everyone at the airport decided they were lucky to have made it!

Harry Tompkins remembered the early fifties, when he left New York by commercial airline in the morning, to compete in an afternoon rodeo in Omaha. He hopped onto another commercial airline to compete that evening in Chicago, and was back in New York by 10:00 P.M. to compete in the bull riding. "We would really cut it short," he reminisced. "The bull riding would already be in session when I walked into the arena."

Tompkins also remembered a memorable flight from Reno to Great Falls, Montana, with Jack Buschbom, Jim Shoulders, Casey Tibbs, and Gerald Roberts. It was very hot in Reno and they couldn't get the plane high enough to cool off. With the heat and the pitch of the plane, Harry said he felt like he was going to get sick. Tibbs spoke up and said, "Hey, I've got some

Harry Tompkins makes an outstanding ride on Earl Hutchison's Mighty Mike to win first in the eighth go-round of the 1960 National Finals Rodeo at Dallas.
— Photo by Devere Helfrich, donated by June and Buster Ivory. Courtesy of the National Cowboy Hall of Fame.

Buck Rutherford, All-Around Cowboy and top bronc rider, 1954.
— Photo courtesy of Stan Searle.

airsick pills I take now and then. Want one?" Harry said he was always leery of Tibbs and his practical jokes, but when Tibbs took two of the pills Harry decided it would be okay, so he took two also. Later Harry learned Tibbs had merely thrown the pills over his shoulder into the seat behind him, instead of swallowing them. Harry said, "I took two—they were laxatives—and I had to go to the bathroom in a paper sack in front of five other cowboys before we landed."[53]

Tibbs was known for his pranks, and you didn't have to know him to be involved. Once on a very rough commercial airplane flight Tibbs noticed the woman next to him was getting a little "green around the gills." He faked airsickness, asked the stewardess for a cup (that was before the neat little airsick bags were available) and gagged a couple of times to fake throwing up in the cup. He held the cup a few minutes. Then he put the cup to his mouth as if to drink the contents! The woman next to him lost it right then. Oh, what a rascal Tibbs could be!

In the *Rodeo Sports News*, August 1, 1958, headlines told that by flying four round-trips between the Nampa, Idaho, and Salinas, California, rodeos and commuting 700 miles by air, the following cowboys got in the money at both rodeos: Deb Copenhaver, George Menkenmaier, Enoch Walker, Marty Wood, Bill Rinestine, Jim Shoulders, Dean Oliver, and Harry Tompkins. Wood won the bronc riding at Salinas and Nampa, and Shoulders won the Nampa All-Around.[52]

A rodeo cowboy spends many hours going "on down the road" or in the sky from one rodeo to the next. The one thing that is complained about the most is the time spent getting to and from rodeos. A lot of cowboys hop in their vehicles after a rodeo and take advantage of the night to avoid traffic and probably keep from having to pay for a room. It doesn't come as a big surprise to learn how many of these western heroes have lost their lives in auto accidents.

An example was related in the September 1, 1958, *Rodeo Sports News*:

> War Paint, twice honored by bronc riders as Bucking Horse of the Year, was led into a silent arena at Redmond, OR. The big pinto head came up, ears forward, eyes rolling

in surprise as the fragrant wreath of flowers was slipped around his neck. He and the lead horse were the only moving things and then as the voice of Manuel Enos sang "There's An Empty Cot In The Bunkhouse Tonight," tears welled to the eyes of spectators and cowboys alike and ran unashamed down the bowed faces of many hardened rodeo hands. Thus, rodeo paid last tribute to one of its best, for early the day before, Friday, August 21, George Menkenmaier, 31, leading contender for the 1958 Saddle Bronc Riding Champion of the world, had met sudden tragic death on a highway Y a mile east of the neighboring town of Prineville, Oregon.

George had been a member of RCA since 1947, but had not ventured out of the Northwest to compete until 1956. He was from Burns, Oregon, and grew up in an area where riding broncs was still part of a cowboy's chores.[52]

Adding a Climax to the Season

One of the highlights of the 1950s was the decision to hold a National Finals Rodeo. Everyone involved with rodeo had talked about it for years, but not until early 1958 did it make inroads to where people started to believe it would actually become a reality. It had been said that in rodeo there was no climax, no smashing end to a season. After building up a competitive race in each event, the end of the year just came to a quiet end. Other sports had a big annual finish, so why did rodeo have to be any different?

As directors, representatives, and officials put their heads together, it was decided to have the seven recognized events at an end-of-the-year rodeo, with the top fifteen competitors of each event in attendance—four performances and four go-rounds. Various stock contractors in the association would provide bucking stock, and the Rodeo Cowboys Association would oversee and supervise the event.

By August 25, 1958, John Van Cronkhite, general manager of the RCA, realized that there was a very high national interest in holding this event, as governors from twenty-six states and mayors from twenty-eight cities had contacted him across the nation. Finally, a historic session was held in San Francisco on November 6 and 7 by the National Finals commission to determine conditions and policies which would govern the event. The site was to be determined between Dallas, Los Angeles, or Louisville, Kentucky. Dallas was chosen for the first National Finals. The National Finals Roping would be held in Clayton, New Mexico.

As 1959 evolved, all plans were put into play, and as each decision was reached, national coverage revealed what was to happen. Records to help select the stock for National Finals were developed by Mike Swift of the Rodeo Information Commission to assure that the most outstanding stock was selected. Stock contractors were required to keep detailed records on each head of bucking stock: where they bucked, what they scored, who rode, how they were rated, and so forth. It was also decided that no stock with less than five times out of the chute could be considered for the National Finals Rodeo. A prize of $3,000 was to go to the top National Finals stock in each of the three roughstock categories: $500 for first place, $300 for second, and $200 for third.

The Baker Hotel in Dallas was selected as National Finals Headquarters. Bill Linderman was chosen as arena director; Cecil Jones as rodeo secretary; Buster Ivory as livestock superintendent; announcers were Cy Taillon and Pete Logan; timers were Flaxie Fletcher of Oklahoma City, Jo Ann Herrin of Dallas, and Muggs McClanahan of Fowler, Colorado.

The bucking stock was finally determined by November, and 210 broncs, bareback horses, and bulls were chosen, with forty more in reserve. Stock contractor Harry Knight had the most head of stock selected, with twenty-nine, followed by Beutler Brothers, with twenty-three. Twenty-five different stock contractors would be represented at the National Finals.

The December 26-30 event was held at the new $2-million coliseum with seating for 8,000 spectators. There were ten performances with the top fifteen contestants in each of the five standard events.[52]

Going into the first National Finals Rodeo, the following were sitting first and second in each of the roughstock events:

Sleeper, a Harry Knight bare-back bronc, was always flashy. Jack Buschbom holds his own as a judge scrutinizes the ride.
— Photo by Devere Helfrich, donated by June and Buster Ivory. Courtesy of the National Cowboy Hall of Fame.

Saddle Bronc—Casey Tibbs and Winston Bruce; Bareback Riding—Jack Buschbom and John Hawkins; Bull Riding—Bob Wegner and Jim Shoulders. Winners of the National Finals Average Champions were Saddle Bronc—Jim Tescher; Bareback Riding—Jack Buschbom; Bull Riding—Jim Shoulders. Jim Shoulders also won the All-Around title.

The 1950s were truly the years of promoting rodeo to the world. Not only did groups go to various foreign countries and hold rodeos, but the media in the United States via magazine articles, newspaper columns, and television programs promoted rodeos. Additionally, statistics showed that more than 14 million spectators bought tickets to see RCA-approved rodeos in 1958. But the highlight, which continues on through today, was the addition of National Finals as the climax to each rodeo season. It was a tremendous way to end the decade.[52]

Broncbusters of the Era (1950s)

GERALD ROBERTS (1919-____) was born in the Flint Hills of Kansas, near Strong City. He left home at thirteen, hitched a ride on a freight train, and went to Perry, Iowa, to

John Hawkins, Champion Bareback Rider of 1963, rides Cream of Kentucky, a Christensen Brothers horse at Red Bluff, California, in 1955.
— Photo by Devere Helfrich, donated by June and Buster Ivory. Courtesy of the National Cowboy Hall of Fame.

join his older brother and sister, Ken and Margie, who were with the Clyde Miller Wild West Show. Miller hired Gerald to ride buckers, but in a short time he got knocked out and Miller sent him home. The following year he returned with a note from his dad saying it was all right if he got knocked out!

At fifteen he tried his first rodeo competition and came up empty-handed. He entered fifteen more shows that season, but winnings were slim. For a while he had an ice cream man talked into paying his entry fee, plus all the ice cream he could eat!

Gerald Roberts won the All-Around Champion of the World for the International Rodeo Association in 1942, and again in 1948 for the RCA. He placed in one of the top five spots nine times in roughstock events from 1945 to 1955. But injuries took their toll on him. He won sixty-seven buckles and seventeen saddles and was inducted into the ProRodeo Hall of Fame in 1990. "I can feel with my spurs, like most people can feel with their hands," claimed Roberts.[53]

CASEY TIBBS (1929-1990) was born in a cabin on the Cheyenne River, in the Mission Ridge area of South Dakota. The youngest of ten children, Casey, at age ten, was helping his dad with the horses he raised. Dad Tibbs didn't like much, except the horses. By the time Casey was thirteen he left home and went to work for the Diamond A Ranch, a cattle outfit. By fourteen, he had entered his first rodeo and never looked back. He had a remarkable talent for riding broncs and liked the rodeo world. From then on, it became his life.

In 1949 he won his first World Champion Saddle Bronc title, and repeated the win five more times, in 1951, 1952, 1953, 1954, and 1959. He was World Champion Bareback Rider in 1951, and won the World Champion All-Around title in 1951 and 1955. His tremendous ability aboard the broncs plus his good looks and devilish personality made him a favorite of fans everywhere. He was always in the news, but not always about his rodeo fetes—his life outside the arena was almost as well known as his wins.

After his second All-Around title, Tibbs didn't rodeo much; his time was taken up with personal appearances. The money was coming in and he was living high. His cowboy friends called him a "hot dog," but he didn't care. "I knew I could still ride better'n most of them and they knew it, too," he remarked. In 1958 he signed with a Wild West group that went to the World's Fair in Brussels, Belgium. The program bombed and the show went bankrupt, leaving more than 200 cowboys, cowgirls, and Indians on their own to make their way back to the United States. Following this episode he went back to rodeoing and won his last World Championship in saddle bronc.

The next year he moved to Hollywood and spent time in movies and television as an actor, stunt man, and consultant, and even received an award from the National Cowboy Hall of Fame for a documentary film he produced called *Born To Buck*.

In a taped interview with Lyle Graves, rodeo announcer from Billings, Montana, in 1961, Tibbs said: "I ride a bucking horse the way it fits me, the way it feels. I learned real early that you get more points by spurring, so I started out learning that way." He was asked a question about "floating a bronc" and his answer was: "I never floated a horse in my life. I rode with balance and my spurs."

He was extremely serious about his profession and always prepared himself for each ride. But he also had a tremendous wit and was able to think up and perform the wildest schemes, such as running over hitchhikers' suitcases with his purple Cadillac, soaking his new saddle in the only bathtub on the floor of his rooming house (leaving other residents out in the hall), and faking airsickness while in turbulent skies!

Tibbs spent his life promoting rodeo. Even when he was not near an arena he continued to recommend new concepts and ideas for the betterment of rodeo. He was truly a great ambassador of the sport.[7, 11, 35, 52, 65]

JIM SHOULDERS (1928-____), of Tulsa, Oklahoma, spent many hours on his grandfather's farm during his young years. His first rodeo was in Oiltown in 1943, and he won $18. He won his first World Championship title in 1949 as All-Around Cowboy of the World. He racked up a total of sixteen World Championships by the time he was through competing: five All-Around Championships (1949, 1956, 1957, 1958, and 1959); four Bareback Riding Championships (1950, 1956, 1957, and 1958); and seven Bull Riding Championships (1951, 1954, 1955, 1956, 1957, 1958, and 1959).

After Shoulders retired from competition, he was the first to begin schools to teach roughstock riding. He also got into the stock contracting business. His famous bull, Tornado, was ridden only once, in six competitive seasons, by Freckles Brown. The bull is buried on the grounds of the National Cowboy Hall of Fame.[35]

When asked what he saw as the biggest changes in the bronc riding events since he started in the business, he said he felt the current bareback rigging design is not helpful to the event. "It holds on to the man instead of the man having to hold on to it. It gets too many cowboys hurt and breaks the egg in them," he remarked. ("Egg" is a cowboy term to define a cowboy's determination). "When I competed I rode bareback and bulls primarily because I could win more and get to more rodeos because there were more bareback competitors so you

Jim Shoulders, holder of sixteen world titles, losing his balance on Harry Vold's great mare, Necklace, at the Houston Astrodome, 1966.

— Photo by Ferrell, donated by
June and Buster Ivory.

generally only got one head at a rodeo. In those days there were less saddle bronc riders and they generally had two head of stock," Shoulders explained. "Today there are twice as many saddle bronc riders, as bareback competitors."

Still active in the rodeo world through advertising and promotions, Shoulders is often seen at rodeo functions across the country.

HARRY TOMPKINS (1927-____), a native of Peekskill, New York, went to work for the Cimarron Dude Ranch near his home. They held frequent rodeos on the ranch, and when a rodeo was not in session Tompkins practiced riding all the ranch steers. His job also required him to test out the horses for the dudes. He tried many. In 1946 the Cimarron entered him in the Madison Square Garden Rodeo. Although he says he bucked off most of his stock, he won $316.

Harry Tompkins, All-Around Champion Cowboy of the World in 1952 and 1960, on Steiner's Zip Code at St. Louis in 1967.

— Photo by Bern Gregory.

The thrill of rodeo appealed to Tompkins, and soon he was on the circuit. He was known for his natural ability, coordination, and balance. He won the World Champion All-Around title in 1952 and 1960, the World Championship Bull Riding in 1948, 1949, 1950, 1952 and 1960, and the World Champion Bareback Riding in 1952.[61]

He credits Come Apart as one of the best bucking horses during his era. Colborn's #32 bull also gets a vote for toughness. In the 1956 *Rodeo Sports News Annual*, the reporter said of Tompkins: "Seldom has a cowboy been bitten as hard by the swelling virus of the rodeo bug, and seldom has anyone made good in such a hurry."[52]

BENNY REYNOLDS (1936-____) was born in Twin Bridges, Montana, and the youngest of three boys. His father, Frank, put on rodeos in the 1930s and 1940s, and his mother broke horses until she was sixty-three years old.

Reynolds was a big boy, could run like the wind, and high school coaches from the surrounding communities were relieved when he made rodeoing his sport, and quit outrunning their track athletes. He was strong and possessed a heart full of "try." He became the RCA Rookie of the Year in 1958. From 1958 through 1967, he scored among the top fifteen for All-Around Cowboy, except 1965. He also ranked in the top fifteen in bareback for six years, 1958 through 1963, and in bull riding and steer wrestling several years, as well. He won the World Champion All-Around Cowboy title in 1961.

Reynolds was a versatile competitor. He was the first recipient of the Linderman Memorial Award, which was started in 1966, for winning over $1,000 in three or more events.

The National Old Timers Rodeo Association, which later changed its name to National Senior Pro Rodeo Association, awarded Reynolds the All-Around Championship from 1984 through 1991. He suffered a broken shoulder in 1992 on a bareback horse, and has not competed in roughstock events since then.[11, 53]

Broncs of the Era (1950s)

CRAZY ONE was owned by Bobby Estes. He came from Joe Chase in North Dakota, who sold a truckload of bucking horses to Estes. This little dark brown horse had been missing on the reservation for four years, and just before the truck left South Dakota for Estes' ranch, in Baird, Texas, he turned up. Estes named the brown Easy Money, and bucked him in the bareback string. He was anything but "easy" and fought the chute. A week later, back on the ranch, Estes and his wife, Marianne, were branding the new stock with rodeo numbers and when they heard a commotion in the holding pen she asked, "Is that the crazy one?" The name stuck.

So skittish that he was too difficult to saddle, Crazy One remained in the bareback string for two years, and wasn't ridden until late 1955 by Bernis Johnson at Carthage, Texas. In 1956 Estes took his rodeo to Europe for ninety days and eighty performances. Crazy One was out twenty times and was ridden only five times. In 1957 he was bucked exclusively as a saddle bronc. He fired every time, and was seldom ridden. Estes traded him to Harry Knight. He went to the National Finals Rodeo many times. When Knight sold out, Billy Minnick of Fort Worth got the brown horse.[11]

WILD SWEDE, owned by Bob Barmby, was bucked as a saddle bronc. His last time out he was ridden at the Cow Palace in 1957, by Bill Ward. He bucked so hard he tore open his stomach and died a few days later.[52]

SCHOOL BOY ROWE was owned by Ken and E. C. Roberts. At the Pony Express Rodeo, at St. Joseph, Missouri, in 1949, which they produced, they advertised that Gerald Roberts would ride the wildest bunch of horseflesh in their string—a chunky blood bay, an unpredictable freak. In six years of competition only four cowboys rode him, and 150 broncstompers "bit the dust." Gerald stayed on the outlaw for nine seconds of the ten seconds required for a qualified ride, before the horse's head shot down and over he tumbled.[7]

MISS KLAMATH was a Mack Barbour horse, which later sold to Christensen Brothers. Bill Ward had made the first qualified ride on her at Klamath Falls. Just a few days later she had just unseated Manuel Enos at Ogden when the mare's front feet slipped and she fell, breaking both hind legs. She had to be destroyed.[52]

MISS NEWHALL was owned by Andy Jauregui. "She ducked and dodged the worst I ever saw," said Glenn Ohrlin. "Hutch Hutchison tried to make a stock horse out of her, and he was an artist at making it happen, but he couldn't ride her. She broke Smoky Snyder's back. The two wildest bareback rides I saw were on her. Jack Spurling and Slugger Sloan. They both spurred wide open through all her ducks and turns, it looked impossible. On the other hand, Gene Rambo could ride her with no trouble."[11]

9

REBELLION IN THE 1960s

The country went a little crazy in the sixties. "Flower children" protested and staged sit-ins to express their dissatisfaction with the world. "Peace" was their by-word. They picked communal living instead of the tried and true single family homes their parents and grandparents had enjoyed. The favorite diversions on college campuses were pot smoking and bra-burnings. Meanwhile, rodeo got bigger and better. The flower children could have been a planet away, as these dissenters usually were not in the rodeo family.

The growth and improvement of rodeo continued, but it took numerous cowboys dedicating many hours to subjects ranging from television coverage of rodeo, better insurance for competing cowboys, and specific details involving rule infractions and changes in the rodeo arena. The RCA by-word seemed to be "improve"!

In 1961 the Rodeo Cowboys Association board of directors met for five long days during the National Western Stock Show in Denver on controversial matters. Many areas of rodeo were labored over, including a new rule on specifications of the bronc saddle that was issued. The saddle bronc director announced its use would be strictly enforced. In 1962 headlines called the Fourth of July weekend the "Cowboy Christmas," with thirty-four rodeos in nineteen states and two Canadian provinces. The largest purse that weekend was at Camdenton, Missouri, with $14,000 to be divided in eight performances. By 1963, rodeo was setting attendance records, the RCA approved five regular season rodeos to be

139

shown on national television, and the National Finals Rodeo was moved to Los Angeles for one year. By the end of 1963, RCA had 583 approved rodeos for a payoff of $3,496,739.52. This was an increase of forty-six approved rodeos and $416,000 over 1962.[52]

But not the entire rodeo world was on the upswing. As rodeo officials, directors, and members attempted to improve the sport, there were some who learned how to work the angles. A November 15, 1963, issue of *Rodeo Sports News* reported that Paul Mayo, of Grinnell, Iowa, and R. C. "Judge" Tolbirt, of Columbus, Texas, were suspended indefinitely from the Rodeo Cowboys Association by the board of directors. Both men were fined $500, and Mayo's name was stricken from the championship standings. He was in the lead for the bareback riding title until the action was taken. The article stated:

> Riding judges Don Fedderson and Tex Martin discovered Tolbirt cheating in Mayo's favor during official drawing of bucking stock for the Memphis, Tenn., rodeo in mid-September. The judges reported the fix to RCA officials who then placed Tolbirt and Mayo under bond pending final hearing before the full board of directors at their regular fall meeting. Tolbirt admitted his guilt. He said Mayo instigated the plot to provide the Iowa cowboy with the best bucking horses at rodeos where he, Tolbirt, was employed as arena secretary.
>
> Mayo denied all charges, but evidence examined by the RCA Board resulted in both men being found equally guilty.
>
> Rodeo stock contractor Tommy Steiner, Austin, TX, who had the Memphis contract, had no knowledge the men were cheating in the draw, and assisted in exposing the deal. He cooperated with the Board to the fullest extent and is entirely blameless. No stigma should be attached to Tommy Steiner or his rodeo outfit as a result of this matter.
>
> Mayo had won $16,829 this season in his bid for the bareback bronc riding title, making an almost $3,000 edge over the next man, when the storm broke. He had taken the event's national lead in August from elder brother, Don Mayo, after the latter had been injured seriously in a July 4th motor car accident. Don Mayo remains paralyzed from the waist down as a result of the crash.

Paul Mayo joined the RCA in the fall of 1959 after winning the National High School Rodeo Association's all-around cowboy title earlier that year. He also was 1958's N.H.S.R.A. bareback bronc riding champion.

Tolbirt had not competed professionally but took part in college rodeo while attending the University of Texas. He joined the RCA as an arena secretary in 1961.[52]

In the June 15, 1964, *Rodeo Sports News*, it was reported: "Paul Mayo and Judge Tolbirt Re-instated. . . . Two members of the Rodeo Cowboys Association, who were suspended eight months ago for cheating in competition, were officially re-instated at the RCA Board of Directors' Las Vegas meeting, May 20.

"Paul Mayo, 22, of Grinnell, Iowa, and R. C. 'Judge' Tolbirt, 26, Columbus, Texas, were given 'another chance' after full consideration by the 12-man board. 'They didn't like to hand out a life sentence for a first mistake,' said Dale Smith, RCA President."[52]

In 1965 Mayo placed second in bareback riding winning $16,990 against Jim Houston's $17,631. He also was sixth in the All-Around and fifteenth in the bull riding. In 1966 he became Bareback Riding World Champion with $25,473—$8,000 more than Houston, who was in second place. He also placed third in the All-Around. In 1967 Mayo placed second, to Clyde Vamvoras' win in the bareback event. Mayo won the Bareback Riding World Championship again in 1970, and placed somewhere in the top five places in the event every year from 1965 through 1971.[61]

In 1964 Cy Taillon, well-known rodeo announcer, captured a man impersonating Casey Tibbs during the Fort Worth rodeo. Taillon noticed this man, whom he did not recognize, signing autographs behind the announcer's stand. When Taillon inquired he learned the gent was signing as Casey Tibbs. It turned out the mystery man had been in prison and while there had written about Tibbs' life. Apparently he had come to believe he was the famous bronc-riding champion. [52]

In the *Rodeo Sports News* of May 1, 1967, a headline read: "Association Formed in Opposition to RCA." The article reported that Bob Wegner, World Champion Bull Rider of

Enoch Walker is not doing a handstand on saddle bronc Apache, owned by Jiggs and Elra Beutler.
— Photo by Ferrell, donated by
June and Buster Ivory.

1964, had been suspended due to actions detrimental to the best interests of RCA. He incorporated, in the state of Washington, an organization named American Cowboys Association, which was to be composed of twenty men teams which would compete as home teams in a newly formed league. In an October issue of *Rodeo Sports News* it was reported Wegner had filed suit and was asking for $300,500 from the Rodeo Cowboys Association and George Williams of *Rodeo Sports News*, for damage to his reputation in controversy over team rodeo competition.[52] According to Wegner, the case was settled out of court. Wegner received $25,000 and a promise his name would be removed from RCA's blacklist. For one issue of the *RSN* his name was removed from the list, but in the next issue it was back, despite the court decision. Wegner filed suit against the Rodeo Cowboys Association again, this time for $1 million. In 1969 another out-of-court settlement was made. Wegner received $7,500 and his name was removed from the blacklist permanently.

In 1974 he reinstated his RCA card and competed at sanctioned rodeos. The *Wegner vs. RCA* case set a precedent toward allowing athletes, in various major sports, to act as free agents.

Publicity and Change

Meanwhile, the RCA had other problems. The association was continually answering to humane societies in various states, which were up in arms over the treatment of animals in rodeo. Anti-rodeo bills were introduced in West Virginia and Connecticut. But in 1967 it was reported the Ohio law that abolished rodeos from the state for two years was unconstitutional. Also, a bill in California to outlaw cattle prods, the hot shot used to move animals, was killed in committee.[52] Even the *Wall Street Journal* included an article on the issue, stating that if the animals were not performing in rodeos they would probably be in a can—as dog meat. The RCA directors knew that most complaints were lodged from extremists who had not investigated properly and were unaware of the facts. However, each criticism had to be addressed, and many hours were spent informing animal activists on the true perspective of animals used in rodeos, and the good care they received, compared to what might have been their destiny.

Rodeo was receiving plenty of publicity, though some of it was not positive. The board of directors of the RCA made changes and additions, and new rules continued to be announced. In 1964 a notice to saddle bronc competitors warned: "Any contestant using any sort of adhesive preparation on chaps or saddle shall be disqualified at that rodeo immediately." And for bareback riders: "Any contestant using finger tucks or finger wraps shall be disqualified at that rodeo immediately."[52]

The 1967 *Official Rule Book* offered the following new rules pertaining to rough stock: "Any animal that becomes excessively excited so that it gets down in the chute repeatedly, or tries to jump out of the chute, or in any way appears to be in danger of injuring itself, should be released immediately." And:

Bob Eidson gets a re-ride ruled by the judge as Devil's Partner, Harry Knight's bareback horse, goes down.
— Photo by Devere Helfrich, donated by June and Buster Ivory. Courtesy of the National Cowboy Hall of Fame.

"Sheepskin lined flank straps shall be placed on the animal so the sheepskin covered portion is over both flanks and the belly of the animal." And: "A one inch thick pad must be used under bareback rigging if stock contractor requests its use. Stock contractor must have pads available if rider does not have one." And: "Cinchas on bronc saddles and bareback riggings shall be made of Mohair and shall be at least five inches wide."[52]

One can only surmise that Humane Society criticism might have caused some of these changes and additions.

Another major change was in the implementation of Rodeo Foundation Judging Schools, which were mandatory for RCA judges and prospective judges, as of 1966. The schools were conducted by Bill Fedderson and were held initially in Sidney, Iowa; Pueblo, Colorado; Coffeyville, Kansas; Huron, South Dakota; Louisville, Kentucky; Pendleton, Oregon; Omaha, Nebraska; and San Francisco, California.

The RCA was making every effort to improve professional rodeo and create an atmosphere as fair and equal for all competitors as possible. Judging of roughstock events is purely a personal opinion. But fair and impartial judges, demanded RCA, must ignore competitors.

By 1964, the RCA had new and larger headquarters in Denver. In 1965 the top fifteen saddle bronc riders collected $193,189. The top fifteen bareback riders collected $165,783. A total of 382 rodeos sent in attendance totals of 5,331,985 fans. Adding to this total, rodeos not sending in attendance information, it was estimated that 9.5 million people attended RCA-approved rodeos. There were 10,696 bareback entries and 7,095 saddle bronc entries at RCA rodeos. [52]

In 1966, Houston moved the rodeo to the Astrodome and the following year they added $10,000 to the purse. Headlines in 1968 reported "Year's Biggest Money Pie at Houston, $89,240!"[52]

A Sport . . . Or Not a Sport?

In the midst of all the changes being made in professional rodeo, in 1966 the *Denver Post* announced they had established an editorial policy placing national news of professional rodeo and current World Champion Standings on the sports page. The RCA board had been working toward this end with newspapers since 1950.

On February 25, 1968, a free-lance writer, John White, wrote in the *Portland Oregonian*'s *Northwest Magazine*:

> For 361 days a year the village of St. Paul in the Willamette Valley south of Portland is friendly but reasonably drowsy. But for 3 or 4 days a year there is bedlam as the nation's finest professional cowboys take over for the St. Paul Rodeo, a fixture for the past 32 years.
>
> July 3rd, 12,417 fans attended. And on July 4th, despite oppressive heat, 10,192 watched.
>
> Now if hockey's Portland Buckaroos draw back-to-back sellouts, the sports page headlines scream. If the baseball Beavers attract a two-day total of 22,609, the columnists have a ball (ouch!) for days. Draw 22,609 for a pair of pro-basketball games in Memorial Coliseum, and there would be major league talk for months.
>
> So naturally there were large headlines on the sports pages of Portland after the St. Paul Rodeo mob made the scene.
>
> Right? Forget it! There wasn't a line on the sports page.

There were stories in news sections. But there was nothing in sports. The reason is absurdly simple. Rodeo is not a sport! Who says rodeo is not a sport? Those who run the sports pages say so, that's who! And that's who counts. Now don't look for any "message" inciting rodeo fans to arise. They don't need it. They arise early and stay late.

From the standpoint of ground rules, however, the decision that rodeo is not a sport is a bit puzzling. Big-time professional golfers play what is called a "tour." In each tournament, they compete for prize money. The Professional Golfers Association keeps meticulous records of total earnings. And the sports pages dutifully publish them. The professional bowlers do the same thing, although at times, before a mere handful of real live spectators. But the sports pages mention their exploits. Well, gee whiz, professional cowboys do the same things. But sports pages look the other way, because rodeo is not a sport. In a technical sense, too, the decision is puzzling. Rodeo is not a sport?

The bronc rider has exactly 10 seconds to live or die financially—and take a chance on the other way. And as in the "sports" of diving or ski jumping form counts heavily in determining winners.

The bounce of a football, in bounds or out of bounds, can decide a championship. So can a skittish calf which heads straight for the exit at track-record speed, then swerves at a 90-degree angle, leaving a roper broke for the move to the next town.

Speed, endurance, courage, toughness, touch, skill, quickness—all are terms applied to stars of professional football, basketball, hockey and baseball. The stars of professional rodeo are endowed with or learn the same qualities.

But let's not get carried away. Rodeo is not a sport, and that's that. Shut up, kid, eat your snow cone and watch the "entertainment."

It doesn't matter in the slightest that *Sports Illustrated*, with the largest circulation of any national sports magazine, has recognized rodeo as a sport since early publication days when winners of the Pendleton Round-Up were listed. You had better believe that *Sports Illustrated* isn't going to tell any newspaper sports editor what to do. Besides, the magazine really can go a bit berserk at times with accounts of such "sports" as fireplug-painting and rock-collecting.

Roller, owned by Frank Prunty, gives Allan Hicks proof he was a horse to ride at the Cow Palace, 1964.

— Photo by Devere Helfrich, donated by June and Buster Ivory. Courtesy of the National Cowboy Hall of Fame.

Sportswriters thought rodeo was not a sport?? Look at the acrobatics by Mike Isley and saddle bronc Rawhide, a Beutler Brothers horse, at Denver, 1962.

— Photo by Devere Helfrich, donated by June and Buster Ivory. Courtesy of the National Cowboy Hall of Fame.

Kenny McLean on Jack Fettig's Calcutta at the 1968 National Finals in Oklahoma City. A high score was always possible on this bronc.

— Photo by Ferrell. Donated by
June and Buster Ivory.

Colt 45, Rodeo Inc.'s saddle bronc, puts a little daylight under him trying to dislodge Jim Moore at a Kankakee, Illinois, rodeo in 1968.

— Photo by Bern Gregory.

Neither does it matter that national television networks have recognized rodeo as a sport, with millions of viewers watching championship finals. If *Sports Illustrated* isn't going to tell newspaper sports pages what to do, then it's for by gum certain that no television personality is going to have the slightest influence.

So let's temporarily forget rodeo, except for one final inquiry prompted by sheer stupidity. The long-established and widely respected Bill Hayward Banquet of Champions is a sports function, right? The banquet annually honors Oregon's outstanding athletes, right? The newspaper sports pages support and publicize, with considerable and justifiable pride, the Hayward Banquet, right? Then if rodeo isn't a sport, how in the name of bronco-busting did a cowpoke named Larry Mahan become one of the ten finalists for the Hayward Award this year and a year ago?[52]

White went on at length, comparing other sports and spoofing the newspaper sports page editors for not recognizing rodeo. It was a shot in the arm for rodeo and well appreciated. Rodeo did have an uphill battle that to present times has not been totally resolved.

In 1959 the Rodeo Information Foundation worked diligently to revise and improve new media packets to educate and inform the media and interested rodeo committees. A second writer was approved for the foundation to hire. Randy Witte, of Lakewood, Colorado, a journalism major who rode bulls and was learning to steer wrestle, was hired. His priority was to write hometown stories on cowboys and pick up more human-interest stories to circulate to the media.

Meanwhile, sports editor John Wendeborn, of the *Enterprise-Courier* in Oregon, had written an article admitting that rodeo was not his bag; he considered it a yearly show that came to Oregon communities once a year, bringing a bunch of "hard ridin', hard drinking cowboys—fugitives from some less-disciplinarian past."[52] When reports of rodeo results came across his desk he equated it to wrestling or roller derbys—mainly entertainment, but not sport. His opinion changed, however, after his exposure and education regarding rodeo clarified for him what and who make up rodeo.

Harry Knight's big stout Pee Wee could stand a rider on his head. Tex Martin found out in San Antonio, 1968.
— Donated by June and Buster Ivory.

Big Bend Rodeo's Trade Winds tosses another rider, Max Griffin, at the Cow Palace in the 1960s. The saddle bronc was top horse in 1964, 1965, and tied with Major Reno for the top spot in 1969.
— Donated by June and Buster Ivory.

Wendeborn admitted that competition is the key word to rodeo being classified a sport. He also learned that a rodeo cowboy competes against a bucking bronc or bull, the clock, himself, and other cowboys. Professionalism in the sport of rodeo had been honed to a fine degree. Cowboys in 1969 were not range cowboys looking for an easy buck. They were making a living—working hard to stay in their chosen trade. Wendeborn said rodeo definitely belonged on the sports page![52]

More Perils On the Road

While serious effort was being expended to convince everyone rodeo was a bona fide sport, cowboys were trekking on down the road. Unfortunately, some didn't make it to the next rodeo. Bert France was killed in a highway crash near Mobridge. Smoky Snyder was killed in a car accident in Kern City, California. Don Mayo, leading bareback rider, broke his back in a three-car collision en route from Belle Fourche, South Dakota, to the Camdenton, Missouri, rodeo. There were about forty-six pro-rodeos over that Fourth of July weekend in 1963, and not one cowboy got injured in the arena. On the road, they weren't so fortunate.

Not all roads in the 1960s, however, were covered with asphalt. The number of rodeos and distance between arenas made cowboys become more creative in figuring ways to get to as many rodeos as they could. Flying seemed to be the logical answer.

An article in a 1967 *Rodeo Sports News* reported:

> Rodeo utilizes the light plane better than any other professional sport and there hasn't been a guy—especially if he's title-happy—who hasn't given general aviation a serious thought, unless he's the kind who figures rodeo keeps his feet off the ground enough without getting airborne outside the arena.
>
> Because most cowboys are naturally well coordinated, they make good fliers. Yet, the sport demands such mobility there have been cases of flight planning, prompted by compulsion rather than judgment, so that rodeo's flying-history

isn't exactly the kind of story for which the FAA would write a glowing forward.

Some twenty years ago, Gerald Roberts and Casey Tibbs acquired a surplus Bamboo Bomber, a twin engine Cessna which Casey said, "had been patched so many times it looked like a crossword puzzle coming at you."

The outfit had trouble keeping paying passengers; they could handle six—and it took at least that to split the gas—but after one of their more hair-raising trips, the permanent riders lost their permanency. Casey said, "I'd have to shanghai me a new bunch, usually out of the bar, after dang near every rodeo."

Once they ran out of gas in Idaho and landed on the highway close to a filling station. The sheriff sirened out to meet them, heard their tale, shook his head. The exact laws broken puzzled him. "I just don't know what to do with you boys," the sheriff said. Jim Like, a bronc rider clutching his saddle, squirmed out with eyes widened by fear and sputtered, "I don't give a damn what you do to me as long as you don't make me get back in that plane."

One moonless night, trying to get from Sidney, Iowa, to Los Angeles, the Bamboo Bomber fought headwinds with decreasing success. East of Denver they had to set down due to fuel starvation. Lee Harris, often the pilot, saw a clearing through the ground haze, but he did not see the two fences and road they hit as they tried to make it to the clearing. They totaled the bomber.

But today, there's close to seventy cowboys with licenses and a squadron of producers and announcers that use flying. Larry Mahan, with the help of a Comanche 250, has brought both his flying ability and rodeo record to remarkable peaks. Jim Bausch flew Jim Houston and Shawn Davis, both to World titles. Houston to World Champion Bareback Rider in 1964 and 1965, and Davis to World Champion Saddle Bronc Rider in 1965, 1967 and 1968.[52]

Bill Linderman, secretary of RCA, was killed in a United Airlines Boeing 727 plane crash on November 11, 1965, near Salt Lake City. His untimely death was a shock to the rodeo world. In his memory, the Bill Linderman Memorial Buckle, first presented in 1966, goes to the cowboy winning the most prize money in three or more events—one being a roughstock event

Bill Linderman, RCA president and top All-Around Cowboy.
— Photo by Lucille Stewart, courtesy of Stan Searle.

and one being a timed event—and he must win at least $1,000 in each event. The first recipient was Benny Reynolds. Also in 1967, Bob Scriver of Browning, Montana, was chosen to sculpt a life-size bronze of Linderman for the National Cowboy Hall of Fame in Oklahoma City. It was unveiled in December 1969.

Rodeo was well on its way in the 1960s. The growth in attendance, number of cowboys competing, and purse money was making each season better than the last one. A higher percentage of competitors were making a living by rodeo alone. The *Rodeo Sports News* and *Hoofs and Horns* were full of advertisements for bronc saddles and bareback riggings made by respected saddlemakers. Jim Houston and Larry Mahan advertised their own designs.

The "flower children" eventually waned, but rodeo kept on truckin'. It hadn't solved all the problems of the sport, but it had come a long way from those first rodeos when contestants had to bring their own bronc and to win required riding until the outlaw quit bucking.

Broncbusters of the Era (1960s)

LARRY MAHAN (1943-____) was born on a farm near Salem, Oregon. At ten he was employed by an amateur-roping club to take care of their calves. He also learned to ride them, unknown to club members. He entered the calf riding at a Redmond rodeo two years later.

In 1961, while working on a ranch, a part-time rodeo cowboy took him to the Stockton, California, rodeo. Mahan entered the bull riding. The bull's hoof shattered his jaw and it had to be wired shut. Mahan learned to ride bulls. He also attended Ken McLean's riding school. McLean said of Mahan, "What impressed me most was that he couldn't get on enough stock. He must have climbed on 45 head. He was having trouble with horses that cut back to the right. When he left, he'd improve on that kind of horse."

Mahan won All-Around Cowboy of the World in 1966, 1967, 1968, 1969, 1970, and 1973. He was fourth in bareback riding in 1966, 1967, and 1970, second in saddle bronc riding in 1968, 1969, and 1973, and won the bull riding in 1965 and 1967.

Mahan worked out in gyms to stay in shape. He flew his own twin engine Cessna 310 to get to the many rodeos he needed to make to compete for top spot. His business ventures have been varied, including writing *Fundamentals of Rodeo Riding* and having his own brand of western wear. He was one of a "new breed" of cowboy who became successful businessmen in a variety of endeavors, in addition to their rodeo skills. [66, 19]

MARTY WOOD (1933-____), from Alberta, Canada, learned his balance and ability on broncs from riding jumping horses for his father. He first competed in rodeo in the United States in 1953 at Omaha, and won the saddle bronc event.

When he entered his first rodeo, he tried bareback riding and bull riding, but didn't like it. He decided to make saddle bronc riding his event. Subsequently, he became Champion of the World in 1958, 1964, and 1966; was four times runner-up; three times Canadian Rodeo Cowboy Association Saddle Bronc Champion; and average winner at numerous rodeos in the U.S. and Canada. He learned his "classic" style of bronc riding from watching others and going through the school of hard knocks. He had a slashing style of spurring, and nobody reached out any farther or used the full spread with more vigor.[52]

His career lasted from 1957 to 1974, and he was inducted into the ProRodeo Hall of Fame in 1992, the Canadian Hall of Fame for Rodeo in 1993, and the Alberta Hall of Fame for Sports in 1994.[53]

BILL SMITH (1941-____), from Cody, Wyoming, entered

the professional rodeo circuit in 1961. He competed seventeen years, and for fourteen of those years went to the
National Finals in saddle bronc riding. He won the World
Championship in 1969, 1971, and 1973. Injuries have
plagued him, mostly a pinched nerve in his back. He ran a
nightly rodeo at North Platte, Nebraska, where youngsters
could learn to ride from a champion. He served as PRCA saddle bronc director for 1972 and 1973, and retired from rodeo
in 1979. Today he lives in Thermopolis, Wyoming, and raises
quarter horses.[53]

SHAWN DAVIS (1941-___), from Whitehall, Montana,
began riding at four years old with his uncle, Sam Kissock. At
eleven he was breaking colts for cash. He won the Montana
State High School Bareback Championship, and while at
Western Montana College of Education he won the National
Inter-Collegiate Rodeo Saddle Bronc title. He turned professional in 1963. As a saddle bronc rider, he won the 1965,
1967, and 1968 World Champion title. At the time he won
the third Saddle Bronc World Championship, he was in an elite
group: Bill Smith and Marty Wood had tied him with three
saddle bronc wins, Pete Knight had won four, and Casey Tibbs
had won six. In 1966 he went cold. He was vice president of
RCA for a time, and in 1968 he was named Montana
Professional Athlete of the Year.

He suffered a crippling back injury in May 1969, on a
bareback horse, when he was again leading for the saddle
bronc title. He was told never to ride again but finished
twelfth at the end of the year. He then made the Finals in
1971. Between 1963 and 1974, he qualified for the Finals
every year but 1970.

Still competing in the late seventies, Davis ran the rodeo
and horse program at the College of Southern Idaho at Twin
Falls, when not at a rodeo. Mental attitude was Davis' long
suit, and he taught students this title-winning key. Southern
Idaho put out some top-flight rodeo contestants. In the 1979
National Finals, Davis rode Beutler and Sons' saddle bronc
Strychnine, to the high point ride of the Finals—an 83-point
score.[53]

WINSTON BRUCE (1938-____) was born and raised in Canada. Before he could walk, his dad, a stock contractor and former bronc rider, put him on horses. While a kid, as his ability to ride improved, so did the horse's buck. (Unknown to young Bruce, his dad kept upgrading the ability of the horse to match him.) It is said he rode so well spectators thought he always drew the easy horses. Years of practice perfected his style. He was the Canadian Saddle Bronc Champion in 1957 and 1958. He became the World Saddle Bronc Champion in 1961. From 1959 through 1968, he qualified for the National Finals.

In 1968, he became the assistant arena director at the Calgary Stampede. Later he became a division manager for rodeo, and supervises the animal-breeding program as well as the annual Calgary Stampede rodeo.[53]

Broncs of the Era (1960s)

DESCENT was foaled on the Art Douglas ranch, northeast of Browning, Montana. His sire was a government thoroughbred stallion by Plentipotentiary, a half-brother to Man-O-War. Eddie Vaughn got him from Douglas and sold him to Cremer, who for the first few years didn't do much with him. Beutler Brothers and Cervi bought him from Bud Cremer. In 1966 the ten-year-old palomino gelding was ridden once in twenty-one attempts. He was 1,300 pounds and sixteen hands and was chosen as Bucking Horse of the Year in 1966-1969, 1971, and 1972.

Mike Cervi kept track of Descent's performance and he was ridden every fourth time out. He never had a pattern to his bucking; never bucked the same way twice. Bill Smith, World Champion Saddle Bronc Rider for 1969, 1971, and 1973, drew Descent nine times in his career. He rode him to the whistle five times. "He was the greatest bucking horse I ever rode," said Smith.[53]

SHEEP MOUNTAIN, born on the Tooke Ranch near

Ivan Daines on Descent, Beutler Brothers and Cervi's famous bronc, at National Finals, 1969. Descent won the PRCA Stock of the Year Award six times, 1966 through 1969 and again in 1971 and 1972.

— Photo by Ferrell, donated by
June and Buster Ivory.

Alvin Nelson on Crazy One at San Antonio, Texas, 1964.

— Photo by Ben Allen. Courtesy of Alvin
and Kay Nelson.

Ekalaka, Montana, was the son of General Custer, who was son to Prince, the son from Tooke's original big Shire named King Larego. In 1967 Sheep Mountain was voted top saddle bronc of the National Finals Rodeo. Feek Tooke accepted the plaque from Clem McSpadden in 1968, and rode to the saddling area outside the arena and died of a heart attack.

TRAIL'S END was a Morgan-bred sorrel gelding, weighing 1,200 pounds. In the early 1950s he was a packhorse known as Dexter in the Bitterroot Mountains. Once he got away with the pack and was not found until the next year. Oral Zumwalt discovered him at a sheep-raiser's ranch. He first bucked at Missoula, Montana. After the bucking he had done so well that Zumwalt said, "That's the end of the pack trail for you, old fella." Sonny Linger said he was the most perfect bucking horse, when he had his day.

Trail's End had no set pattern to his bucking, and had a lot of ways of going. Benny Reynolds said he was never ridden when he turned back to the right. He was gentle to handle. Zumwalt used to take the saddle off of him, in the arena, after he had bucked someone off, to show how gentle he was. Trail's End was chosen as the Bucking Horse of the Year in 1959. He was also judged the best saddle bronc horse at the National Finals for 1959, 1960, and 1961.

After Zumwalt's death, at the dispersal sale, Trail's End sold for $4,400 to Big Bend Rodeo Company of Wilbur, Washington. When Big Bend sold out, Bud King of Odessa, Washington, retired him, and he lived for three years near Oklahoma City, on George Williams' ranch. He died in February 1980.[11]

BIG JOHN came out of Saskatchewan in 1960 as part of a work team. Jack Bloxham slipped him in the bareback string for a high school rodeo when one of his "regulars" got sick. Big John nearly flung his rider over the grandstand. The next day Bloxham tried the big, 1,400-pound, bay gelding in the saddle bronc event, and the same thing happened. Harry Knight bought him in 1961.

Big John was gentle to handle and quiet in the chutes. He

Jim Ferguson on Rodeo Inc.'s Major Reno at Kankakee, Illinois, 1969.
— Photo by Bern Gregory.

The retirement of Trail's End, 1959 Saddle Bronc of the Year, an Oral Zumwalt horse, at National Finals Rodeo, 1976, held by George Williams.
— Photo by Bern Gregory.

was picked twice as Bucking Horse of the Year, 1963 and 1964. In September 1968, a freak accident killed him. He cut his jugular vein on a section of corrugated tin, part of a windbreak, in one the Knight corrals. Knight also lost Sage Hen and Misty Mix that year when they died of toxic poisoning during Cheyenne Frontier Days.[52]

CENTENNIAL started in rodeo in 1949. Doc Sorenson bucked him as a saddle bronc first. He ran head on into a fence at Idaho Falls and knocked himself out. Everyone presumed he was dead and he was sledded out of the arena, but after the rodeo was over he came to and was fine, except for a broken nose. After he healed, Doc put him in the bareback string and then sold him to Oral Zumwalt in 1950. Harry Vold bought him in 1964 through an auction in Missoula, Montana. The 1,500-pound, sorrel gelding qualified for six National Finals rodeos. In fourteen starts he had six firsts, two seconds, one fourth, three buck-offs, and one trip out of the money.[52]

Centennial died during the Dallas All-Star Rodeo in 1966. John Edwards had just ridden to mark 69, good for second in the first day money, when Centennial suffered a heart attack and died. He was twenty-one years old.

10

SCHOOLS AND SPONSORS IN THE 1970s

The 1970s introduced many changes, and the efforts to accomplish more for rodeo were beginning to be seen. The Rodeo Cowboys Association, using the pyramid-style program, had more levels of their membership working on improving professional rodeo. Event representatives had area directors, which covered problems and answered questions on rodeo, within their area of the country.

Judging of events continued to improve. The pro-judging seminars were used, which were modeled after a program used in the National Football League and found successful. The program required prospective judges to pay $100, attend a stringent four-day program, and be tested and interviewed regarding their rodeo experience, attitude, and knowledge.

Publicity for rodeo was still a foremost concern of the RCA. In 1971 and 1972, the RCA hired a New York public relations firm, but in 1973 the firm's contract was not renewed. By early 1974, the RCA discovered they had more publicity without the New York firm. Several movies had been made featuring rodeo or the cowboy life. Casey Tibbs produced a movie on a wild horse round-up he staged in 1967 in South Dakota, entitled *Born to Buck*, and received an award from the National Cowboy Hall of Fame for it. The movie *The Great American Cowboy* was given an Academy Award for being the best feature-length documentary of the year. And Cliff Robertson, actor, starred in a movie entitled *J. W. Coop*, which was the story of a cowboy, and the world premiere was held in Oklahoma City during the National Finals in 1971.

161

The movie theater has given our country a look at the western hero since the beginning of movies. However, the cowboy of the Roy Rogers/Gene Autry era was unrealistic in many ways. The movies of the 1970s were grounded in realism, and gave a more honest view of cowboys and rodeo.

Other publicity included the formation of International Rodeo Writers Association, which in conjunction with sponsor Levi-Strauss held an annual competition for the best rodeo coverage and writing. One of the first winners, Carmen Anthony, from Spain, viewed a rodeo from behind the chutes at Calgary. Dusty and weary after the rodeo, she wrote, in part: "I think rodeo is a great sport. It takes skill, physical conditioning, physical ability and technical knowledge. The men are so attractive and appealing, too . . . that helps as a spectator sport." She went on to say, "It makes football look rather dull . . . just fighting for a touchdown."[52]

A short film entitled *Match of Champions*, narrated by Larry Mahan, was made available to television stations across the country. Justin Boot Company put out a sixteen-page booklet, "Rodeo: The All American Sport," which contained action photographs of six rodeo greats giving their personal experiences and opinion about rodeo. They were Larry Mahan, Jim Shoulders, Freckles Brown, Marty Wood, Jack Roddy, and Pete Logan, all members of Justin's advisory board on boot styling. Justin received thousands of requests from all over the country and all around the world for this booklet.

Radio stations were beginning to cover rodeo information. Some of the earliest to do so were WBAP of Fort Worth; KROE from Sheridan, Wyoming; KDGR of Deer Lodge, Montana; and KBLF out of Red Bluff, California. Added publicity for the local rodeos, often a golf game matching local golfers with cowboys competing in the rodeo, were staged. These seemed to be well received and spread to various locales across the country. At Steamboat Springs, Colorado, a skiing competition was held prior to the National Western Stock Show in Denver, where cowboys pitted their abilities against skiers. And, in Edmonton, Alberta, they even held an ice hockey contest, pitting cowboys against hockey players on ice, along with the rodeo. It was so successful it was repeated several times.

Joe Alexander, seven-time Bareback World Champion, on Swanny Kerby's Hoot Owl at Gooding, Idaho, 1970.
— Photo by James Fain.

Newspaper reporters are either lauded for their rodeo reporting or cussed and discussed. Jim Murray, a syndicated sports columnist of the *Los Angeles Times,* took a different approach. Known for his satire and subtle wit, his description of the Golden States Rodeo Company's twenty-three-year-old paint horse, Cheyenne, went like this: "He's overweight, swaybacked, his ancestry is as dubious as a unicorns. He's turning gray in spots, and he looks like something led into town on the end of a frayed rope by an old Indian. He'd eat sugar out of the hand of a little old lady from Pasadena, he's about 90 years old, as humans would reckon age, and he should have been on a shelf in cans long ago. He's as mournful as a coyote's howl. If he were human, you'd get him a cane. Man-O-War would bite him."

Murray's "disrespect" was tongue-in-cheek, as he went on to point out that literally hundreds of thousands of dollars had been won off his "buzzsaw" back. "Cheyenne was on his way to the slaughterhouse when Andy Jauregui, a rodeo livestock contractor, who keeps closer tabs on the equine underworld than the FBI does on the criminal element, heard of him. Andy is kind

*Andy Jauregui's twenty-five-year-old Cheyenne
still bucks like a colt. Rider is Mike Adams.*
— Donated by June and Buster Ivory.

of the Godfather of the switchblade set of horses, the despera-
does of the tanbark," credited the dry-witted Murray. [53]

And Now a Word from Our Sponsor!

A major improvement to rodeo was the increase and
development of rodeo sponsors. Winston Tobacco Company in
1971 implemented an incentive program and gave $105,000
a year to top cowboys in six events. The program paid the
incentives twice a year.

In 1977 the Black Velvet Stock Contractor Awards were
providing bonus incentives that allowed each stock contractor
to nominate at the beginning of each season one saddle bronc,
one bareback horse, and one bull to be eligible to receive the
Black Velvet Bonuses throughout the year. This was done to ele-
vate the pro rodeo stock to the same level as the winning cowboys. The program gave the stockmen $25 each time the Black
Velvet animals were bucked during a paid PRCA performance.
Contractors also received $250 for each BV-nominated animal

Beutler Brothers and Cervi's Frontier Airlines won Top Horse of the Year in 1975.
— Donated by June and Buster Ivory.

selected for National Finals, $500 for each selected as the best at National Finals, $300 for each selected as the best in each of the twelve circuits throughout the country, $3,000 for the best Saddle Bronc, Bareback Horse and Bull of the Year, and $5,000 for any animal nominated to the Black Velvet program for the first time and selected as a bucking animal of the year, that same year.[53]

By 1978, headlines reported "Corporate Sponsorship Reaches Two Million." Sponsors included R. J. Reynolds, Schlitz, Frontier Airlines, Huebelin Distillers, Justin Boot Company, Prior Shirt Company, Bailey Hat Company, Hesston, Blue Bell, Inc., Levi Strauss, H. D. Lee Company, Simco Saddlery, McDonald's, Rodeo America, and Morgan Products.

Growth Brings Change

The Rodeo Cowboys Association became the Pro-Rodeo Cowboys Association in 1975. Other significant changes in the 1970s era included dues going up to $50 a year, from $35, and *Rodeo Sports News* rates climbing from $1 to $6 a year. In an economic survey done through questionnaires sent to all readers of the *Rodeo Sports News* in 1972, it was reported that members of RCA annually spent $24,288,101 on rodeo-related expenses. The readership spent $82,252,033 on rodeo-related expenses. This was evaluated from 852 reporting members and 4,121 readers completing the survey. In a breakdown, members (competing cowboys) annually spent $5,776,039 on vehicle expense; $3,104,756 on food and lodging; telephone, $1,891,451; western wear, $2,165,478; tack, $1,481,513; insurance, $3,262,182; and horses and horse trailers, $3,124,960. Cowboys traveled 119,835,217 miles per year.

PRCA reported in 1977 that an estimated 14 million spectators watched professional rodeo, not including those who watched it on television. Prize money was at $7 million annually. There were 4,322 members in the PRCA, and 3,026 permit holders.[53]

Rules were continually being questioned and discussed to determine if they should be changed, added to, or deleted for the improvement of the sport. The most important changes made during this time were to change the ten-second saddle bronc ride to an eight-second ride in 1972. Another rule enforced at that time was that the pickup men were to stay clear of the rider and the bronc until after the whistle sounded. It seems that on occasion the pickup men, trying to do their job most efficiently, would get in the way of the judges' ability to see and score the ride.[52]

Rodeo schools began to be taught by cowboys in various areas of the country. Jim Shoulders held the first rodeo school in the early sixties, at his ranch in Henryetta, Oklahoma. He had all three roughstock events, while Shoulders taught the basics. He often had Bill Fedderson and others, in later years, working with the saddle bronc riders. By the early 1970s, *Rodeo Sports News* advertisements were chocked full of schools: Bynums College of Doggin' Knowledge; Gary Leffew Bull Riding; Olin Young Calf Roping; Walt Arnold Steer Roping; Lee Cockrell Roping and Horsemanship; Mahan Rough Stock; Glen Franklin, Joe Alexander, and Bill Smith Bareback and Saddle Bronc; Rodriguez and Luman Team

Bill Smith, Saddle Bronc Champion in 1969, 1971, and 1973, tops Kesler's Short Crop, the National Finals Top Bucking Horse that year and again in 1983, in the seventh go-round of the 1977 National Finals Rodeo.
— Photo by James Fain, courtesy of June and Buster Ivory.

Heading for the sky, Bobby Berger, 1977 and 1979 Saddle Bronc Champion, keeps his seat atop Hoss Inman's Big Buck at the Naitonal Finals Rodeo.
— Photo by Bern Gregory.

Roping; and others. Shawn Davis scheduled the first rodeo school for Indian youth. He also advertised a mechanized bucking machine. Davis also commented that during his rodeo career he saw a big change from seeing a top-flight rodeo cowboy come along about once every five years, then change to the day when top-flight rodeo cowboys were ten-deep in each event. He attributed the difference in the fact that in the earlier days it was all trial and error and competitors had to learn for themselves. Once the rodeo school came into being, the novice competitor had the opportunity to be trained by a proven champion in the event, and he could practice, practice, practice![53]

Unfortunate Events

Tragedy always creeps into everyone's world, and rodeo has had its share.

Bill Stevenson, a saddle bronc rider from Staten Island, New York, making his home in Greeley, Colorado, hit the ground wrong at a Vernon, Texas, rodeo in 1973 and broke his neck. The spinal cord was severed and he died in an Arlington, Texas, hospital. Also that year, while traveling to Cheyenne Frontier Days, a car pulled out in front of a Harry Vold truck, near Longmont, Colorado, and the driver had to turn into the median and rolled the truck, which was carrying twenty-four of Vold's top broncs. Four were killed: Grey Cup, Tall Timber, Mother Goose, and Geronimo. Fourteen more were crippled. In 1978 seven of Bob Barnes' broncs were killed in a truck wreck at Peterson, Iowa.

In 1979 four Canadian PRCA cowboys were reported missing when their single-engine airplane en route from Salem, Oregon, did not reach its destination of Las Vegas. Searches were held for weeks to no avail. Brian Claypool, Gary Logan, Lee Coleman, and Calvin Burney just disappeared. Nearly four months later the remains of the plane were found in northern California.[53]

Another disappointment in the rodeo world was the stock market crash of 1970 that caused the failure of Rodeo Far

West, a $3-million production of rodeo people touring in Europe for nine months, performing in Italy, Switzerland, France, Holland, Germany, Belgium, and Austria. Sponsors were Wrangler, Ford, Coca-Cola, and Marlboro.

But when near-tragedies occur, and all the information is gathered, you can only shake your head in amazement that it wasn't any worse than it was. A November 15, 1972, *Rodeo Sports News* headline reported: "Five Hands Escape Bad Injury." While going from Evanston, Wyoming, to San Francisco to a rodeo, traveling at speeds of over 100 miles per hour, the car the cowboys were in rolled several times in the median strip of freeway. Saddles, riggings, and other items bronc riders and bull riders need were scattered for hundreds of yards down the highway. Shawn Davis was the least hurt; Rusty Riddle had cuts and bruises, a concussion and was unconscious for over an hour; T. R. Wilson, John Holman, and Pete Gay sustained some injuries, none serious.[52]

Keep on Truckin'

In spite of the ups and downs, rodeo continued its course. The National Western Stock Show and Rodeo started the 1970 season with 564 cowboys entered. In 1971, Cheyenne Frontier Days had the biggest payoff in its history, with a $96,700 purse. The rodeos across the country over the "Cowboy Christmas," July 4, paid out over a quarter of a million dollars in 1973. The National Finals Rodeo in 1975 sold out all performances. In 1977 there were 579 PRCA rodeos in thirty-seven states and four Canadian provinces.[53]

Cowboys are noted for their willingness to help one another, even though often they may be competing against one another in the rodeo arena. Such is a rodeo fact, and has been repeated too many times for anyone to doubt it. Larry Burgess, a saddle bronc veteran and native of Wyoming, said this about the long, tedious hours spent traveling from rodeo to rodeo:

Some time ago I was in Gladewater, Texas, for a night performance and had to get to Grover, Colorado, in time for the saddle bronc riding the next day. Direct flights from

Clyde Vamvoras, 1967 and 1968 World Champion Bareback Rider, has both feet on the left side of Grand National's neck, but is still aboard, Fort Worth, 1971. Buster Ivory took this horse on his European rodeo tour, then sold him to Harry Vold.
— Photo by Ferrell. Courtesy of June and Buster Ivory.

Gladewater to Grover are non-existent, and I was afoot. The only person I could find still in Gladewater who was through that night was Jerome Robinson. Jerome wasn't up at Grover until the day after I was, and he was suppose to pick up Gene Beghtol somewhere in Oklahoma that night. But he took pity on me, and after the bull riding we jumped in the "bullmobile" and were on our way.

We picked Gene up sometime around midnight, and he and Jerome drove the rest of the night, replying to my offers to drive with, "You rest, you're up." We pulled into Grover just as the bareback riding ended. Jerome and Gene had driven over 1,100 miles in about 19 hours to get me there, even though they weren't up until the next day.

Now I like to count Jerome and Gene as friends, and I sure hope they feel the same about me; but I don't really believe that's why they did it. I have a sneaking suspicion they would have done the same for any cowboy—going down the road.[52]

In 1973 Casey Tibbs and Billy Myers finished first and second in the saddle bronc riding at the Las Vegas Helldorado rodeo. After the rodeo they went to Binion's Horseshoe Casino. Benny Binion made it a rule that his casino always catered to cowboys. Casey and Billy cashed their win checks and proceeded to lose every dime they had won. At a Texas rodeo the following week, someone asked Casey who won at Las Vegas. Casey's answer was, "Well Benny Binion won first and second in the bronc riding."

One hundred years had gone by since the sport of rodeo had begun during the trail drive era. What had developed in the arena sport was astonishing, but the "try" of a determined cowboy wanting to win his event is the same "try" that made such changes and improvements a reality. Space travel and electronic devices had become commonplace, and yet the curiosity and interest in watching a bronc-y horse and an ingenious cowboy try to outwit each other could still draw a crowd.

Broncbusters of the Era (1970s)

JOE ALEXANDER (1943-____) was raised on a ranch near Cora, Wyoming. He attended Casper Junior College and started competing then. In 1966 he won the National Intercollegiate Rodeo Association Bareback title. Encouraged by neighbor and saddle bronc champion Bill Smith, Alexander

Joe Alexander rides High Tide, the 1975 National Finals top bareback horse at Filer, 1976.
— Donated by June and Buster Ivory.

began in 1970 on the pro-rodeo circuit and wound up fifth in bareback riding that year.

He won the World Champion Bareback Riding title from 1971 through 1975 and the PRCA Champion Bareback title in 1976 and 1977. He had a spurring lick that was virtually unbeatable. He would sit upright a little more than some riders, and he tried his hardest on every horse, jerking his spurs clear up to his rigging with each jump.

Alexander hated to travel and had to be prodded to leave home. The last rodeo of the season was the Grand National at San Francisco, and then he would lay off for a month until the National Finals. Consequently, he never had a very good Finals because the first few mounts would make him sore. In 1975 he and Rusty Riddle were neck-and-neck for the championship going into the Finals. Alexander stayed in shape. It paid off. [52]

BRUCE FORD (1953-____) is a native of Kersey, Colorado. When he was nine years old he was in a terrible school bus accident. The driver of the bus failed to see an oncoming train at a railroad crossing. The bus was cut in two, and twenty students were killed, including Ford's thirteen-year-old brother, Jimmy. His brother Glen was injured, and Bruce was unconscious for seven days. Needless to say, when the Ford boys wanted to rodeo, their dad was hesitant to agree. He was afraid a blow to the head might cause serious problems for Bruce. Their dad finally gave in.

Bruce became World Champion Bareback Rider in 1979, 1980, and 1981. The second championship was more of an achievement to Ford because he came from behind. He said the hardest part was taking the title away from one of his best friends, Mickey Young. In 1981, Ford led all year long. But it can happen both ways. In 1977, Ford came up to the last performance of the National Finals with hopes of winning the World Championship, then Jack Ward scored an 80 on a reride and beat him.

Ford's style of bareback riding is copied somewhat from the Jay Himes way of topping a bronc—he likes to gap wide, spur hard, and expose himself as much as possible each time the horse makes a jump. In his bucking school Ford tells his

Bruce Ford on Yellow Fever during the second go-round at the 1977 National Finals Rodeo. He won the Bareback Championship the next three years.
— Photo by James Fain.

students they can't copy him or anyone else; they have to do what is natural. He said the basic rules are: 1. chin down; 2. feet set in the neck; 3. stay focused; 4. doesn't matter what you do with the upper body; 5. don't let the horse take your form away from you. "When your feet hit his neck at the exact time his front feet hit it acts as sort of a shock absorber, and you get a hold of the horse. Then you will try to get a lot of drag with your feet. This even straight drag back to your rigging, while holding your feet in the neck, is what pulls your butt back down on your bareback rigging," Ford explained.[53] He believes a rider should try to win on every horse, and be a showman whether the horse bucks or not. Lewis Feild told Ford bareback riding is being out of control and yet being in control, and Ford agrees.

Ford conducts riding schools at his indoor arena with five students for three days. Some of the graduates from his school include Marvin Garrett, Dave Appleton, C. R. Kemple, Jeff Hart, and Pete Hawkins. He also was bareback representative to PRCA. Inducted into the ProRodeo Hall of Fame in 1993, he entered the Pikes Peak or Bust Rodeo bareback event at Colorado Springs the same day as his induction. During an interview at the hundredth anniversary of Cheyenne Frontier Days in 1996, just prior to the bareback competition in which he was entered, he said out of the nine rodeos he had entered that year he had placed at six.

MONTY "HAWKEYE" HENSON (1952-____) grew up in Mesquite, Texas, with Don and Pete Gay as friends. His dad was a policeman. Monty began his rodeo career by riding prospective bulls at the Mesquite arena, unknown to his family. When he tried his first bronc it was a natural, and from that time on his favorite event was saddle broncs, with bull riding a second. He used Neal Gay's forty-year-old bronc saddle. Gay would let him use it, but wouldn't sell it to him. Observers say "Hawkeye" won because he could fit the same stylish ride on any kind of horse, rank or easy. He reaches for the neck with each jump and the spurs are back clear to the cantle.

Henson won the World Champion Saddle Bronc title in 1975, and the PRCA Saddle Bronc Championship in 1976. He won money at seventy rodeos that year. In the 1979 National Finals, Henson experienced a bittersweet incident. He was awarded the champion buckle, only to be asked to give it back twenty minutes later, when it was awarded to Tom Miller. Then a few minutes after that it was taken from Miller and awarded to Bobby Berger. There was only $305 separating the three, and someone doing the figuring didn't wait for the final tally. Berger won it that year—by $5.28! Henson did win the World Champion Saddle Bronc buckle again in 1982.[53]

JAMES CHARLES "J.C." TRUJILLO (1948-____) was born and raised in Prescott, Arizona. He began rodeoing when he was six. He went to Eastern Arizona Junior College on a football scholarship and finished at Arizona State, graduating with a degree in elementary education.

Trujillo joined the RCA while in college. In 1973 he cracked out hard. He won the World Champion Bareback title in 1981. From 1973 through 1985, Trujillo was in the top fifteen in the bareback event, except in 1984. His best score ever was at the Cow Palace in 1978 on Rosser's #12. At National Finals in 1978, Double Jeopardy broke his jaw and busted his lower lip, requiring thirty-eight stitches.

Trujillo compares rodeoing to professional skiing, another sport at which he excels. They are both individual sports and the bottom line in both is competition. On the subject of rodeo, he said, "A guy complains about all the traveling, going and going all the time, spending money and being gone from home; but then when I'm up on the chute and running my hand into the bareback riggin' there's a space right there that I really thrive on; that's when I know why I'm there; to compete. To put my personal, individual skill into competition against that horse, and at the same time of course, I'm in competition against the other bareback riders."[53]

Broncs of the Era (1970s)

ANGEL SINGS, a registered quarter horse mare, was turned over to a professional horse trainer when a young filly. She was found to be untrainable. After one saddling, she blew up and the trainer refused to have anything more to do with her. A college rodeo stock contractor in Texas, Charley Thompson, bought her. At the Texas Tech Rodeo in 1977, Harry Vold leased the horse and could hardly believe his eyes when he saw her buck. He asked Thompson if that was the way she bucked every time, and he was assured that it was. Vold tried to buy her. Thompson said no at first, but eventually Vold made the deal.

The brown, heavy-muscled mare, at 1,050 pounds, stood tall for a saddle horse, at fifteen hands. In 1978 she was out thirty times. How many riders she bucked off was not available, but she became the Saddle Bronc of the Year for the 1978 season, and tied with Sutton's Deep Water for Saddle Bronc of the Year in 1979. Bronc rider Rick Wharton said, "She is fast, kicks hard and won't allow you any mistakes."[53]

Sippin' Velvet, Champion Bareback Horse many times over, owned by Bernis Johnson, and listed in the Guinness Book of World Records.

— Donated by Bernis Johnson.

SIPPIN' VELVET was sired by a thoroughbred running horse that won more than $300,000 on the track. His dam was a Belgian bucking mare. Bernis Johnson acquired him from Hoss Inman. He tried to shoe him only once. "He didn't want anyone to put their hands on him," recalled Johnson. The horse had to be sedated so much to get the job done that Johnson decided the bronc deserved to go without shoes, and Johnson found other ways to keep his feet in shape. The bald-faced sorrel was halter broken, but that is as far as he would let anyone go. He was never under a saddle.

Sippin' Velvet had been in competition for four years when the eight-year-old bronc was picked as the Bareback Horse of the Year in 1978. He was drawn forty times and ridden twice, once by Paul Mayo. He was picked again as Bareback Horse of the Year in 1983, 1984, 1986, and 1987.[53] This feat is listed in the *Guinness Book of World Records*.[74]

Sippin' Velvet died at twenty-seven years of age, with colic, in early January 1996. He is buried in the Johnsons' backyard. The bronc's twenty-two-year career in rodeo included five

Reg Kesler's outstanding bronc, Three Bars, won the National Finals Rodeo's Top Bareback Horse award in three different decades—1967, 1973, and 1980.
        — Photo by Allen, courtesy of Reg Kesler.

Bareback Horse of the Year titles, five National Finals top stock awards, and six Bareback Horse of the Year awards in the Texas Circuit. He bucked at the National Finals eighteen years. "No cowboy that drew him ever turned him out," said Johnson proudly. "Everyone wanted to ride him. He had a lot of heart."

CRYSTAL SPRINGS qualified for the National Finals Rodeo fifteen times. Her first Finals was in 1972, and Ned Londo set a record eighty-eight points on her. She was chosen Saddle Bronc of the Year in 1977. Everyone who got her either won or failed to qualify. She died at age twenty-seven at Iowa State University in Ames, Iowa, in 1987. She was buried at the Barnes Rodeo Company's family ranch.[53]

THREE BARS was owned by Reg Kesler, who bought him from a man who was going to sell her for dog food. Kesler tried her as a saddle bronc, but she didn't do much. As a bareback horse she was impossible! Three Bars was chosen as Top

Bareback Horse at the National Finals in three different decades: 1967, 1973, and 1980.[61, 63]

RODEO NEWS, a Reg Kesler saddle bronc, was picked as 1970 Bucking Horse of the Year. The dam was a range mare, which bucked a few times. The sire was veteran arena performer Rattler, who later sold to Calgary Exhibition and Stampede.

11

"I Ain't Hurt, There's No Bones Showin'"

The 1980s saw professional rodeo become big business. Sponsors were spending more money on the sport, and more invitational rodeos where top cowboys could win additional money were being held. From 1976 to 1981, prize money increased 79%. Corporate sponsorship, including promotions, administrative costs and television, reached $9 million in 1981, up more than *$8 million* from 1977, when the prize money totaled only $900,000. Even more astounding: *More tickets were sold to PRCA rodeos than to National Football League games in 1981*.[53]

By 1989, 4,031 contestants had won money at PRCA rodeos. Membership increased to 5,560, permit holders to 3,584. There were 741 rodeos that year and 2,128 performances. Prize money totaled $16,879,429.[53]

Sponsors that provided financial as well as promotional support to professional rodeo by the end of the 1980s included Wrangler, Dodge Truck, Coors Beer, Coca-Cola, Copenhagen/Skoal ProRodeo, Resistol Hats, Justin Boots, Gist Engravers, Binion's Horseshoe Casino, Rodeo America, Award Design Medals, National Car Rental, Bull's-Eye Barbecue Sauce, the American Quarter Horse Association, and United Airline Travel Program.

New competitions added during this era included the Rodeo ProTour, sponsored by the PRCA-established production company that picked five regular PRCA rodeos to be televised, then climaxing the year with a televised finals expected to offer $100,000 to $150,000 in prizes. The Coors Chute Out

Rodeos added extra dollars as well. The Calgary Exhibition and Stampede introduced their $50,000 Showdown Round. And the XV Olympics Winter Games, held in Calgary, held a Challenge Cup pitting the United States rodeo team against the Canadian team. Wrangler Showdown, held in Scottsdale, Arizona, also had the United States rodeo team competing against Canada for $220,000.[53]

The National Finals Rodeo moved to Las Vegas, Nevada, in 1985, and gave to "the city of lights" a shot in the arm. December was generally slow in the casinos, hotels, and show-bars. Once National Finals Rodeo settled in, that problem ended, and a contract was soon signed to keep it there through 1994.

Meanwhile, back behind the chutes, the cowboys were handling life just as they had for some time. One reporter asked what the good and bad points of rodeoing were. Todd Little, a bareback rider, replied, "The money, the women and the good times." Shawn Frey, another bareback rider, said, "The money, the freedom and the friends." Gary McDaniel said, "It was the ability to make your own decisions and the friends you made—and the bad, you got to wear your car out!"[53]

When asked what the major difference was between roughstock riders and timed event contestants, one roughstock contender from San Marcos, Texas, said, "We don't fall off intentionally like bulldoggers do. Plus they watch Wheel of Fortune and we watch Jeopardy."[53]

A New Style in Bareback

During the 1960s, the bareback riding event had begun to see some significant style alterations. Don Mayo, top-ranked bareback rider of 1963, until the automobile accident that took him out of contention, competed by using a laid back style that kept his body almost horizontal with the bronc's back. It looked as though his head was hitting the rump of the bronc. His brothers, Paul, Bob and Roger, also used the same technique and found they won their event or placed in the money often. Others followed. Jim Houston, another bareback rider, began making a bareback rigging with a more flexible handhold, which allowed the rider to lean back farther than the traditional handle.

Through the 1970s others tried this laid back style. By the 1980s, the newer bareback riding style was quite popular, and many competing cowboys chose it. Contestants and spectators from earlier times were critical of the new position. In fact, Harry Tompkins, roughstock champion from the 1950s, was asked by a *ProRodeo Sports News* reporter to comment on the style, and he said: "The way the cowboys fall back and let the rump of the horse hit them in the back doesn't call for a lot of coordination. If the great horse, Come Apart, were around today, they'd all be on the ground—crippled, too."[53]

Don Mayo, when asked about the style that he made famous, admitted when he started riding he had not been to a rodeo to see how bareback riders rode. He and his younger brothers, Paul and Bob, practiced on some calves on their Iowa farm. In trying to recall, he believed he rode that way because the calves had no shoulders and he couldn't keep his feet up on the neck to spur without leaning back, so "Good old farm boy logic told me to throw my body back and it would throw my feet forward. I guess when I rode my first bronc, at 14, I just did what I had practiced at home." At seventeen he went into professional rodeo. His brothers followed, using the same style, and it worked for them as well. They were top contenders. "Paul was the best," said Don. "Bob and I weren't even in his league, and it was obvious when Paul was 12 years old."

Don admitted the different style did get attention, and at times it got a lot of criticism. He said the crowd seemed to like it. Some judges did not like the style. Mayo said that one time he went to Louisiana to rodeo. No one knew him, and he drew a good little horse. He had a good ride; the horse jumped, kicked, and made a circle. The scores were not announced, but Mayo just knew he had won the bareback event. "I didn't even place," he said. "I knew it was because of my style of riding." A week later he was at another Louisiana rodeo, using the same stock. He went to a fellow who worked for the contractor and asked if he could be put on the labor list. He also asked if the guy would pay Don's entry fee in the bareback riding, promising to give him half his winnings. The guy agreed. Don drew the same little horse, rode him the same way, and won the event.

Not all judges disapproved of Don's style of riding, but the ones who did would not score Don to win no matter how well he rode. He would call ahead, at times, and see who was judging to determine whether he should enter or not.

In time, Don said he learned to adjust his riding to accommodate a judge who was critical of the laid back style. He also said when he competed in California he saw some riders from that area who had a style similar to his. As with many new ways, they often may be happening in various areas simultaneously. Only those who get in the winner's circle, however, are the ones others hear about.

T. J. Walter, director of rodeo administration for PRCA, said when asked about this bareback form, and how the judges evaluate different styles: "There are bareback riders who do lay back, but when the horse comes down, some riders come back up to a sitting position. The judges should be watching the spurs, the stroke and the length of the spurring. The position of the rider should not matter." In reviewing the top riders in the event today, Walter determined at least half a dozen were of the "old school" that did not lay back. Both styles are capable of winning the event. Walter related, "Leonard Lancaster once told Paul Mayo, when he was competing, if he had a spur on the back of his head he'd win first every time."

Sports Medicine and the Controversial Helmet

The bronc rider was battered and bruised. He'd been in a "wreck" on his last mount and he was walking mighty careful. The trip to Cheyenne had been long and the car was crowded with roughstock riders, saddles, and gear. When they finally piled out, he limped toward the rodeo office. One of his buddies said, "Where you goin'?" He said he had to enter the bronc riding. "Why are you goin' to ride if you're hurt?" asked his friend. "Because it's Cheyenne!" he said.

The "Daddy of 'em all" has a way of doing that to every cowboy who has ever entered. Whether they were at their best or not, they just couldn't be there without being entered. Cowboys have competed in their event with busted ribs, broken legs and arms, and God knows what else. But cowboys have a way of ignoring injury and pain—especially the closer they get to being up in their event.

A cowboy is going to get hurt. It is not a maybe, but a given. You can't put a 150-pound cowboy on a 1,200-pound animal that doesn't want him there and expect no one to get hurt. Timed event competitors also fight injuries, but not as often as roughstock riders do.

EMS (Emergency Medical Services) workers who cover the rodeos have commented that they have never seen the likes of a cowboy. Even when he is injured, he is still trying to convince himself he can continue to compete. They have said there is no other sport where the participants are so determined. Whether it is the adrenaline flow during the competition, or the sheer determination of the independent hand that refuses to admit pain, there is something that sets the cowboy a breed apart.

Nevertheless, by 1980, there was an area of rodeo being covered that had never officially been addressed, and that was cowboy injury. Everyone knew it happened, and everyone who competed got hurt and had to heal, but finally some interest was being put forth to assist the 'busters with their bruises and breaks.

The Justin Boot Company sponsored a program called the "Justin Heeler," which was the brainstorm of Dr. J. Pat Evans and Don Andrews, both sports medicine gurus. They brought to rodeo medical expertise as applied to athletes. The primary rationale in sports medicine is to work with the injury to allow the athlete to get on with competition as quickly as possible. Unlike many doctors who require that, or believe, an injured patient must stop participating, sports medicine specialists realize the importance of continuing to compete.

Dr. J. Pat Evans was the team doctor for the Dallas Cowboys football team and the director of the Sports Medicine Clinic of North Texas. His understanding of the cowboy and

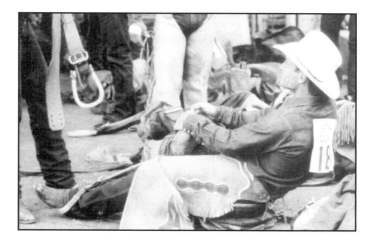

Clint Johnson, 1980, 1987, 1988, and 1989 Saddle Bronc Champion, stretches before the 1991 Pikes Peak or Bust Rodeo, Colorado Springs, Colorado.
— Photo by Susan Lambeth.

his attitude toward competing was based on personal experience: he had competed in rodeo and played high school and college sports. Evans and Don Andrews, who put together the proposal for the Justin Heeler Program, recognized that rodeo provides some of the most intense physical punishment of any professional sport, yet it had a complete lack of sports medicine personnel so common in other sports.

The sports medicine program for rodeo began at a tournament-style rodeo held in Fort Worth in 1979. Don Andrews helped as many cowboys as he could with their injuries; however, they didn't have a trailer or a sponsor. John Justin committed to sponsor the program in 1980. In 1982 Andrews went to twenty-two rodeos, where he wrapped, taped, gave treatments, and directed cowboys to doctors like Dr. Evans.

Several cowboys were interviewed in the *ProRodeo Sports News* about their experience with the Justin Heeler Program. Bob Brown, a saddle bronc rider, said he had injured his leg. Don Andrews said it was a pulled hamstring and treated it with an electrical stimulator. The leg improved. Clint Johnson, also a saddle bronc rider, strained some ligaments in his knee

Swanny Kerby's Alley Cat tosses Ivan Daines at Douglas, Wyoming.
— Photo donated by June and Buster Ivory.

two weeks earlier. Andrews taped his knee and gave him a galvanic treatment. Jim Dunn, bareback rider, jammed his hand into the front of his rigging and bruised his knuckles. Ultrasound and an electrical muscle stimulator were used and the hand improved. Butch Knowles had hyperextended his knee earlier and then reinjured it during a bronc ride. The "Heeler" taped his leg before every go-round, which helped to limit it from hyperextending again.[53]

In early 1980s issues of *ProRodeo Sports News,* Dr. Bruce F. Claussen discussed various parts of the anatomy, common injuries, and how to care for them. Several issues covered the knee and various injuries to it. Other issues covered ankle injuries. It was obvious that as the sport was increasing financially in prize money, as well as bonuses from various sponsor groups, the athlete was becoming more aware of his vulnerability and attempting to prevent injuries from occurring—not just counting on luck to keep him whole. When a rodeo cowboy gets injured the paychecks stop. The cowboy must get back on the road as quickly as possible as a simple means of economic survival.

Dr. J. Pat Evans is a nationally known and well-respected

Derek Clark, thirteen-time National Finals Saddle Bronc rider, won the fourth go-round on Flying U's Buckskin Velvet at the 1983 National Finals.
— Photo donated by Imogene Beals.

orthopedic surgeon. If surgery is required to correct an injury, he will prepare the injured cowboy by telling him just what to expect. He believes surgery comprises 40% of the positive results, and the other 60% comes from the proper physical therapy. Dr. Evans tells the cowboys exactly when they can be back at their competition; and if they are smart, they will comply with what he prescribes. Several have jumped the gun and returned sooner than he recommended, only to find they had reinjured themselves. Dr. Evans has kept many top cowboys in working order.

By 1984, the Justin Heeler Program had two rigs, and was making forty rodeos a year. Jacki Romer joined the group. Her bachelor's degree in exercise technology, master's degree in exercise physiology, and a subsequent internship earned her an athletic trainer certificate. Before a rodeo, a long trail of bareback riders could be found taping their arms and taking advice from Romer for their special problem. Her ultimate goal was to keep them rodeoing, in spite of injury.

Headlines on the front page of the *ProRodeo Sports News*, September 14, 1988, asked: "Is it time to consider safety gear?" Two separate accidents in the rodeo arena had taken the lives of two bull riders shortly before the article. Don Andrews, of course, was consulted, and his reply was: "The solution isn't as simple as it appears. If everyone wore a helmet, we might reduce head and skull injuries. But what we've found in other sports is that with helmets, we see a greater rate of spinal injuries. Whenever there's a force delivered, it has to be transmitted to another area. The helmet takes the force, but it transports it to the spine." Andrews suggested that more study, in laboratories, be done before any quick decision, based on emotion, be made.

In bareback riding, wearing a helmet or some type of protective gear would be appropriate, as it would in bull riding. However, "Adding the weight of a helmet to the snapping motion of a bareback rider's neck would magnify that snapping motion," Andrews explained. "When you increase the load on the end of a lever, the head in this case, you're asking for a neck injury."

Cowboys interviewed were not in favor of protective gear. They said the public comes to see cowboys compete in dangerous sports and would be disappointed if they wore protection. However, it was also felt that it would become a reality sometime in the future. The opinion was that more cowboys had developed their own training programs. Strengthening the muscle groups around knees, shoulders, ankles, and the neck helped them keep their bodies in working order and prevent injuries.

It was not until the mid-1990s that protective vests and helmets were seen in the arena. Such gear was primarily used by bull riders, but on occasion bronc riders were seen in them, specifically if they had suffered a recent head or neck injury. In 1996 a helmet made of titanium, and weighing only one and a half pounds, was advertised in the *ProRodeo Sports News*. Although many professional cowboys are still up in the air about the use of protective gear, it is beginning to be required at youth rodeos throughout the country.

Broncbusters of the Era (1980s)

BRAD GJERMUNDSON (1959-____) was born and reared in North Dakota. He joined the PRCA in 1980, and won the World Champion Saddle Bronc title in 1981, 1983, 1984, and 1985. He qualified for eight straight National Finals, 1981 through 1988. But in 1994 he pocketed $81,405 at the National Finals, ending up third for the year. It wasn't as if he had retired between 1988 and 1994, but he cut down to fifty or sixty rodeos a year and spent more time with his family. The 5'5, 145-pound bronc rider ranches when not rodeoing.

Gjermundson thinks the major difference in the event from 1980, when he started professionally, and now is the number of rodeo schools available. He also thinks everyone pays a great deal more attention to their equipment, and keeping it updated, than they did in earlier days. If he could change one thing in rodeo, it would be to have sponsors for all cowboys. He said his sponsor had been very good to him.

In his opinion, some of the best broncs were Try Me, of Rex Logan's string, No Savvy and Angel Sings.[53]

CLINT JOHNSON (1956-____) is from Spearfish, South Dakota, and grew up on a ranch in the Black Hills. His dad liked good bucking stock, so they went to many rodeos. He won the High School Saddle Bronc title in 1974, and joined PRCA in 1975. He won the World Championship Saddle Bronc title in 1980, 1987, 1988, and 1989. He did not miss a National Finals competition between 1978 and 1989.

Johnson tries not to complicate saddle bronc riding. He took Bill Smith's bronc riding school, and feels he learned more from Smith than from anyone else in the business. Johnson tries to keep in his head and concentrate on the basic things Smith taught in his school. He was on the PRCA board of directors from 1986 through 1989 and now lives near Amarillo.[53]

LEWIS FEILD (1956-____) grew up around Elk Ridge, Utah. He won the All-Around World Championship in 1985,

*Marvin Garrett, 1988, 1989, 1994, and 1995
Bareback World Champion, shows his style of riding
at Cheyenne Frontier Days, 1991, after much rain.*
— Photo by Susan Lambeth.

1986, and 1987, and the Bareback Riding World Championship in 1985 and 1986. He qualified for the National Finals eleven straight times. The 5'6, 150-pound cowboy won well over a million in his career earnings. He retired at the end of 1991 to become a stock contractor (Lewis Feild Diamond G Rodeos).[53]

MARVIN GARRETT (1963-____), while growing up around Aladdin, Wyoming, watched rodeo on TV and determined Bruce Ford had more fun than anyone did. When Garrett started riding bareback, he learned to lean back. He said it gave the bronc absolute freedom to attempt to toss his rider. "Riding and leaning way back works as long as you are lifting exactly right," he said, "but if you're not lifting right you can fall to the side and be thrown off." Garrett said the basics work for everyone: Keep your shoulders behind your hips, your chin down, and set in your feet, because that is where the controls are.

He won the 1988, 1989, 1994, and 1995 World Champion Bareback Riding titles. The '89 title was touch-and-go to the end. That year he said he used a combination of consistency and recklessness to win the title. "I made sure of my

Robin Burwash, bareback rider, shows how much strength is required in the arm that holds the rigging.

— Photo by Susan Lambeth.

spur-outs," he said, "then I tried to get a little wild and sneak into that first place spot."[53]

Garrett had just finished riding a Kesler bronc, Buckskin Billy, at the 1996 Calgary Stampede (for a 77 score) when interviewed and he said, "Don't ever think you are the best, because you can always get better." When not competing he is on his ranch tending to his 100 cows and 30 bucking horses. He also wants to give back to the sport by teaching kids how to ride bareback horses.

ROBIN BURWASH (1958-___), from Okotoks, Alberta, was chosen to be part of the Canadian team at the Calgary Stampede Rodeo 1988 Challenge Cup, an exhibition rodeo competition between the Canadian and the United States top competitors in each event. Burwash, a bareback rider, felt this rodeo would show fans from across the world, many of whom had never seen a rodeo before, the very best of the business.

Twenty-four hours before the '88 Challenge Cup was to begin, Burwash received notice, while rodeoing in Houston, Texas, that his ailing father's health was slipping. He rushed home, only to find that his father had died minutes before he arrived. His father had been one of Burwash's biggest fans, but also his best critic. Burwash could have resigned from the upcoming competition and no one would have questioned his decision, but Burwash competed. He scored 80 points in the first go-round. For seven rounds the competition was keen. Going into the last round, Burwash was leading the bareback event with 225 points. Bruce Ford was second with 215. Burwash finished with three firsts, and had never finished worse than tied for second. He accepted the gold medal in front of 80,000 fans, and his only regret was that his dad, Don Burwash, was not there to see it.[53]

Broncs of the Era (1980s)

HIGH TIDE, a great-grandson of Man-O-War, one of the most famous thoroughbreds in racing history, was a ranch horse until he took to bucking. Archie Anderson purchased him from the McCleary ranch in Winnemucca, Nevada. He was sold to Cotton Rosser's Flying U Rodeo Company when he was about fourteen years old.

High Tide was selected for twenty-one consecutive years to compete in the National Finals Rodeo. He was Bareback Champion Horse at the 1975 Finals, and Reserve Champion several other years. Rosser retired him from the arena at the 1986 Finals after twenty-three years of active bucking.

He was known for his consistency and altitude. If a bareback rider's arm could hold out against his strength, and he spurred in rhythm with the horse, he would go to the pay window. If not, however, he would find himself somewhere in the arena dirt. He had been considered to be a classic bucking horse. Bruce Ford drew him six times and always won money on him.

High Tide died August 5, 1987, and is buried at Rosser's Marysville, California, ranch. J. C. Trujillo is quoted as describing High Tide as "one in a million." High Tide was inducted into the ProRodeo Hall of Fame in 1993, only the second bareback horse to be inducted.

CHEYENNE was found in 1951 by Andy Jauregui in Nevada. Out of an entire truckload of bucking prospects this spotted gelding was the only one to work out. He had a twenty-six-year bucking career, and in 1977 was named as the winningest bareback horse ever. He was retired at the Cow Palace, the same place he began his career when Casey Tibbs bucked him out of the chutes twenty-six years earlier. Tibbs said, "Cheyenne was a crowd pleaser, but to the cowboys he was an honest bucker and got better with age. He did his best all the time."

The Flying U Rodeo Company hauled him the last twelve years. The day of his retirement some of the hands decided they should get the stains off this old horse before the ceremony. But Cheyenne had other plans; he was not about to start bathing at thirty years of age! He was led into the arena, stains and all. Jauregui, the oldest active stock contractor in California, took the lead shank of Cheyenne's silver halter and tried to hold on while Archie Anderson attempted to place a huge wreath of flowers around the snorting horse's neck. This was another first that was not going to happen. Cotton Rosser, Flying U's head honcho, finally took the wreath and placed it around Jauregui's neck.[35]

Retired, Cheyenne went back to Jauregui's Newhall, California, ranch, and was turned out to pasture with Whiz Bang, another old bronc. In earlier years, the two horses had been inseparable buddies when hauled together. Cheyenne saw Whiz Bang immediately, threw his head in the air, and trumpeted a shrill hello and dashed straight to him. One day, when the two geldings were celebrating with a run along a rain-soaked canyon rim, the trail gave way beneath Cheyenne, and he tumbled to the canyon floor, fracturing a leg. He had to be put down.[11]

SKOAL'S ALLEY CAT was foaled by saddle bronc Cool Copenhagen, formerly named Cool Cat, at the Kesler ranch near McGrath, Alberta. The dam delivered the highest scored ride at the 1986 National Finals Rodeo, an 82 by Bud Munroe.

Skoal's Alley Cat won the Saddle Bronc of the Year in

Hyrum Special, a Swanny Kerby saddle bronc, went to twenty consecutive National Finals Rodeos from the early 1960s to the 1980s. Aboard in this Jim Fain photo is Clair Palmer at Preston, Idaho, 1966.
— Courtesy of Swanny and Bud Kerby.

1988, at age nine. In fifteen trips out of the chute, he allowed only two riders to qualify: Jack Nystrom and Kyle Wemple. Kesler said that if Alley Cat were a baseball player he would be called a "utility player" which means being capable of playing more than one position.

He began his career as a bareback horse and qualified for National Finals in 1985 and 1986, but his size soon made it necessary for him to become a saddle bronc. Over sixteen hands and weighing 1,350 pounds, he was simply a hard horse to ride. Out of a possible 25 points, Alley Cat always scored at least 23 or better.[53]

TOMBSTONE *a.k.a.* BIG BUD *a.k.a.* ALL VELVET *a.k.a.* THE LEGEND, owned by Sutton Rodeo, Inc., was purchased from Bud Cooper and lived his life in South Dakota. The 1,425-pound, tall dun gelding was used in saddle bronc events. He was the top saddle bronc at the Wolf Point Match of Champions, but he started spinning and was switched to the bareback event. He won the top bareback horse at the

Black Velvet Tournament of Champions in the early 1980s; therefore, his name was changed to All Velvet. Later, Wrangler did some advertisements using legends including Wrangler Jeans and Willie Nelson, and All Velvet's name was changed to The Legend. His last stint with a sponsor was for Tombstone Pizza Company, and his name was changed again, to Tombstone.

Tombstone treated all cowboys the same—amateurs and champions—for buck-offs or hang-ups. Jack Ward, J. C. Trujillo, and Steve Carter all hung up on him. Bruce Ford drew him eleven times and won money eleven times.[53] He was the PRCA Bareback Horse of the Year in 1985. Sutton retired him in 1994 at the Black Hills Rodeo at Rapid City, at age twenty-five. Bruce Ford was at the retirement of the bronc that carried him to victory so many times. He made some comments while action shots were shown on LamaVision of Ford riding Tombstone. The old bronc died in the summer of 1996, and Sutton buried him above the Missouri River beside some other top Sutton stock, Yellow Jacket, War Drums, Half Velvet, Country Music, and six-time Badlands Bull of the Year, Wipe Out Skoal.

12

COMPUTERIZED COWBOYS IN THE 1990s

As the last decade of the twentieth century began, the 150-year-old sport of bronc riding was becoming as technically up-to-date as any major sport or business. Although in the arena the broncbuster tests his ability against a bronc the same way as the earliest bronc rider, the administrative end of the business has become state-of-the-art computerized technology.

Today the computerized ProCom program is used. All PRCA contestants call to enter any PRCA-approved rodeo in the country. Dates to register for each upcoming rodeo are posted. Cowboys phone during that time and give the PRCA representative their preferred dates for various rodeos, as well as contesting cowboys they travel with so that dates coincide. They also designate which rodeo points, if they win, go toward their year's final tally. PRCA roughstock competitors currently can have 125 rodeos count for championship points. Timed event competitors can choose only 100 rodeos. The representative will give the cowboy a time to call back after the entries close, when they can get confirmed dates of when they are up and what stock they have drawn.

Kevin Ward, PRCA director of management information systems, worked with the U.S. Olympics Committee for eight and a half years before coming to the association. The system of entering rodeos prior to 1976 was for competitors to call individual rodeos and enter with the rodeo secretary. Later the cowboys called the PRCA office, but information was taken by hand and transferred to other places. Information regarding each member was not readily available, nor was information regarding the rodeos always at hand. It caused cowboys to spend a lot of unnecessary time on the telephone without getting much accomplished. The ProCom system has been on-line since January 1990. The bugs are still being worked out and the system is being improved, because in the computer world, nothing remains constant.[53] In 1995 the ProCom system received 700,000 calls. All calls are recorded, and if a discrepancy occurs the call is reviewed by a supervisor and resolved promptly.[61]

Additionally, the ProOfficials Judging System has been developed, and Jack Hannum, PRCA supervisor of ProOfficials and circuit coordinator, conducts twelve seminars for judges annually. There are eight full-time judges, who receive a salary and expenses, and more than 150 reserve officials. They are allowed to mingle with the cowboys, but do not drink with them or travel with them. No matter how much the judging is improved, the roughstock scoring is still a personal opinion.[53]

George Gibbs, a Wrangler official, interviewed by Ron Gullberg of the *Casper Star Tribune* while working the Central Wyoming Rodeo, said, "We watch for humane issues because contestants themselves don't want to ride an animal that may be injured or sick." They also make sure competitors get the animals they have drawn.

The roughstock's score, by the judge, when scoring a competition, is determined by a variety of actions; buck drop, power, height of kick, change in direction, spin, front-end movement, and rhythm or lack thereof.

According to Gibbs, "In bareback bronc riding there is a spurring motion that the cowboy rolls back and forth from the neck back to the hand hold as fast as he can. He wants to get as high in the neck as he can." Regarding saddle bronc riding, Gibbs explained, "The spurring motion comes from the neck back through the sides of the horse's body and then back up front again. What determines the ride is how high the cowboy puts his feet up the neck of the horse. The timing and the rhythm of the horse and the length of the spur motion are important. And very important is the contact of the feet and spurs, which we call drag. You just don't want a swiping motion where the cowboy's not getting a lot of contact with the neck and body."[69]

High-Tech Rodeo

The world of computerized technology is increasingly edging into rodeo. One example is the Copenhagen/Skoal ProRodeo Scoreboard. Two scoreboards were designed and introduced in 1990, by Daktronics, Inc., of Brookings, South Dakota. The scoreboards provide quick scores and times on cowboys and cowgirls as the rodeo progresses, and adds to the overall enjoyment of a rodeo.

Today there are three scoreboard teams on the road 312 days a year, going from rodeo to rodeo, being hauled in forty-five-foot trailers. The team consists of a systems operator who mans two computers. One takes care of all the rodeo statistics; the other takes care of all graphics and logo displays. A person in the arena with a telephone headset relays information from the rodeo judges to assist the operator.[53]

In 1992 at Reno, Tony Lama introduced two high-resolution state-of-the-art screens that showed video replay of the ride or timed event that had just occurred in the arena. This allows the audience to see and review a ride. But an additional bonus is the opportunity for a good announcer to explain and show the audience where the ride went wrong or what caused a competitor to fail in his attempt. This educational boon to the industry has aided many spectators in becoming more knowledgeable of the sport.

The most recent addition to PRCA in this ever-changing world of sophisticated electronics happened on June 12, 1996, when Professional Rodeo went on-line. ProRodeo.com in computer language is the official website of the Professional Rodeo Cowboys Association, and anyone connected to the Internet can draw information on a multitude of PRCA subjects, such as National Finals, ProRodeo Hall of Fame, Event Descriptions, PRCA publications, humane facts, sponsor information, and so on. Other major sports also have this ability—and PRCA is not to be outdone![53]

New Events in the '90s

In addition to the approved annual rodeos, the PRCA sanctioned other rodeos, which were conducted like one-time tournaments or an annual event but based on scores of the competitors as to who could participate. Many of these events were sponsored by some of the major supporters of professional rodeo.

For example, in 1989, Wrangler Jeans held a United States versus Canada Rodeo Showdown and offered $220,000 to the participants. It was held in Scottsdale, Arizona. The top five participants in each event made up each team. In the saddle bronc event the competitors were Clint Johnson, Lewis Feild, Kent Cooper, Dan Etbauer, and Derek Clark for the United States. Duane Daines, John Smith, Wayne Powell, Denny Hay, and Mel Coleman represented Canada. In the bareback event, the U.S. team consisted of Marvin Garrett, Clint Corey, Bruce Ford, Chuck Logue, and Lewis Feild. The Canadian team was composed of Steve Dunham, Robin Burwash, Bill Boyd, Darrell Cholach, and Jim Dunn. The results found the U. S. team winning over Canada. In the saddle bronc, it was Kent Cooper winning top award, and Bruce Ford tops in bareback, plus winning the average championship.

In 1992 the first Original Coors-sponsored Rodeo Showdown was held. Cowboys competed individually instead of the team concept that Wrangler used. Craig Latham won the saddle bronc event, and Denny McClanahan won in bareback.

Walt Garrison's All Star Rodeo for Multiple Sclerosis continued to be a major attraction. Begun in 1976, this rodeo has always been quite successful. Garrison's main wish was that a cure for the illness could be found so there would be no need for this fundraiser. So far that has not happened.

Another rewarding event of the 1990s was the Exceptional Rodeo. Cowboys and cowgirls participated in thirty-five to forty of these rodeos around the country each year. The Exceptional Rodeo, generally held prior to the regular rodeo performance, matches cowboys and cowgirls with physically and mentally challenged children in "special" rodeo activities. The children obviously enjoy interacting with these heroes of the rodeo arena, but one look at the faces of the cowboys and cowgirls who participate shows they are just as thrilled to be able to assist these young "buckaroos" in a taste of arena fun.

In 1975 the PRCA Circuit System was founded. It divided the country into twelve divisions, called circuits. The purpose was for those PRCA members who have talent, but don't have time to travel and compete with the PRCA's biggest stars, to have a chance to win at circuit level. Cowboys are required to designate one of the twelve circuits as their "home" circuit. When participating at rodeos, in that circuit, each win of money earns points toward that circuit's finals. The winners of each circuit finals are then invited to the Dodge National Circuit Finals Rodeo. The Finals created in 1987, and operating under a tournament-style system, are held in Pocatello, Idaho, each spring.[53]

It'd Be a Short Ride Without the Sponsors

Sponsors add megabucks to rodeo, making payoffs much better. If it were not for such committed sponsors, many rodeo events could not be held. Many sponsors choose to be involved in various venues, giving not only financial assistance but in other ways as well. The Justin Heeler Program celebrated ten years of service to rodeo and continues to aid injured contestants. The Justin Cowboy Crisis Fund assists financially when a cowboy is killed or injured in a rodeo accident, and is not able to compete. Chuck Simonson, a bull rider injured at Caldwell, Idaho, was the first to receive financial assistance. The fund covered the cost of his rehabilitation for one year, reduced his medical expenses and offset his living expenses, it was reported in January 1991. Later that year PRCA donated $75,000 to the Fund, putting the balance at $230,000. Many events are held each year to benefit this worthy cause. [53]

Other sponsors—Dodge, Coca-Cola, Coors, Copenhagen/ Skoal, Wrangler Jeans, Sharp Electronics, Tony Lama, MCI, Resistol, Rodeo America, Crown Royal—and many others have poured tons of money into the sport of rodeo at various levels from local rodeos to National Finals to special sponsored competitions.

For example, Wrangler Jeans and Shirts rewards PRCA world and circuit champions and stock contractors. Bonuses are given to the top three animals in each roughstock event at all ten NFR rounds. Wrangler, a long-time rodeo sponsor, also helps fund the ProOfficial Judging Program. They sponsor the Wrangler Circuit Series, National Final Steer Roping and the Dodge National Circuit Finals Rodeo, and the Wrangler World of Rodeo, a series of PRCA rodeos featured on ESPN television. One of Wrangler's most popular sponsored programs is the Wrangler Jeans ProRodeo Bullfight Tour, which has been going on since 1981. In addition to rewarding the participating bullfighters, they give bonuses to the owners of the top three fighting bulls in the event.

Without these corporate giants, many cowboys would still be struggling to get their winnings, above their expenses. In 1995 PRCA cowboys competed for $25.4 million at 739 PRCA-sanctioned rodeos. Cowboys are quick to say there are still not enough sponsors. "If there were more sponsors in rodeo more cowboys could go 'on down the road'," said Bob Logue, bronc rider, former bronc rider representative, and currently contest director, on the PRCA board.

The Modern Cowboy's Perspective

Meanwhile, the bronc riders keep taking care of their end of the business—traveling back and forth across the country, attempting to win money, and adding up points toward getting to National Finals. Several of the top cowboys, when asked what advice they would pass on to youngsters interested in following in their boots, gave advice that was sound. Ty Murray: "Don't just want to win on the weekend or at the rodeo, want it all the time." Robert Etbauer: "It requires determination and TRY." Lewis Feild said, "Have patience. Come into rodeo with a 'Look, Listen and Learn' attitude. Try high school, college and amateur rodeo before becoming a PRCA member." Bruce Ford: "Learn to ride safe before you try to be great."[53]

Denny McLanahan readies his bareback rigging at the 1995 Salinas, California, rodeo.
— Photo by Susan Lambeth.

Deb Greenough, 1993 World Champion Bareback Rider, and nine-time National Finals contestant.
— Photo by Susan Lambeth.

Bob Logue, 1991 Original Coors Fans' Favorite Cowboy and PRCA contestant director, giving a good bareback ride. In 1982 Logue placed at more than 100 rodeos.
— Photo by Susan Lambeth.

In 1992 cowboys were asked who their childhood rodeo heroes had been. Eudell Larsen, a saddle bronc rider from Laramie, Wyoming, said, "Clint Johnson and Tom Miller. Clint's school got me on the right track and taught me the basics." Bud Longbrake, a saddle bronc rider from Dupree, South Dakota, said, "Tom Miller, he always said to mark your horse out two jumps and lift on your rein, and everything will work out after that." Marvin Garrett, bareback rider from Belle Fourche, South Dakota, said, "Bruce Ford, Phil Lyne and Mahan. Bruce dominated when I started, he did it different than everyone else, he was wild and aggressive."[53]

Currently, rodeos still range from the small-town rodeo, where local cowboys compete against any top-level competitors that rodeo full-time, to the major attractions such as Houston Livestock Show and Rodeo, Calgary Exhibition and Stampede, and Cheyenne Frontier Days. Calgary's 1996 total purse was $650,400; 1995's rodeo attendance passed 131,938. Cheyenne Frontier Days celebrated its hundredth anniversary in 1996.

Several top cowboys have opinions for improved changes in professional rodeo. Derek Clark, saddle bronc rider, stated he would like to see the top fifty rodeos invite the top fifty competitors in each event. "Good bucking horses are getting more scarce every year. I think a less experienced rider should have to earn his way to get to compete against proven competitors," said Clark. Bob Logue said he would like to see professional judges specialize in one or two events, not try to judge all rodeo events.

What will change in the rodeo of the future remains to be seen. But we know there will be change. For example, when the Cowboys' Turtle Association had been in operation only four years they had a twenty-eight-page handbook, which included twelve pages of members, leaving sixteen pages to list rules and other important information. Today the PRCA rulebook weighs half a pound, has fourteen chapters of by-laws, eleven sections of official rodeo rules, and a sixty-four-page judges' handbook appendix.

It is hoped by many that rodeo will not change so drastically that the following words, written by Gene Lamb in 1954 for a book he had planned, will no longer apply to rodeo:

> There is no place in the competitive part of Rodeo for the man who needs security to keep down his fears for the future. There is no paycheck each week. There is no retirement plan. There is no unemployment insurance. But in Rodeo there is personal independence and FREEDOM!
>
> The cowboy who contests professionally in Rodeo for a living goes where he pleases. He is not "booked" into a town; he just arrives. He may be in Florida one week and Oregon the next. He may drive a Cadillac with a two-horse trailer behind, or he may hitch a ride with one of his friends, or with the stock contractor's truck. He rodeos 12 months out of the year—and when he goes to pay his taxes he may find he has won $20,000, or, if he's the best, it may be $40,000. He also may find that he hasn't won back expenses and entry fees. But either way, if he belongs to Rodeo, he has had a successful year.
>
> The Rodeo Cowboy is generally an educated man. He may have stopped school in the third grade, or he may be a college graduate; he may be a scholar with several books to his credit, or he may have difficulty in sending a telegram to enter a Rodeo. Which ever, he has an education in living, and in people, and in living with people. He's at home in Joe's Beanery in Wideplace, Montana, or in New York's Copacabana. He has been in both, and knows how to act in both.
>
> He works hard, and plays hard. He will fight if necessary, and is polite by nature. He takes off his hat in elevators. He will go to any lengths for a friend, and almost as far for an acquaintance—if the acquaintance belongs to Rodeo. His faults are many and varied—so are his virtues. He may tell a big lie just for the hell of it—he has no need for small lies.
>
> The Rodeo Cowboy has the same fierce independence of the old frontiersman, and in the rodeo arena he has a similar dependence on his friends.
>
> The man who helps him set his saddle is probably competing against him in the same event. The same man may have told him how many reins to give the saddle bronc he is about to get on; what the horse is apt to do. In fact, he has done everything possible to help the other fellow beat him.
>
> Rodeo is the last Frontier for the individual.[53]

Gene Lamb, founder and first editor of the *Rodeo Sports News*, and author of several rodeo books, passed away January 11, 1996.[53]

Broncbusters of the Era (1990s)

ROBERT (1961-___), DAN (1965-___) AND BILLY (1963-___) ETBAUER. These brothers were reared on the family ranch in Ree Heights, South Dakota. Billy lives in Edmund, Oklahoma, and Robert and Dan now reside in Goodwell, Oklahoma. All three boys learned bronc riding from their father, Lyle, and then attended John McBeth's bronc riding school several years straight.

Robert first competed at a 4-H rodeo, and won. He had his first bronc saddle when he was barely sixteen, and rode with it for ten years. Dan started as a bull rider, but a bull knocked Robert's front teeth out, so the folks made Dan quit riding bulls and bought him a bronc saddle.

Robert joined PRCA in 1985, and was Resistol's Saddle Bronc Rookie of the Year. Dan joined in 1987, and was runner-up to the Saddle Bronc Rookie of the Year.

The similarities end in their bronc riding after the spur outs, says Robert. "We all have strong spur outs, but Dan really drives the iron to them, and rides with a lot more strength than I do. Billy reaches farther. He can set his feet on top of a horse's neck."

Dan says he was never a natural, and has had to work for everything he has achieved. Dan says he watched his brothers and Brad Gjermundson ride to learn and improve his bronc riding.

The trio left the 1991 National Finals Rodeo with fourteen checks totaling $117,323. Robert had won the World Champion Saddle Bronc title for a second time, having won it first in 1990. In 1992 Billy won the World Champion Saddle Bronc title. In 1993 they left the National Finals with $160,402, including Billy's $101,531—the most any cowboy ever won at a single rodeo and at National Finals Rodeo.

Their mother handles their money and is wisely investing

The Etbauer brothers talk shop with Derek Clark and friend behind the chutes before the 1995 Salinas, California, rodeo.

— Photo by Susan Lambeth.

for them. They started out, as most cowboys, with very little financially. In fact, friend and banker John Koller, from Moorcroft, Wyoming, had faith in them and loaned them money. At one time the debt was large, but a few wins and it was paid off. Billy, however, had saved $20,000 before he started his rookie year rodeoing. At the end of the year he had $5,000 left. Billy won the World Champion Saddle Bronc title in 1993, and broke an annual earnings record in saddle bronc with $184,675.

In 1995 about thirty would-be bronc riders tested their abilities and learned from the best. The three Etbauers, plus Craig Latham, Paul Peterson, and Bret Franks, conducted the Deke Latham Memorial Bronc Riding School. Deke, Craig's brother, was killed in a car accident shortly after the 1986 National Finals, where he finished fifth. He attended Oklahoma Panhandle State University, and the proceeds from the bronc riding school go to the school's rodeo team.[53]

On January 15, 1995, Robert Etbauer got his foot caught in the stirrup during a saddle bronc ride at Denver. While he hung upside down the bronc stepped on his thumb and tore it off. Robert got loose, picked his thumb up, walked out of the arena, and was taken to Saint Luke's Medical Center. After eight hours of surgery the thumb was re-attached to his riding hand. By March, he was "back in the saddle" and competed at San Angelo. Since then, he has regained the feeling in his thumb and the surgery was successful.[53, 61]

Billy Etbauer won the 1996 World Saddle Bronc Championship by earning $190,257, a single-event record, and set an average record by scoring 805 points in ten rounds of the National Finals. He also hit the million-dollar mark in earnings during the tenth round of the NFR, with career earnings of $1,005,529. Dan ended the year in third place and Robert came in twelfth. And to top it all off, they are three of the nicest representatives in the world of rodeo today.

TY MURRAY (1969-____) was reared in Glendale, Arizona. As a child he looked up to his dad, a cowboy, and Murray admits he wanted to be just like him, and still does. During high school, Murray took gymnastics, with the idea in mind that it would help his rodeo ability. He learned strength and to be limber, and now he says it helps him in all three roughstock events. He tries to keep equal ability in all three events. If he feels he is not doing as well in one event, he will practice on it until he has improved that event to the same level as the other two.

Cody Lambert and Murray took on 125 rodeos in 1988. They flew more places than they drove. Lambert was the teacher, Murray admits, and kept things on an even keel, allowing them both to succeed. They flew first class and arrived refreshed; thus they rode better and won more money.

Murray won the Resistol Rookie of the Year award in 1988. At the awards banquet, he thanked Lane Frost, Tuff Hedeman, Cody Lambert, and Jim Sharp, all competitors, but friends too. He said that he was the only one who wasn't a champion. Just watching and being with them had cut his learning time more than half. He also thanked his family, whom he said had been behind him for twenty years. "Every time I get on a mount, I try as hard as I can," he said.

Murray grew up on the back of an old red roan horse. At five years old he and his mother went rodeoing. She would keep

Ty Murray, six-time All-Around Cowboy of the World, uses this Susan Lambeth photo for his exclusive fan club photo.

— Photo courtesy of
Ty Murray Fan Club.

$15 out of the grocery money so she would have enough money for entry fees for him. He craved it. When his mom was exhausted and ready to head for home after a busy weekend, Murray would be wishing for another rodeo. When they would arrive home, friends and neighbors would ask how he had done, but Murray would just say he had done all right. When his mother tried to explain that his friends were just interested, he said, "Mom, if you're good you don't have to tell everybody. They'll know it."

At twelve his dad, who worked at a racetrack, got him a summer job as a flagger. He saved all his money and bought a bucking machine. He rode it until his legs were raw. He even had his mother put padding on his legs so he could continue to practice. He attended Brad Gjermundson's bronc riding school.

He won the PRCA All-Around World Champion title from 1989 through 1994, and the Bull Riding World title in 1993. His first All-Around was won when he was only twenty. He also became rodeo's seventh millionaire through rodeo in 1993; however, he made his money in half the time it took the other six.

In 1995 he had knee surgery, and took the proper time off to heal. In 1996 he was back to compete, but in May he tore a shoulder ligament that required four to six months to heal. Dave Appleton gave Ty one of the greatest compliments when he said, "Ty is an exceptional cowboy—a real throwback to the old cowboy era. He knows his limitations, however, and he will return to the arena when it's right."

Murray did return but, unfortunately, in February 1997 he dislocated his right shoulder during a bull-riding event and had to undergo surgery. Dr. Tandy Freeman, of Justin Sportsmedicine, said they had to reattach the ligaments to the bone. Months of physical therapy followed.[53] At the start of the 1998 season, Murray was first in All-Around.

DAN MORTENSEN (1968-____) is from Manhattan, Montana. His dad is an electrician and his mother a schoolteacher. He is the youngest, and has three sisters. He gives Ike Sankey, rodeo coach at Northwest Community College in Powell, Wyoming, credit for being most instrumental in his bronc-riding success. "Besides technique he taught me three simple goals to shoot for," Dan said. "Always do better, have fun and keep a good attitude." He was the Resistol Saddle Bronc Rookie of the Year in 1990. He was the World Champion Saddle Bronc Rider in 1993, 1994, 1995, and 1997. He was World Champion All-Around Cowboy in 1997. His winnings for 1997 were $184,559.

In the third round of the '95 Finals, the judge ruled Mortensen touched his bronc with his free hand. His response was, "That's rodeo—there is nothing you can do. The judges have a job to do, and so do I. I shouldn't have put myself in that position, where I got into trouble for that possibly to happen. But you have to leave it in the arena."[53, 61]

During an interview with the author at Calgary, he hurriedly packed his saddle. He moved to the front of the saddle bronc riding, at the semifinals, after scoring 83 on Red Sky. When asked how his bronc riding had changed, he said, "I've gotten consistent and I don't waste chances." His bronc saddle is a Broken Arrow made by Allan Pursley of Great Falls, Montana.

Broncs of the Era (1990s)

KINGSWAY SKOAL was born and raised on the Verne Franklin ranch near Bonnyville, Alberta. He was picked the 1988 Bareback Bucking Horse of the Year, the 1987 and 1988 National Finals Bareback Bucking Horse of the Year, the Olympic Exhibition Rodeo gold medal winner, and the 1988 Calgary Stampede Bucking Horse of the Year. At the 1988 National Finals, Dave Appleton drew him in the tenth round. Appleton came into the Finals at third, and was in desperate need of a good score, for which Kingsway obliged him. They made an 81 score and a piece of rodeo history. Appleton did win the All-Around title thanks to that final ride. When final points were announced in the locker room after the rodeo, Appleton and Feild, who were both competing for the top All-Around title, immediately congratulated each other. Appleton beat Feild by $644.

Kingsway Skoal won the 1995 and 1996 PRCA Saddle Bronc of the Year, as well as the National Finals Saddle Bronc title. His versatility in both bareback and saddle bronc makes him unique. Franklin says the sixteen-hand, 1,300-pound bronc is on the wild side. "He's as snake-y as they make them. He's always been a hard bucking horse, since day one. You really have to bear down on him to ride him."[53]

LONESOME ME SKOAL was bought from Rex Logan in 1984 at the Hobbema, Alberta, Bucking Horse Sale by Calgary Stampede. In 1984 he tied with Skoal's Sippin' Velvet for Bareback Horse of the Year, and was top bareback horse at the National Finals in 1984, plus top bucking horse in Canada that year. In 1989 and 1990 he became PRCA Saddle Bronc of the Year, 1990 and 1991 Canadian Saddle Bronc of the Year, and in 1994 PRCA Bareback Horse of the Year.

No two trips are alike for this bronc. This fact makes it extremely difficult for riders to figure out because they never know what to expect. Winston Bruce, director of Calgary Stampede stock, said, "He has four different patterns that he changes up all the time. He's never the same, which is what makes him one of the greatest horses of all time."[53]

KHADAFY SKOAL was raised on a ranch at Jackson Hole and purchased from Ray Sunburn by Hank Franzen of Powder River Production Company. The 14.5-hand, 1,100-pound blue roan gelding is halter broken and easy to catch. His bucking was described as "electric." He was bucked first as a saddle bronc, then changed to bareback. Bruce Ford was the first bareback rider to try him and he scored an 84 at Cheyenne Frontier Days in 1989. Ford said, "He is best in the bucking world. He's the champ!" He was Bareback Horse of the Year in 1990, and National Finals top bareback horse in 1994 and 1996. In 1995 he moved back into saddle bronc competition and was picked 1995 Saddle Bronc of the Year. In 1996 he was the PRCA Bareback Horse of the Year—a very versatile champion.[53]

BOBBY JOE SKOAL was foaled around 1985 out of Vold stud, Custer. The sixteen-hand, 1,300-pound brown gelding was raised on the Vold ranch. He won the Saddle Bronc of the Year in 1991, 1992, and 1993, and was the National Finals Saddle Bronc of the Year in 1991. Billy Etbauer scored 86 on him in the tenth round of the 1991 National Finals Rodeo. However, he dumps more than he helps score. In 1991 he dumped Dan Mortensen in the first round; in 1990, at the Finals, he dumped Robert Etbauer in the tenth round.[53] Of all his stock up to this time Harry Vold feels Bobby Joe Skoal is the most outstanding. Vold starts his three-year-old colts at Cheyenne Frontier Days in the Rookie Bronc riding event. He feels the most important attribute in a bucking horse is their disposition, heart, determination, and consistency.

PAWNEE, a red roan, is owned by Calgary Stampede and weighs 1,200 pounds. A spoiled saddle horse, he first year in the rodeo arena was 1984. In seven years she had been in the chutes 101 times—forty-six cowboys placed on her, thirteen bucked off. She bucked off Robert Etbauer at the Home on the Range Matched Bucking, and Billy Etbauer at Pendleton.

Butch Small claims she is one of his favorite horses. Bob Patterson, who trucks horses, said, "She's plumb gentle. You can walk out in the pasture, put a twine around her neck and

Harry Vold's champion saddle bronc Bobby Joe Skoal attempts to rid himself of Toby Adams at the tenth performance of the 1992 National Finals Rodeo.
— Photo by Dan Hubbell. Courtesy of the ProRodeo Hall of Fame and Museum of the American Cowboy.

lead her back to the corral, and you can pick up her feet and work on them. She's got the biggest heart in rodeo."[53]

HIGH CHAPARRAL COPENHAGEN—Don Peterson of Bar T Rodeo Ltd., of McCord, Saskatchewan, bought the gray gelding in 1987 for $1,000 and some National Finals Rodeo tickets from Mike Shapely, a rancher from Maple Creek, Saskatchewan. The 16.2-hand, 1,350-pound bronc began in the PRCA in 1987, and went to National Finals in 1988. He was the PRCA 1989 and 1992 Bareback Horse of the Year, and in 1991 and 1992 the National Finals best bareback horse. He is gentle to handle and quiet in the chutes. The horse bucks strong and turns back, but he is impossible to predict.

Don Peterson sold him to Mike Cervi in 1995. Peterson's decision to sell him was because he needed to be at big rodeos. The deal included seven horses, but it was estimated the cost of twelve-year-old High Chaparral Copenhagen was around $30,000. It was reported he had won $41,000 in bonuses and year-end awards. He is called "the gray man-eater" and is not popular with the cowboys. Recently, in Canada, he went out twelve times, and there were four buck-offs and four turnouts. In 1993, at the Canadian Finals, he "ripped it out" of Steve Dunham, and left the five-time champion helpless for the remaining four rounds. In an October 4, 1995, *ProRodeo Sports News* article asking bareback riders to talk about "baddest" horses they had encountered, five out of six picked High Chaparral Copenhagen. Those riders included Eric Mouton, Clint Corey, Jeffrey Collins, Bill Boyd, and Deb Greenough. [53]

Clint Corey at 1995 Salinas, California, rodeo, holding his own.
— Photo by Susan Lambeth.

Epilogue

The curtain is closing on the Old West—but you can still get a glimpse of the past when watching a bronc and his rider at a rodeo.

It is said the past provides clues about the future. The frontiersmen were people of independence, not afraid of the unknown, willing to work hard and determined to make a better life. Those same traits are found in those who compete in the rodeo arena. They are saving a unique piece of American heritage for future generations.

Some of those same attributes are present, however, in the men and women responsible for inventing and developing space travel, computerization, and electronics. What is in store for us in the future remains only with those who dare to dream.

Although the rodeo cowboy has adapted his profession to computerized data and corporate sponsors, he still keeps the lore and legend of the early American West alive. And as Too Slim, from the popular musical group Riders in the Sky, said, "The West is the only place big enough to hold all your dreams."

Ross Loney tries to stay on Fox Face, owned by Beutler and Sons, as he bucks straight toward the sky at Burwell, Nebraska, in 1967.
— Photo by Ferrell, courtesy of Imogene Beals.

Appendix

CHAMPION ALL-AROUND COWBOYS

1929	Earl Thode, Belvedere, SD
1930	Clay Carr, Visalia, CA
1931	John Schneider, Livermore, CA
1932	Donald Nesbit, Snowflake, AZ
1933	Clay Carr, Visalia, CA
1934	Leonard Ward, Talent, OR
1935	Everett Bowman, Hillside, AZ
1936	John Bowman, Oakdale, CA
1937	Everett Bowman, Hillside, AZ
1938	Burel Mulkey, Salmon, ID
1939	Paul Carney, Galeton, CO
1940	Fritz Truan, Long Beach, CA
1941	Homer Pettigrew, Grady, NM
1942	Gerald Roberts, Strong City, KS
1943	Louis Brooks, Pittsburg, OK
1944	Louis Brooks, Pittsburg, OK

(The above winners were named by the Rodeo Association of America.)

1947	Todd Whatley

(This champion was named by the Rodeo Cowboys Association, after the season ended at the request of a national trophy donor.)

1948	Gerald Roberts, Strong City, KS
1949	Jim Shoulders, Henryetta, OK
1950	Bill Linderman, Red Lodge, MT

1951	Casey Tibbs, Fort Pierre, SD
1952	Harry Tompkins, Dublin, TX
1953	Bill Linderman, Red Lodge, MT
1954	Buck Rutherford, Lenapah, OK
1955	Casey Tibbs, Fort Pierre, SD
1956	Jim Shoulders, Henryetta, OK
1957	Jim Shoulders, Henryetta, OK
1958	Jim Shoulders, Henryetta, OK
1959	Jim Shoulders, Henryetta, OK
1960	Harry Tompkins, Dublin, TX
1961	Benny Reynolds, Melrose, MT
1962	Tom Nesmith, Bethel, OK
1963	Dean Oliver, Boise, ID
1964	Dean Oliver, Boise, ID
1965	Dean Oliver, Boise, ID
1966	Larry Mahan, Brooks, OR
1967	Larry Mahan, Brooks, OR
1968	Larry Mahan, Salem, OR
1969	Larry Mahan, Salem, OR
1970	Larry Mahan, Brooks, OR
1971	Phil Lyne, George West, TX
1972	Phil Lyne, George West, TX
1973	Larry Mahan, Dallas, TX
1974	Tom Ferguson, Miami, OK
1975	(tie) Tom Ferguson, Miami, OK
	Leo Camarillo, Oakdale, CA
1976	Tom Ferguson, Miami, OK*
	Tom Ferguson, Miami, OK
1977	Tom Ferguson, Miami, OK*
	Tom Ferguson, Miami, OK
1978	Tom Ferguson, Miami, OK*
	Tom Ferguson, Miami, OK

(From 1976 through 1978, world championships were determined by the highest amount of money won at the NFR, signified by *. PRCA championships were also awarded based on total season earnings.)

1979	Tom Ferguson, Miami, OK
1980	Paul Tierney, Rapid City, SD
1981	Jimmie Cooper, Monument, NM

1982	Chris Lybbert, Coyote, CA
1983	Roy Cooper, Durant, OK
1984	Dee Pickett, Caldwell, ID
1985	Lewis Feild, Elk Ridge, UT
1986	Lewis Feild, Elk Ridge, UT
1987	Lewis Feild, Elk Ridge, UT
1988	Dave Appleton, Arlington, TX
1989	Ty Murray, Odessa, TX
1990	Ty Murray, Stephenville, TX
1991	Ty Murray, Stephenville, TX
1992	Ty Murray, Stephenville, TX
1993	Ty Murray, Stephenville, TX
1994	Ty Murray, Stephenville, TX
1995	Joe Beaver, Huntsville, TX
1996	Joe Beaver, Huntsville, TX
1997	Dan Mortensen, Manhattan, MT
1998	_____
1999	_____
2000	_____

SADDLE BRONC RIDING CHAMPIONS

1929	Earl Thode, Belvedere, SD
1930	Clay Carr, Visalia, CA
1931	Earl Thode, Belvedere, SD
1932	Pete Knight, Crossfield, Alberta
1933	Pete Knight, Crossfield, Alberta
1934	Leonard Ward, Talent, OR
1935	Pete Knight, Crossfield, Alberta
1936	Pete Knight, Crossfield, Alberta
1937	Burel Mulkey, Salmon, ID
1938	Burel Mulkey, Salmon, ID
1939	Fritz Truan, Long Beach, CA
1940	Fritz Truan, Long Beach, CA
1941	Doff Aber, Wolf, WY
1942	Doff Aber, Wolf, WY
1943	Louis Brooks, Pittsburg, OK
1944	Louis Brooks, Pittsburg, OK

(From 1929 through 1944, champions were named by the Rodeo Association of America.)

1945	Bill Linderman, Red Lodge, MT
1946	Jerry Ambler, Glenwood, WA
1947	Carl Olson, Calgary, Alberta
1948	Gene Pruett, Tieton, WA
1949	Casey Tibbs, Fort Pierre, SD
1950	Bill Linderman, Red Lodge, MT
1951	Casey Tibbs, Fort Pierre, SD
1952	Casey Tibbs, Fort Pierre, SD
1953	Casey Tibbs, Fort Pierre, SD
1954	Casey Tibbs, Fort Pierre, SD
1955	Deb Copenhaver, Post Falls, ID
1956	Deb Copenhaver, Post Falls, ID
1957	Alvin Nelson, Sentinel Butte, ND
1958	Marty Wood, Bowness, Alberta
1959	Casey Tibbs, Fort Pierre, SD
1960	Enoch Walker, Cody, WY
1961	Winston Bruce, Calgary, Alberta
1962	Kenny McLean, Okanagan Falls, BC
1963	Guy Weeks, Abilene, TX
1964	Marty Wood, Bowness, Alberta
1965	Shawn Davis, Whitehall, MT
1966	Marty Wood, Bowness, Alberta
1967	Shawn Davis, Whitehall, MT
1968	Shawn Davis, Whitehall, MT
1969	Bill Smith, Cody, WY
1970	Dennis Reiners, Scottsdale, AZ
1971	Bill Smith, Cody, WY
1972	Mel Hyland, Surrey, BC
1973	Bill Smith, Cody, WY
1974	John McBeth, Burden, KS
1975	Monty Henson, Mesquite, TX
1976	Mel Hyland, Surrey, BC*
	Monty Henson, Mesquite, TX
1977	J. C. Bonine, Hysham, MT*
	Bobby Berger, Norman, OK
1978	Joe Marvel, Battle Mountain, NV*
	Joe Marvel, Battle Mountain, NV

(From 1976 through 1978, world championships were determined by the highest amount of money won at the NFR, signified by *. PRCA championships were also awarded based on total season earnings.)

1979	Bobby Berger, Lexington, OK
1980	Clint Johnson, Spearfish, SD
1981	Brad Gjermundson, Marshall, ND
1982	Monty Henson, Mesquite, TX
1983	Brad Gjermundson, Marshall, ND
1984	Brad Gjermundson, Marshall, ND
1985	Brad Gjermundson, Marshall, ND
1986	Bud Munroe, Valley Mills, TX
1987	Clint Johnson, Spearfish, SD
1988	Clint Johnson, Spearfish, SD
1989	Clint Johnson, Spearfish, SD
1990	Robert Etbauer, Ree Heights, SD
1991	Robert Etbauer, Goodwell, OK
1992	Billy Etbauer, Ree Heights, SD
1993	Dan Mortensen, Billings, MT
1994	Dan Mortensen, Manhattan, MT
1995	Dan Mortensen, Manhattan, MT
1996	Billy Etbauer, Ree Heights, SD
1997	Dan Mortensen, Manhattan, MT
1998	_____
1999	_____
2000	_____

BAREBACK RIDING CHAMPIONS

(No bareback champions named until 1932.)

1932	Smoky Snyder, Bellflower, CA
1933	Nate Waldrum, Strathmore, Alberta
1934	Leonard Ward, Talent, OR
1935	Frank Schneider, Caliente, CA
1936	Smoky Snyder, Bellflower, CA
1937	Paul Carney, Galeton, CO
1938	Pete Grubb, Salmon, ID
1939	Paul Carney, Galeton, CO

1940	Carl Dossey, Phoenix, AZ
1941	George Mills, Montrose, CO
1942	Louis Brooks, Pittsburgh, OK
1943	Bill Linderman, Red Lodge, MT
1944	Louis Brooks, Pittsburg, OK

(From 1932 through 1944, champions were named by the Rodeo Association of America.)

1945	Bud Linderman, Red Lodge, MT
1946	Bud Spealman, Fort Worth, TX
1947	Larry Finley, Phoenix, AZ
1948	Sonny Tureman, John Day, OR
1949	Jack Buschbom, Cassville, WI
1950	Jim Shoulders, Henryetta, OK
1951	Casey Tibbs, Fort Pierre, SD
1952	Harry Tompkins, Dublin, TX
1953	Eddy Akridge, Midland, TX
1954	Eddy Akridge, Midland, TX
1955	Eddy Akridge, Midland, TX
1956	Jim Shoulders, Henryetta, OK
1957	Jim Shoulders, Henryetta, OK
1958	Jim Shoulders, Henryetta, OK
1959	Jack Buschbom, Cassville, WI
1960	Jack Buschbom, Cassville, WI
1961	Eddy Akridge, Midland, TX
1962	Ralph Buell, Sheridan, WY
1963	John Hawkins, Twain Harte, CA
1964	Jim Houston, Omaha, NE
1965	Jim Houston, Omaha, NE
1966	Paul Mayo, Grinnell, IA
1967	Clyde Vamvoras, Burkburnett, TX
1968	Clyde Vamvoras, Burkburnett, TX
1969	Gary Tucker, Carlsbad, NM
1970	Paul Mayo, Fort Worth, TX
1971	Joe Alexander, Cora, WY
1972	Joe Alexander, Cora, WY
1973	Joe Alexander, Cora, WY
1974	Joe Alexander, Cora, WY
1975	Joe Alexander, Cora, WY

(From 1976 through 1978, world championships were determined by the highest amount of money won at the NFR, signified by *. PRCA championships were also awarded based on total season earnings.)

1976	Chris LeDoux, Kaycee, WY*
	Joe Alexander, Cora, WY
1977	Jack Ward, Jr., Springdale, AR*
	Joe Alexander, Cora, WY
1978	Jack Ward, Jr., Springdale, AR*
	Bruce Ford, Evans, CO
1979	Bruce Ford, Evans, CO
1980	Bruce Ford, Kersey, CO
1981	J. C. Trujillo, Steamboat Springs, CO
1982	Bruce Ford, Kersey, CO
1983	Bruce Ford, Kersey, CO
1984	Larry Peabody, Three Forks, MT
1985	Lewis Feild, Elk Ridge, UT
1986	Lewis Feild, Elk Ridge, UT
1987	Bruce Ford, Kersey, CO
1988	Marvin Garrett, Gillette, WY
1989	Marvin Garrett, Gillette, WY
1990	Chuck Logue, Decatur, TX
1991	Clint Corey, Kennewick, WA
1992	Wayne Herman, Dickinson, ND
1993	Deb Greenough, Red Lodge, MT
1994	Marvin Garrett, Belle Fourche, SD
1995	Marvin Garrett, Belle Fourche, SD
1996	Mark Garrett, Spearfish, SD
1997	Eric Mouton, Weatherford, OK
1998	_____
1999	_____
2000	_____

PRCA STOCK OF THE YEAR

1956	*Warpaint*, Christensen Bros.
1957	*Warpaint*, Christensen Bros.
1958	*Warpaint*, Christensen Bros., and
	Joker, Harry Knight

1959	*Trail's End*, Zumwalt Rodeo Co.
1960	*Jake*, Harry Knight
1961	*Jesse James*, Hoss Inman
1962	*Big John*, Harry Knight
1963	*Big John*, Harry Knight
1964	*Wanda Dee*, Calgary Stampede
1965	*Jake*, Harry Knight
1966	*Descent*, Beutler Brothers & Cervi
1967	*Descent*, Beutler Brothers & Cervi
1968	*Descent*, Beutler Brothers & Cervi
1969	*Descent*, Beutler Brothers & Cervi
1970	*Rodeo News*, Reg Kesler
1971	*Descent*, Beutler Brothers & Cervi
1972	*Descent*, Beutler Brothers & Cervi
1973	*Sam Bass*, Jiggs Beutler

(In 1974, changed to pick one animal in each roughstock event.)

Saddle Bronc	**Bareback Horse**
1974 *Checkmate*, Christensen Bros.	*Moonshine*, Reg Kesler
1975 *Frontier Airlines*, Beutler & Cervi	*Stormy Weather*, Steiner
1976 *Sarcee Sorrel*, Harry & Wayne Vold	*Moon Rocket*, Calgary Stampede
1977 *Crystal Springs*, Bob Barnes	*Mr. Smith*, Christensen
1978 *Angel Sings*, Harry Vold	*Sippin' Velvet*, Bernis Johnson
1979 *Angel Sings*, Harry Vold, and *Deep Water*, Jim Sutton	*Smith & Velvet,* Christensen Bros.
1980 *Brookman's Velvet*, Cervi	*Smith & Velvet*
1981 *Rusty*, Harry Vold	*Classic Velvet*, Flying U
1982 *Buckskin Velvet*, Flying U	*Smith & Velvet*
1983 *Alibi*, Dell Hall	*Sippin' Velvet*, Johnson
1984 *Try Me,* Wayne Vold	*Sippin' Velvet,* and *Lonesome Me,* Calgary
1985 *Blow Out,* Beutler & Son	*Tombstone*, Jim Sutton
1986 *Wrangler Savvy*, Harry Vold	*Sippin' Velvet*, Johnson
1987 *Challenger & Skoal*, Beutler, and *Kloud Grey Skoal*, Calgary	*Skoal's Sippin' Velvet*

1988 *Skoal's Alley Cat*, G. Kesler	*Kingsway Skoal*, Franklin
1989 *Lonesome Me Skoal*, Calgary	*High Chaparral Copenhagen*, Don Peterson
1990 *Lonesome Me Skoal*	*Khadafy Skoal*, Powder River Production Co.
1991 *Bobby Joe Skoal*, Harry Vold	*Satan's Skoal*, Dorenkamp
1992 *Bobby Joe Skoal*	*High Chaparral Copenhagen*, Bar T Rodeo
1993 *Bobby Joe Skoal*	*Skoal's Airwolf*, Franklin
1994 *Skitso Skoal*, Sankey Rodeo	*Lonesome Me Skoal*
1995 *Khadafy Skoal*	*Kingsway Skoal*
1996 *Khadafy Skoal*	*Kingsway Skoal*
1997 *Skitso Skoal,* Sankey Rodeo	*Spring Fling*, Big Bend Rodeo Co.
1998 _____	_____
1999 _____	_____
2000 _____	_____

LINDERMAN AWARD WINNERS

(To qualify, a cowboy must earn at least $1,000 in each of three separate events, at least one of which must be roughstock and one a timed event. This award began in 1966, and was named for Bill Linderman.)

1966	Benny Reynolds, Melrose, MT
1967	Kenny McLean, Okanagan Falls, BC
1968	Paul Mayo, Grinnell, IA
1969	Kenny McLean
1970	Phil Lyne, George West, TX
1971	Phil Lyne
1972	Phil Lyne
1973	Bob Blandford, San Antonio, TX
1974	Bob Blandford, San Antonio, TX
1975	Chip Whitaker, Chambers, NE
1976	Phil Lyne, Artesia Wells, TX
1977	Chip Whitaker

1978	Chip Whitaker
1979	Chip Whitaker
1980	Steve Bland, Trent, TX
1981	Lewis Feild, Peoa, UT
1982	Tom Erikson, Innisfall, Alberta
1983	Marty Melvin, Holabird, SD
1984	Marty Melvin
1985	Tom Erikson, Innisfall, Alberta
1986	Bob Schall, Arlee, MT
1987	Tom Erikson
1988	Lewis Feild
1989	Philip Haugen, Williston, ND
1990	Bernie Smyth, Jr., Crossfield, Alberta
1991	Casey Minton, Redwood City, CA
1992	Bernie Smyth
1993	Casey Minton
1994	No contestant qualified
1995	Chuck Kite, Monfort, WA
1996	No contestant qualified
1997	Kyle Whitaker, Chambers, NE
1998	_____
1999	_____
2000	_____

PRCA RESISTOL ROOKIE OF THE YEAR

1956	John W. Jones, San Luis Obispo, CA
1957	Bob A Robinson, Tuttle, ID
1958	Benny Reynolds, Melrose, MT
1959	Harry Chartiers, Melba, MT
1960	Larry Kane, Big Sandy, MT
1961	Kenny McLean, Okanagan Falls, BC
1962	Jim Houston, Omaha, NE
1963	Bill Kornel, Salmon, ID
1964	Jim Steen, Glenn's Ferry, ID
1965	Dan Willis, Aquila, TX
1966	Tony Haberer, Muleshoe, TX
1967	Jay Himes, Beulah, CO

1968	Bowie Wesley, Wilderado, TX
1969	Phil Lyne, George West, TX
1970	Dick Aronson, Tempe, AZ
1971	Kent Youngblood, Lamesa, TX
1972	Dave Brock, Goodland, KS
1973	Bob Blandford, San Antonio, TX
1974	Lee Phillips, Carseland, Alberta
1975	Don Smith, Kiowa, OK
1976	Roy Cooper, Durant, OK
1977	Jimmy Cleveland, Hollis, OK
1978	Dee Pickett, Caldwell, ID
1979	Jerry Jetton, Stephenville, TX
1980	Jimmy Cooper, Monument, NM
1981	John W. Jones, Jr., Moro Bay, CA
1982	Clark Hankins, Rock Springs, TX
1983	Jackie Gibbs, Ivanhoe, TX
1984	Sam Poulous, Julian, CA
1985	Joe Beaver, Victoria, TX
1986	Jim Sharp, Kermit, TX
1987	Tony Currin, Heppner, OR
1988	Ty Murray, Odessa, TX
1989	David Bailey, Tahlequah, OK
1990	Fred Whitfield, Cypress, TX
1991	Brent Lewis, Pinon, NM
1992	Rope Myers, Athens, TX
1993	Blair Burk, Durant, OK
1994	Cody Ohl, Orchard, TX
1995	Curt Lyons, Ardmore, OK
1996	Shane Slack, Idabel, OK
1997	Mike White, Lake Charles, LA
1998	_____
1999	_____

SADDLE BRONC RIDING ROOKIE OF THE YEAR

1982	Kip Farnsworth, Anderson, CA
1983	Terry Carlon, Lawen, OR
1984	Guy Shapka, Spruce View, Alberta

1985	Robert Etbauer, Goodwell, OK
1986	Tom Wagner, Buffalo, WY
1987	Kyle Wemple, Milford, CA
1988	Craig Latham, Kaycee, WY
1989	Rod Hay, Mayerthorpe, Alberta
1990	Dan Mortensen, Billings, MT
1991	Toby Adams, Red Bluff, CA
1992	Kenny Taton, Mud Butte, SD
1993	Kelly Palmer, Stigler, OK
1994	Glen O'Neill, Strathmore, Alberta
1995	J. T. Hitch, Stilesville, IN
1996	Scott Johnston, Boorall, Australia
1997	T. C. Holloway, Eagle Butte, SD
1998	_____
1999	_____
2000	_____

BAREBACK RIDING ROOKIE OF THE YEAR

1982	Steve Carter, Klamath Falls, OR
1983	Stephen Smith, Hollywood, CA
1984	Marvin Garrett, Gillette, WY
1985	Tom Henrie, Mesquite, NV
1986	Colin Murnion, Jordan, MT
1987	Ken Lensegrav, Meadow, SD
1988	Ty Murray, Odessa, TX
1989	D. J. Johnson, Hutchinson, KS
1990	Jack Sims, Hutchinson, KS
1991	Vern Millen, Rapid City, SD
1992	Beau Mayo, Dublin, TX
1993	Jason Jackson, Nespelem, WA
1994	Mark Gomes, Florence, AZ
1995	Davey Shields, Jr., Hanna, Alberta
1996	Dusty McCollister, Acworth, GA
1997	Scott Montague, Fruitdale, SD
1998	_____
1999	_____
2000	_____

NATIONAL COWBOY HALL OF FAME
Oklahoma City

RODEO HALL OF FAME HONOREES

Aber, Doff
Akers, Ira
Altizer, Jim Bob
Appleton, Dave
Arnold, Carl
Askin, Bob
Austin, Tex
Beeson, Fred
Bell, Ray
Bennett, Hugh
Blackston, Vick
Blancett, Bertha
Blevins, Earl
Boen, Ken
Bolen, Bernice Dossey
Bond, Paul
Bowman, Lewis Ed
Bowman, Everett
Bowman, John
Brady, Buff
Brennan, Harry
Brooks, Louis
Brown, Freckles
Beutler, Elra
Beutler, Lynn
Burk, Clyde
Burmeister, A. H. "Hippy"
Burrell, Cuff
Byers, Chester
Bynum, James
Caldwell, Lee
Camarillo, Leo
Canutt, Yakima

Carney, Paul
Carr, Clay
Carroll, J. Ellison
Christensen, Hank
Clancy, Foghorn
Clark, Bobby
Clark, Gene
Colborn, Everett E.
Colborn, Alva
Connelly, Lex
Cooper, Jimmie B.
Cooper, Roy
Copenhaver, Deb
Cornish, Cecil
Cox, Breezy
Crosby, Bob
Curtis, Andy
Curtis, Eddie
Davis, Sonny
Davis, Gordon
Decker, Tater
Dightman, Myrtis
Doubleday, Ralph R
Elliott, Verne
Eskew, Colonel Jim
Eskew, Junior
Estes, Bobby
Feild, Lewis
Ferguson, Tom
Fletcher, Kid
Fort, Troy C
Gale, Floyd
Gamblin, Amye

Gardner, Joe
Garrett, Sam
Goodspeed, Jess
Goodspeed, Buck
Greenough, Turk
Griffith, Dick
Hancock, Bill
Hancock, Sonny
Hastings, Fox
Hefner, Hoytt
Helfrich, Devere
Henson, Margie Greenough
Holcomb, Homer
Irwin, C. B.
Ivory, Buster
Jauregui, Andy
Johnson, Ben Sr.
Jones, Cecil
Kirnan, Tommy
Knight, Harry
Knight, Pete
Lefton, Abe
Lewallen, G. K.
Like, Jim
Linder, Herman
Linderman, Bill
Linderman, Bud
Lindsey, John
Logan, Pete
Long, Hughie
Lowry, Fred
Lucas, Tad
Lybbert, Chris
Lyne, Phil
McCarty, Eddie
McClure, Jake
McCrory, Howard
McGinty, Rusty
McIntire, John

McGinnis, Vera
McGonagill, Clay
McLaughlin, Don
McSpadden, Clem
Mahan, Larry
Mansfield, Toots
May, Harley
Merchant, Richard
Merritt, King
Mills, George
Montana, Montie
Mulkey, Burel
Mulhall, Lucille
Mullens, Johnnie
Murray, Leo "Pick"
Murray, Ty
Nesbitt, Don
Nesmith, Tom
Oliver, Dean
Orr, Alice Greenough
Oropeza, Vincente
Pickens, Slim
Pettigrew, Homer
Pickett, Bill
Pickett, Dee
Porter, Willard H.
Privett, "Booger Red"
Pruett, Gene
Rambo, Gene
Randall, Glenn
Randolph, Florence
Reynolds, Benny
Richardson, Nowata Slim
Riley, Lanham
Riley, Mitzi Lucas
Roach, Ruth
Roberds, Coke T.
Roberts, E. C.
Roberts, Gerald

Roberts, Ken
Robinson, Lee
Roddy, Jack
Rollens, Rufus
Ross, Gene
Rowell, Harry
Rowell, Maggie
Rude, Ike
Rutherford, Buck
Ryan, Paddy
Salinas, Juan
Sawyer, Fern
Schneider, Frank
Schneider, Johnie
Shaw, Everett
Shelton, Dick
Shelton, Reine Hafley
Sheppard, Chuck
Shoulders, Jim
Smith, Dale D.
Sorenson, Doc
Sorrels, Buckshot
Sowder, Thad
Stahl, Jesse
Steele, Fannie S.
Steiner, Buck
Steiner, Tommy
Stillings, Floyd
Strickland, Hugh
Strickland, Mabel
Stroud, Leonard

Sundown, Jackson
Snyder, Smokey
Taillon, Cy
Tegland, Howard
Thode, Earl
Tibbs, Casey
Tierney, Paul
Tompkins, Harry
Todd, Homer
Truan, Fritz
Truitt, Dick
Tucker, Harley
Veach, C. Monroe
Walker, Enoch
Ward, Leonard
Weadick, Guy
Webster, Shoat
Weeks, Guy
Welch, Joe
Whaley, Everett "Slim"
Wharton, Ray
Whatley, Todd
White, Vivian
Whiteman, Hub
Whiteman, Jim
Wilcox, Don
Worrell, Sonny
Yoder, Phil
Zumwalt, Oral

NATIONAL COWBOY HALL OF FAME
TRAIL OF GREAT BUCKING HORSES

BlueJay
Chief Tyhee

Five Minutes to Midnight*
Hell's Angels
Midnight*
Steamboat
No Name AKA Fox AKA Reservation
Tipperary
Trail's End
Made in Germany
Come Apart

(* Buried at the National Cowboy Hall of Fame site.)

PRO-RODEO HALL OF FAME HONOREES
Colorado Springs

All-Around
Everett Bowman
Louis Brooks
Clay Carr
Lewis Feild
Bill Linderman
Phil Lyne
Larry Mahan
Gene Rambo
Benny Reynolds
Gerald Roberts
Jim Shoulders
Casey Tibbs
Fritz Truan

Saddle Bronc
Bobby Berger
Winston Bruce
Deb Copenhaver
Shawn Davis
Brad Gjermundson
Monty Henson
Sharkey Irwin

Clint Johnson
Pete Knight
Gene Pruett
Bill Smith
Mike Stuart
Earl Thode
Marty Wood

Bareback
Eddy Akridge
Joe Alexander
Jack Buschbom
Bruce Ford
Marvin Garrett
John Hawkins
Jim Houston
J. C. Trujillo
Sonny Tureman
Jack Ward

Bull Riding
Freckles Brown
Lane Frost

Don Gay
Dick Griffith
Tuff Hedeman
George Paul
Ken Roberts
Johnie Schneider
Smokey Snyder
Harry Tompkins

Steer Wrestling
Hugh Bennett
Ote Berry
James Bynum
Roy Duvall
John W. Jones, Sr.
Harley May
Homer Pettigrew
Bill Pickett
Jack Roddy
Gene Ross

Calf Roping
Barry Burk
Clyde Burk
Roy Cooper
Troy Fort
Glen Franklin
Toots Mansfield
Don McLaughlin
Dean Oliver

Team Roping
Jake Barnes
Leo Camarillo
Ben Johnson
John Miller
Clay O'Brien Cooper
Jim Rodriguez
Dale Smith

Steer Roping
Jim Bob Altizer
Sonny Davis
Clark McEntire
Ike Rude
Everett Shaw
Shoat Webster
Olin Young

Contract Personnel
Ellen Backstrom
Bobby Clark
Gene Clark
Jazbo Fulkerson
Dudley Gaudin
Chuck Henson
Homer Holcomb
Mel Lambert
Montie Montana
George Mills
Chuck Parkinson
Wick Peth
Wilbur Plaugher
Glenn Randall
Jimmy Schumacher
Andy Womack

Notables
Malcolm Baldridge
Josie Bennett
Benny Binion
Lex Connelly
Bob Crosby
Eldon Evans
Bill Hervey
John Justin
Buster Ivory
Harry Knight
Tad Lucas

Clem McSpadden
Dave Stout
Cy Taillon
W. R. Watt, Sr

Stock Contractors
Walt Alsbaugh
Gene Autry
Bob Barnes
Lynn Beutler
Henry and Robert, Sr.,
    Christensen
Everett Colborn
Leo Cremer
Verne Elliott
Neal Gay
C. B. Irwin
Andy Jauregui
D. A. "Swanny" Kerby
Reg Kesler
Cotton Rosser
Harry Rowell
James Sutton
Harry Vold

Stock
Baby Doll
Baldy
Bullet
Come Apart
Crooked Nose
Descent
Five Minutes to Midnight
Hell's Angels
High Tide
Midnight
Miss Klamath
Old Spec
Oscar
Peanuts
Poker Chip Peake
Red Rock
Steamboat
Tipperary
Tornado

Rodeo Lifetime Achievement
Sonny Linger

PRCA NATIONAL FINALS AVERAGE CHAMPIONS

Saddle Bronc Riding

1959	Jim Tescher, Medora, SD
1960	Enoch Walker, Cody, WY
1961	Alvin Nelson, Sidney, MT
1962	Alvin Nelson, Sidney, MT
1963	Jim Tescher, Medora, ND
1964	Ken McLean, Okanagan Falls, B. C.
1965	Bill Martinelli, Oakdale, CA
1966	Marty Wood, Bowness, Alberta
1967	Larry Mahan, Brooks, OR
1968	Ken McLean, Okanagan Falls, B. C.

1969	Buzz Seely, Roosevelt, WA
1970	Ivan Daines, Innisfall, Alberta
1971	Ken McLean, Okanagan Falls, B. C.
1972	Marvin Joyce, E. Helena, MT
1973	Dennis Reiners, Scottdale, AZ
1974	Joe Marvel, Battle Mountain, NV
1975	Tom Miller, Faith, SD
1976	Monty Henson, Mesquite, TX
1977	No average
1978	Joe Marvel, Battle Mountain, NV
1979	Tom Miller, Faith, SD
1980	Bobby Berger, Lexington, OK
1981	Tom Miller, Faith, SD
1982	Monty Henson, Mesquite, TX
1983	Brad Gjermundson, Marshall, ND
1984	Monty Henson, Mesquite, TX
1985	(tie) Bud Pauley, Shepherd, MT and Monty Henson, Mesquite, TX
1986	Dave Appleton, Arlington, TX
1987	Butch Knowles, Hemiston, OR
1988	Brad Gjermundson, Marshall, ND
1989	Clint Johnson, Spearfish, SD
1990	Bud Longbrake, Dupree, SD
1991	Robert Etbauer, Goodwell, OK
1992	Billy Etbauer, Ree Heights, SD
1993	Tom Reeves, Stephenville, TX
1994	Dan Mortensen, Manhattan, MT
1995	Robert Etbauer, Goodwell, OK
1996	Billy Etbauer, Ree Heights, SD
1997	Scott Johnson, DeLeon, TX
1998	_____
1999	_____
2000	_____

Bareback Riding

1959	Jack Buschbom, Mobridge, SD
1960	Benny Reynolds, Dillon, MT

1961	Jack Buschbom, Mobridge, SD
1962	John Hawkins, Twain Harte, CA
1963	John Hawkins, Twain Harte, CA
1964	Jack Buschbom, Mobridge, SD
1965	Dennis Reiners, Clara City, MI
1966	Gary Tucker, Carlsbad, NM
1967	Clyde Vamvoras, Burkburnett, TX
1968	Jim Houston, Omaha, NE
1969	Royce Smith, Iona, ID
1970	John Edwards, Red Lodge, MT
1971	Ace Berry, Modesto, CA
1972	Ace Berry, Modesto, CA
1973	Sandy Kirby, Greenville, TX
1974	Jack Ward, Jr., Odessa, TX
1975	Jack Ward, Jr., Odessa, TX
1976	Jack Ward, Jr., Odessa, TX
1977	No average
1978	Mickey Young, Ferron, UT
1979	Bruce Ford, Kersey, CO
1980	Bruce Ford, Kersey, CO
1981	Jimmy Cleveland, Durant, OK
1982	Bruce Ford, Kersey, CO
1983	Larry Peabody, Bozeman, MT
1984	Lewis Feild, Elk Ridge, UT
1985	Chuck Logue, McKinney, TX
1986	Lewis Feild, Elk Ridge, UT
1987	Bruce Ford, Kersey, CO
1988	Dave Appleton, Arlington, TX
1989	Marvin Garrett, Belle Fourche, SD
1990	Chuck Logue, Decatur, TX
1991	Wayne Herman, Dickinson, ND
1992	Deb Greenough, East Helena, MT
1993	Ty Murray, Stephenville, TX
1994	Brian Hawk, Azle, TX
1995	Marvin Garrett, Belle Fourche, SD
1996	Mark Garrett, Spearfish, SD
1997	Eric Mouton, Weatherford, OK
1998	_____
1999	_____
2000	_____

PRCA NATIONAL FINALS TOP BUCKING STOCK

Saddle Bronc	Bareback
1959 *Trail's End*, Zumwalt	*Come Apart*, H. Knight
1960 *Trail's End*, Zumwalt	*Short Fuse*, Flying U
1961 *Trail's End*, Zumwalt	*Come Apart*, H. Knight
1962 *Big John*, H. Knight	*Snappy John*, Beutlers1977
1963 *Jake*, H. Knight	*Devil's Partner*, Knight
1964 *Tradewinds*, Big Bend	*Necklace*, H. Vold
1965 No horse named	No horse named
1966 *Tradewinds*, Big Bend	*Bay Miggs*, Flint Hills
1967 *Tea Trader*, Rodeos Inc.	*Three Bars*, R. Kesler
1968 *Major Reno*, Rodeos Inc	*Necklace*, H. Vold
1969 (tie) *Tradewinds*, Big Bend	*Cindy Rocket*, Calgary
Major Reno, Rodeos, Inc.	
1970 *Big Sandy*, Beutler, Cervi &	*Necklace*, H. Vold
Linger	
1971 *High Ball*, Arizona Pro Rodeo	*Moonshine*, R. Kesler
1972 *Streamer*, B. Minick	*Smokey*, H. Vold
1973 *Rip Cord*, C & E Rodeo	*Three Bars*, R Kesler
1974 *Zone Along,* Calgary	(tie) *Spark Plug*, Alsbau
	Skyrocket, Kelsey
1975 *Old Shep*, Bob Aber	*High Tide*, Golden State
1976 *Sunday Punch*, Stephens	*Strawberry*, S. Linger
1977 *Short Crop*, R. Kesler	*Double Jeopardy*, Aber
1978 *Ekalaka*, Beutler & Cervi	*Sippin' Velvet*, Johnson
1979 *Frontier Velvet* (formerly	*Sippin' Velvet*, Johnson and
Ekalaka), B & C	Markum
1980 *High Roll*, Cervi	*Three Bars,* R. Kesler
1981 *Rusty*, H. Vold	*Dreamboat Annie*, Growney Bros.
1982 *Rusty*, H. Vold	*Sippin' Velvet*, Johnson
1983 *Short Crop*, R. Kesler	*Classic Velvet*, Flying U
1984 *Zippo Velvet*, Circle K	*Lonesome Me*, Calgary
1985 *Angel Blue*, Flying U	*Tom Thumb*, Harper & Morgan
1986 *Angel Blue*, Flying U	*Sippin' Velvet*, Johnson
1987 *Angel Blue*, Flying U	*Kingsway*, Franklin
1988 *Matt Dillon*, Northcott	*Kingsway Skoal*
1989 *Saddle Bags*, Franklin	*Skoal Sippin' Velvet*, BJ
1990 *Sparrow*, Bar T Rodeo	*Mindy*, Dorenkamp
1991 *Bobby Joe Skoal*, Vold	*High Chaparral* Copenhagen, Bar T
1992 *Snydly Skoal*, Sankey	*High Chaparral* Copenhagen, Bar T
1993 *Kingsway Skoal*, Franklin	*River Bubbles,* Calgary
1994 *Copenhagen Blue Jeans*, Pinz	*Khadafy Skoal*, Powder R
1995 *Kingsway Skoal*, Franklin	*Brown Bomber*, Beutler & Cervi
1996 *Copenhagen Blue Jeans*, Pinz	*Khadafy Skoal*, Powder R

1997	*Wyatt Earp Skoal*, Northcott	*Comotion*, Beutler & Gaylord
1998	_____	_____
1999	_____	_____
2000	_____	_____

PRCA CIRCUIT INFORMATION

Circuits Competing

Badlands Circuit
Columbia River Circuit (CR)
First Frontier Circuit (FF)
Great Lakes Circuit (GL)
Montana Circuit (MC)
Mountain States Circuit (MS)
Prairie Circuit
Sierra Circuit
Southeastern Circuit (SE)
Texas Circuit
Turquoise Circuit
Wilderness Circuit

DODGE NATIONAL CIRCUIT FINALS RODEO WINNERS

Saddle Bronc

Bareback

	Saddle Bronc	Bareback
1987	(tie) Clay Jowers, SE and Bud Monroe, TX	(tie) Steve Carter, CR and Todd Little, SE
1988	Dave Appleton, TX	Ken Lensegrav, Badlands
1989	Lewis Feild, Wilderness	Clint Corey, CR
1990	Mike Ramsey, CR	Colin Murnion, MT
1991	Derek Clark, Prairie	Clint Corey, CR
1992	Billy Etbauer, Prairie	Ken Lensegrav, Badlands
1993	Ty Murray, TX	Jeff Collins, Prairie
1994	Dan Mortensen, MT	Chuck Logue, TX
1995	Chance Dixon, CR	Deb Greenough, MT
1996	Dan Etbauer, Prairie	Deb Greenough, MT
1997	Dan Mortensen, MT	Clint Corey, CR
1998	J. T. Hitch, GL	Kelly Wardell, Wilderness
1999	_____	_____
2000	_____	_____

All-Around

1989 Lewis Feild, Wilderness
1990 Joe Parsons, Turquoise
1991 Dee Pickett, Wilderness
1992 Dan Mortensen, MT
1993 Ty Murray, TX
1994 Ty Murray, TX
1995 Speedy Williams, SE
1996 Brian Fulton, Badlands
1997 Tony Curran, CR
1998 Brad Goodrich, CR
1999 _____
2000 _____

RODEO ORGANIZATIONS

Professional Rodeo Cowboys Organization
101 ProRodeo Drive
Colorado Springs, CO 80919

American Junior Rodeo Association
P. O. Box 481
Rankin, TX 79778

Canadian Professional Rodeo Association
223 2116 27th Avenue N. E.
Calgary, Alberta, Canada T2E 7A6

National High School Rodeo Association
11178 N. Huron St., #7
Denver, CO 80234

National Intercollegiate Rodeo Association
2316 Eastgate N. Street. Suite 160
Walla Walla, WA 99362

National Little Britches Rodeo
1045 W. Rio Grande
Colorado Springs, CO 80906

Women's Professional Rodeo Association &
Professional Women's Rodeo Association
1235 Lake Plaza Drive, Suite 134
Colorado Springs, CO 80906

Senior Pro Rodeo National Old Timers Rodeo Association
P. O. Box 419
Roundup, MT 59072

The International Professional Rodeo Association
2304 Exchange Ave.
Oklahoma City, OK 73108

Glossary

All-Around Champion Cowboy: wins the most money for the year in more than one event.

association saddle: a saddle that was considered the most typical bronc saddle, and was originally provided for saddle bronc event contestants by certain rodeos.

average: taking all the scores, by one cowboy, and dividing by the number of broncs he drew, in that event.

bareback event: riding a bronc without a saddle; only a cinch with a handle on it.

bronc: horse that is not broken to ride and bucks whenever anyone attempts to ride him.

bucking machine: an apparatus that is motorized and has the motions of a bronc or a bucking bull.

buck off: when a bronc rider loses his balance during the ride and falls to the ground before the eight-second whistle blows.

chaps: worn by cowboys over their pants, to protect their legs; usually made of leather.

chute: enclosed area with a gate which swings open from the side, and hinges at the bronc's head.

cinch, cinchas: a strap attached to the saddle that goes under the bronc's belly to keep the saddle in place.

circuit: smaller areas divided off in the U.S. so that cowboys could make rodeos in their area, and not travel as far.

Cowboy Christmas: the Fourth of July weekend was called this because there was so much money to be won.

Cowboy Crisis Fund: money set aside by the PRCA, through their efforts and the efforts of various sponsors, to be used in case of injury or death to cowboys in rodeo-related accidents.

day money: winning the event, that day, and being paid for a single ride, not the entire rodeo.

dee ring: metal ring, shaped like a "D," used on saddle's rigging and flank straps.

draw: when all cowboys are entered at an event at a rodeo, they put all the broncs' names in a hat and randomly draw names for each entry.

exhibition ride: instead of competing against other riders, the person rides to please the crowd and is paid by the rodeo producer.

fight a horse: struggle with a bronc, other than bucking, such as to try to control horse's direction.

flank strap: a leather strap, lined with sheepskin, that is placed around the bronc's flank and over his back; just as the rider is ready to buck out of the chute, the strap is tightened and usually makes the bronc buck.

float a horse: to ride a bronc with feet up and not planting spurs.

foaled: a colt is born.

gelding: a male horse that has been neutered.

go-round: most rodeos comprise several go-rounds, with one head of stock for each rider in each go-round; National Finals has ten go-rounds.

hackamore: a bridle that does not have a bit; control of the horse is accomplished with the pressure across his nose.

hands: a hand is used to measure a horse's height—five inches.

hang-up: when a cowboy gets his hand caught in his rigging and can't dismount or get released from the handhold.

hobbled: the stirrups are tied under the horse's belly.

honda: a loop in a rope.

Justin Heeler Program: a medical unit that attends rodeos in customized trucks prepared to treat injured cowboys prior to and during the rodeo.

mark 'em out: a term indicating that a cowboy is required to spur the horse in the shoulder on the first jump out of the chute.

mustang: a wild horse on the North American plains, descended from Spanish horses.

permit holder: a rodeo cowboy is still amateur, holding a PRCA card for $5, until he wins $1,000 in PRCA-sanctioned rodeos; then he is no longer eligible to hold a permit.

pick-up men: usually two cowboys, on horseback, in the arena who are supposed to ride next to a bronc at the end of their eight seconds and assist the rider off the bronc; they also herd the broncs and other stock used in rodeo out of the arena, if necessary.

protective vest: a covering for the chest made specifically to protect a roughstock rider from the brunt of being stepped on, or hooked with a horn, when getting off or being thrown from a bucking horse or bull.

ProCom Program: a computerized program which rodeo cowboys use to enter any PRCA-sanctioned rodeo.

pulling leather: a term used to describe a roughstock rider that touches the animal with his free hand, which automatically disqualifies the rider.

qualified ride: a cowboy that rides a saddle bronc, bareback horse, or bull until the eight-second whistle blows.

re-ride: if a saddle bronc, bareback horse, or bull does not perform fairly during the eight-second ride, or the equipment provided is faulty and breaks, the judges make the determination whether the rider should be allowed a second ride, on another head of stock, or with equipment that does not break.

ridden to a finish: In the early days of rodeo the roughstock events were not timed (eight seconds) but were judged from the time the rider got on the bronc or bull's back until is stopped bucking, or the rider fell off. Many times this went on for a long time, causing the spectators to lose interest. It also discouraged many broncs and bulls from bucking the next time they were tried, which required new stock to be found.

rigging: a leather apparatus that fits around the bronc's belly with a handle-like hold for the rider's hand, used in the bareback event.

rodeo team: a group of cowboys that represent a sponsor, a school, a circuit, or a country and compete against other cowboys in rodeo events.

roughstock: broncs that are used in the saddle bronc event or bareback event, and bulls used in the bull riding event.

round-up: a term used for gathering horses or cows in a group; also used in reference to a rodeo (such as: Pendleton RoundUp).

saddle bronc: a horse that usually bucks better when it is under a saddle; some broncs have been versatile enough to be used in both saddle bronc and bareback events.

scratch: in roughstock refers to spurring the bronc during the ride.

snubbing horse: In early days of rodeo a bronc was brought into the area used as an arena in halter with the halter rope tied closely (snubbed) to a horse ridden by a rider, to keep his head as steady as possible while the rider saddled him and got mounted. Later this method was replaced when chutes were invented and used.

soogan (sougan): cowboy's bedroll, or blanket that goes in bedroll.

spurs: an apparatus made of metal that goes around the heel of the cowboy boot that aids the cowboy in scratching the rough-stock during the event; not dangerous or painful to the horse or bull, but gives a more enthusiastic animal.

spur out: the saddle bronc and bareback riders are required to spur their mount on the neck during the first jump out of the chute, or they are automatically disqualified.

stock contractors: those who supply stock to rodeos, such as saddle broncs, bareback broncs, bulls, roping calves, and steers, and many times supply the hands to run the rodeo.

surcingle: early-day bareback rigging made of leather, with one or more hand holds.

turn out: if a rider draws a head of stock, and he knows the history of the animal, he may opt to not show up at a rodeo or choose not to ride him. This could be if the stock does not have a history of bucking well and the rider does not think he can score highly on it, or if the reputation of the animal is that he has a tendency to intentionally try to hurt the rider.

Wild West Show: Before and after the turn of the century, producers gathered cowboys, cowgirls and oftentimes Indians to depict early-day western events, and held these spectacular presentations in various areas of the country (often the East). The people involved were paid employees, however, and the bronc riding and roping were exhibition and the riders and ropers were not competing for moneyed prizes.

winded: tested a horse's stamina by running it; the horse was culled if unable to withstand long-distance travel at a fast pace.

World Champion Cowboy: From 1929, records were kept and only one World Champion Cowboy was chosen in each event, and the All-Around. Prior to 1929 some rodeos would advertise their events and call the winner the "World Champion"; therefore there could be several different cowboys claiming to have been the World Champion—winning at Cheyenne, or Denver, or Calgary.

wrangler: a cowboy who rode horseback and worked with horses and/or cattle, in herding them, sorting them, and/or keeping them fit.

RESOURCE MATERIALS

[Reference numbers within text refer to this list.]

1. *Mustangs and Cow Horses*, by J. Frank Dobie, Mody C. Boatright, Harry H. Ransom. Published by the Texas Folk-Life Society, Austin, 1940.
2. *The Mustangs*, by J. Frank Dobie. Curtis Publishing Company, 1934.
3. *The Trail Drivers of Texas*, by J. Marvin Hunter. Published by George W. Saunders, 1924.
4. *Pikes Peak or Bust: The First Fifty Years*. Edited by Steve Fleming and Judy Larkin. Published by the ProRodeo Hall of Fame and Museum of the American Cowboy, 1990.
5. *The Cowboys*. The Old West Series, by the Editors of Time-Life Books. Text by William H. Forbis, 1973.
6. *Let 'Er Buck: A Story of the Passing of the Old West,* by Charles Wellington Furlong. Published by G. P. Putnam's Sons, New York and London, 1923.
7. *Hoofs and Horns*, "The Only Rodeo Magazine in the World," Established July 24, 1931.
8. *My Fifty Years in Rodeo*, by Foghorn Clancy. Published by The Naylor Company, San Antonio, Texas, 1952.
9. *American Rodeo, From Buffalo Bill to Big Business*, by Kristine Fredriksson. Texas A&M University Press, College Station, TX, 1985.
10. "History of First Frontier Days Celebration," article by Warren Richardson in the *Wyoming Historical Department Report*, Volume 19, Issue 1, January 1947.
11. *Wild Bunch*, magazine published by Rodeo Hall of Fame, Oklahoma City, OK.
12. *Buffalo Bill and the Wild West*, by Henry Blackman Sell and Victor Weybright. Oxford University Press, 1955.

13. *The 101 Ranch*, by Ellsworth Collings, in collaboration with Alma Miller England, daughter of the founder of the 101 Ranch. University of Oklahoma Press, 1937.

14. *Pawnee Bill: A Biography of Major Gordon W. Lillie*, by Glenn Shirley. University of New Mexico Press, 1958.

15. *Lucille Mulhall, Wild West Cowgirl*, by Kathryn Stansbury. Homestead Heirlooms Publishing Company, Mulhall, OK, 1992.

16. *The Boone Boys, Frontiersmen, and Their Great Wild West Show*, by Pecos Pate Boone. Christoval, TX, 1976

17. "The Greatest Bronc Buster Who Ever Lived," by Jack Burrows, article in *American West* magazine, Volume II, No. 3, May/June 1983.

18. *Rodeos and Tipperary, Including the Life of Sam Brownell*, by Sam Brownell. Big Mountain Press, Denver, CO, 1961.

19. *Who's Who in Rodeo*, by Willard H. Porter, Powder River Book Company, Oklahoma City, OK, 1983.

20. *Steamboat, Legendary Bucking Horse*, by Candy Vyvey Moulton and Flossie Moulton. High Plains Press, Glendo, WY, 1992.

21. "Rodeo's Sundown," by Bob Loeffelbein, article in *Wild West* magazine, February 1994.

22. *Tipperrary, The Diary of a Bucking Horse 1905-1932*, by Paul Hennessey. State Publishing Company, Pierre, SD, 1989.

23. *Man, Beast, Dust: The Story of Rodeo*, by Clifford P. Westermeier. University of Nebraska Press, 1947.

24. *Extra* newsletters, published by the Rodeo Historical Society, Oklahoma City, OK.

25. *Let 'Er Buck: A History of the Pendleton Roundup*, by Virgil Rupp. Pendleton RoundUp Association, 1985.

26. *Cowgirls of the Rodeo, Pioneer Professional Athletes*, by Mary Lou LeCompte. University of Illinois Press, Urbana and Chicago, 1993.

27. *World's Oldest Rodeo, 100 Year History 1888-1988*, by Danny Freeman. Published by Prescott Frontier Days, Inc., Prescott, AZ, 1988.

28. "Some Famous Bucking Horses," by Foghorn Clancy, article in *The Cattleman* magazine, September 1939.

29. "The Saga of Rodeo," by Chuck Martin, article in 1956 *Rodeo Sports News Annual*.

30. *Daddy of 'Em All: The Story of Cheyenne Frontier Days*, by Robert D. (Bob) Hanesworth. Flintlock Publishing Company, Cheyenne, WY, 1967.

31. "The Rodeo, What It Is and Its Inception," article in the 1936

Sixth Annual World's Championship Rodeo at Boston Garden Official Program.

32. "Trailering Forty Years Ago, Texas to Calgary," by Gib Potter. article in *Western Horseman*, July 1968.

33. *Turn Him Loose! Herman Linder, Canada's Mr. Rodeo*, by Cliff Faulknor. Western Producer Prairie Books, Saskatoon, Saskatchewan, 1977.

34. "The Rodeo Train," by Patricia Rodriguez, article in *Fort Worth Star-Telegram*, Sunday, April 25, 1993.

35. *The Ketch Pen*, magazine published by the Rodeo Historical Society, Oklahoma City, OK.

36. "Colonel William Thomas Johnson, Premier Rodeo Producer of the 1930s," article in *Canadian Journal of History of Sport*, by MaryLou LeCompte, Vol. 23, No. 1, May 1992.

37. "It's Been 90 Years Since the First Denver Stock Show," by Walter Dennis, article in *Quarter Horse Journal*, February 6, 1996.

38. *"Here's A Go!" Remembering Harry Rowell and the Rowell Ranch Rodeo*, by Vicki Weiland and Bill Strobel. Published by Rowell Ranch Rodeo, Inc., 1995.

39. *A Brand of Its Own, The 100 Year History of the Calgary Exhibition and Stampede*, by James H. Gray. Published by Western Producer Prairie Books, Saskatoon, Saskatchewan, 1985.

40. *50th Anniversary, West of the Pecos Rodeo*, 1979.

41. *Calgary Stampede: The Authentic Story of the Calgary Stampede, 1912-1964*, by Fred Kennedy.

42. *Cheyenne Frontier Days: "A Marker From Which to Reckon All Events,"* by Milt Riske. Published by the Cheyenne Corral of Westerners International, 1984.

43. *A Hundred Years of Heroes: A History of the Southwestern Exposition and Livestock Show*, by Clay Reynolds. Published by Texas Christian University Press, Fort Worth, 1995.

44. *Episode of the West: The Pendleton Roundup, 1910-1951*, by Pink Boylen. Published by Boylen, 1975.

45. "The History of Bareback Bronc Riding," by Earl Bascom, article in *Western Horseman*, July 1990.

46. "World's Roughest Sport," by Edmund Christopherson, article in *Holiday Magazine*, June 1956.

47. "Jerry Ambler—Rough Ridin' Champ," by Hawk Hyde, article in *The RoundUp Magazine,* February 1947.

48. *Stunt Man: The Autobiography of Yakima Canutt*, by Oliver Drake. Walker & Company, NY, 1979.
49. "Ace Rodeo Rider Tells How He Tames Vicious Broncos," by Johnny Schneider, article in *Popular Science Monthly*, August 1934.
50. *Let's Go! Let's Show! Let's Rodeo! The History of Cheyenne Frontier Days,* by Shirley Flynn. Published by Wigwam Publishing Co., LLC, 1996.
51. *Rodeo Trails,* by Bill King. Published by Jelm Mountain Press, Laramie, WY, 1982.
52. *Rodeo Sports News*, official newspaper of Rodeo Cowboys Association, established 1952.
53. *ProRodeo Sports News*, official newspaper of ProRodeo Cowboys Association.
54. *Mr. Rodeo: The Big Bronc Years of Leo Cremer*, by Patrick Dawson. Published by Cayuse Press, Livingston, MT, 1986.
55. "Paddy Ryan . . . He Lived to Ride Broncs," by J. P. S. Brown. article in *Persimmon Hill*, Vol. II. #2, Spring 1981.
56. *The World Famous Miles City Jaycee Bucking Horse Sale*, Collectors Edition, by John Moore, 1982.
57. Article on Colonel W. T. Johnson's Madison Square Garden Rodeo and the Railroad Train, *San Antonio Light*, November 19, 1933.
58. *10 Karat Hole in a Donut*; Based on the Life of Bert France, by Billy Wilcoxson. Torres Publishing Co., 1973.
59. "They Named Him Hell-To-Set: He Learned to Be," by Stan Frank, article in *Western Livestock Journal*, May 1946.
60. *Rodeo Sports News Annual* (1955, 1956, 1957).
61. *Professional Rodeo Cowboys Association Media Guide*, 1996, Colorado Springs, CO.
62. *Home on the Range 37th Annual Champions Ride Match*, 1993, Sentinel Butte, ND, Program.
63. "Bucking Horses," theme by Randall Witte, 1975.
64. *Rodeo Souvenir Program,* Grover, CO, 1995.
65. "Casey Tibbs, Maybe The Best Bronc Rider Ever," by Bill Gilbert, in *Playboy Magazine*, June 1973.
66. "Best Damn Cowboy in the World," article by James Stewart-Gordon, in *The Saturday Evening Post*, Fall 1971.
67. *50 Years of Rodeo: A Pictorial History of the Red Bluff Round Up*, by George and Marie Froome. 1972.
68. *50 Years of Nebraska's Big Rodeo—Burwell*, by Clare Berney. Published by Rodeo Book Co., 1975.

69. "Rodeo Officials Have Last Word" and "How Roughstock Rides Are Scored," by Ron Gullberg, in *Casper Star-Tribune* newspaper, Casper, WY, July 11, 1996.

70 "The Consummate Cowboy," by Joe Chasteen, in *Wyoming Tribune-Eagle*, Cheyenne, WY, July 21, 1996.

71. *Raymond 1901-1967*, compiled and edited by J. Orvin Hicken, assisted by Kay B. Redd and John L. Evans. Printed by the Lethbridge Herald Company, Ltd., Lethbridge, Alberta, Canada, May 1967.

72. *Col. W. T. Johnson's Sixth Annual World's Championship Rodeo, at Boston Garden, Official Program*, November 2-11, 1936.

73. *The Linder Legend: The Story of ProRodeo and Its Champion*, by Harald Gunderson. Published by Sagebrush Publishing, Calgary, 1996.

74. *Guinness Book of World Records*. Published by Guinness Media, Inc., 1997.

INDEX

248